# PRACTICE THEORY IN ACTION

This book explores intra-team interaction in workplace settings devoted to technological breakthroughs and innovative entrepreneurship. The first set of studies to investigate these economically important institutions through the lens of talk-at-work, this book begins by discussing the ethnomethodological traditions of Conversation Analysis and institutional interaction and linking them to innovation and entrepreneurship.

The book offers rich and detailed empirical accounts of teams talking new technologies and new ventures into being. By focusing on the observable language of teams in action, the book reveals the situated practices that teams use to enact their work, including the means by which team members verbally grapple with the uncertainties inherent in doing work in uncharted domains. The book presents important findings about the conversational accomplishment of work and demonstrates the value of examining the practices of teams in action.

A valuable contribution to studies of talk-in-interaction, as well as entrepreneurship-as-practice, this book can help to bridge the gap between scholarly investigations and the practical experiences of entrepreneurs. The author closes by considering the ways that practice-based studies of entrepreneurial work can improve issues of diversity and inclusion within the entrepreneurial ecosystem. This book is intended to serve as an invaluable sourcebook for scholars and students interested in innovation, entrepreneurship, and organizations as well as those focused on applied Conversation Analysis. The book's insights are presented in a richly detailed manner while remaining accessible to readers who are new to the methodologies and activity contexts.

**Betsy Campbell**, PhD, researches the practices of teams at the forefront of science and technology. As a Penn State faculty member, she leads an initiative focused on the democratization of entrepreneurship. Earlier in her career she founded Harvard Alumni Entrepreneurs, Inc. and co-directed the MIT CI Lab.

# PRACTICE THEORY IN ACTION

Empirical Studies of Interaction in Innovation and Entrepreneurship

*Betsy Campbell*

Routledge
Taylor & Francis Group

LONDON AND NEW YORK

First published 2019
by Routledge
2 Park Square, Milton Park, Abingdon, Oxon OX14 4RN

and by Routledge
52 Vanderbilt Avenue, New York, NY 10017

*Routledge is an imprint of the Taylor & Francis Group, an informa business*

© 2019 Betsy Campbell

*British Library Cataloguing-in-Publication Data*
A catalogue record for this book is available from the British Library

*Library of Congress Cataloging-in-Publication Data*
Names: Campbell, Betsy, 1966– author.
Title: Practice theory in action : empirical studies of interaction in
    innovation and entrepreneurship / Betsy Campbell.
Description: Abingdon, Oxon ; New York, NY : Routledge, 2019. |
    Includes index.
Identifiers: LCCN 2018053389 | ISBN 9781138497832 (hardback) |
    ISBN 9781138497849 (pbk.) | ISBN 9781351017718 (e-book)
Subjects: LCSH: Creative ability in business. | New products. |
    Technological innovations—Management. | Organizational behavior. |
    Entrepreneurship.
Classification: LCC HD53 .C36 2019 | DDC 658.4/21—dc23
LC record available at https://lccn.loc.gov/2018053389

ISBN: 978-1-138-49783-2 (hbk)
ISBN: 978-1-138-49784-9 (pbk)
ISBN: 978-1-351-01771-8 (ebk)

Typeset in Bembo
by Apex CoVantage, LLC

# CONTENTS

# ABOUT THE AUTHOR

**Betsy Campbell**, PhD, focuses her research on the practices of teams at the fore-front of technological innovation and scientific discovery. Earlier in her career she did research at Harvard University and co-directed the MIT Community Innovation Lab. She also was awarded a Ghiso Fellowship to study at the Yale University Center for Bioethics and was a Visiting Scholar at the Hastings Center. She was the founder of two high-tech ventures and one non-profit (Harvard Alumni Entrepreneurs, Inc.), which supports innovators and entrepreneurs around the world. As part of an intrapreneurial business unit, her work helped position an established software company for a $1.5 billion acquisition. She is an active member of the Explorers Club. Previously she served as a sub-committee co-chair for the Harvard Alumni Association Board of Directors. She also has been an invited judge and advisor many times for the MIT Innovation, Development, Enterprise, Action, and Service (IDEAS) venture competition.

# ACKNOWLEDGMENTS

The research that developed into this book began at the University of Exeter. I am thankful for my interactions with Adrian Bailey, Andi Smart, John Bessant, Bill Gartner, and other people who helped me with this work in its early days. More recently I have benefited from my connection with the Krause Innovation Studio at Penn State and its people, including Scott McDonald. Ceasar McDowell at MIT deserves a special note of recognition for his thoughtful feedback and consistent encouragement.

I also am thankful to Kristina Abbots, Chrissy Mandizha, and the entire editorial team at Routledge whose efforts were essential to the completion of this book. Neil Jenkins and Ellen Reeves also deserve a note of gratitude for their guidance on the publishing front.

A special nod of appreciation needs to go to the many teams who allowed me to record and analyze their backstage conversations. And similarly, I want to say thank you to Mark Davis whose generosity and creativity opened up new possibilities for my research.

Last but not least, I want to express my deepest gratitude to Barbara and Glenn Campbell, and my friends and colleagues. Without you, I could not have moved this work from hazy idea to finished book.

# PART I

# Interactions and the innovation workplace

Part I introduces concepts and methodologies relevant to the study of entrepreneurship as practice. It describes the ethnomethodological tradition of Conversation Analysis and the interdependent nature of practices. While it emphasizes the importance of verbal conversations between team mates in context, it also explores the socio-material aspects of interaction in innovative entrepreneurial work.

# 1

# FRAMING A CONTEMPORARY UNDERSTANDING OF WORKPLACE INTERACTION

## Introduction

In 1987 Arthur Rock, a well-respected venture capitalist, asserted that he would rather invest in an A team with a B technology than the reverse (Rock, 1987). He reasoned that a top-notch innovative entrepreneurial team would be able to adapt to the market demands and produce a successful product, whereas a less capable team would fail even with a great product innovation within their grasp. Coming from a context in which failure is the norm (Shane, 2008; Timmons, 1994), Rock's words of wisdom became a guiding practice for investors and innovators. They also helped to inspire a rich body of research that attempts to define the qualifications of an "A team".

For decades, researchers interested in entrepreneurship have explored various aspects of high performance. Most of that research has focused on either the impersonal or the intrapersonal aspects of success. The streams of research aimed at understanding the impersonal aspects have included inquiries into external resources such as access to funding sources and geographical proximity to hubs of innovation. They also have examined the size of entrepreneurial teams in conjunction with their performance. Most recently, they have considered the role that diversity – in terms of core skills and network relations – might have on outcomes.

The streams of research organized around questions of intrapersonal traits have considered the role of psychological orientation and cognitive biases of entrepreneurs in their decisions to start and continue to work on their ventures. Topics such as confidence and attitudes toward risk and failure, for example, have been given significant attention. Many of these inquiries into intrapersonal traits have compared entrepreneurs with managers and have attempted to define an enduring characteristic that sets entrepreneurs apart.

As valuable as these efforts have been, they fail to tell us much about what entrepreneurs actually *do* in the course of their daily work. Many scholars recognize that all professional work is verbal work (Donnellon, 1996), and most practicing entrepreneurs will attest to having pivotal conversations in team meetings that define their products and organizations (Reis, 2011). However, the existing body of entrepreneurial research says little about the ways that entrepreneurial teams talk their innovations and ventures into existence. Few researchers have attempted to examine and describe the conversational work of these teams in action. This book reports on the means by which innovations and innovative new ventures are verbally accomplished. It aims to illuminate the means by which teams actively engage in the "interactional competencies"(Psathas, 1990) associated with being an innovator and doing innovative entrepreneurship.

Before unpacking the importance of studying the observable language used by innovative entrepreneurial teams to enact their work, it is worth pausing to define innovative entrepreneurship. Entrepreneurship has been associated with endeavors of many kinds including self-employment (Shane, 2008; Stevenson, 1983), small business (Gibb, 1996), and franchise operation (Azoulay & Shane, 2001). Even though the entrepreneurship term can be applied to anyone who starts a new venture of any kind (Lazear, 2004), this book draws a distinction between imitative and innovative entrepreneurial endeavors (Baumol, 1986; Cliff, Jennings, & Greenwood, 2006). Most entrepreneurs start imitative ventures (Bhide, 2000): ventures that join an established category in the marketplace. For example, an imitative entrepreneur might start a new dry cleaner or a new restaurant. This book, however, is focused on innovative entrepreneurship. Such ventures are based on significantly differentiated value propositions that often include breakthrough offerings (Dyer, Gregersen, & Christensen, 2008). Consequently, the development of a viable and differentiated product or service (Christensen, 1997) is central to and effectively synonymous with the creation of these new business entities. Facebook and Tesla are contemporary examples of innovative entrepreneurial ventures that might be recognized by most readers.

It is difficult to capture the naturally occurring interactions of innovative entrepreneurial teams at work. Often teams working at the forefront of technological innovation have intellectual property concerns for their emerging products. They also may work in private or otherwise protected settings – from the proverbial home garage to the accelerators on university property. For these and other reasons it is not easy for researchers to be in the right place at the right time with the right permissions to record the authentic conversations of teams in action.

Perhaps because recordings of teams in action are difficult to obtain, researchers interested in the roles of language in the innovation process have tended to study presentations rather than intra-team conversations. Pitches are the name for the presentations given by founders to prospective investors. Sometimes given in private or sometimes given as part of a public showcase, pitches are a standard part of the innovative entrepreneurial journey. However, they are quite distinct from naturally occurring intra-team conversations.

Pitches are constructed, at least in part, from prepared and rehearsed points and tend to be monologues more than dialogues. Presentations also are given to inform or influence a listener rather than invite collaboration. By studying pitches, researchers can illuminate the communicative skill of persuasion that may be beneficial for teams in this one particular context. However, the staged language of pitches can tell us little about the ways that teams verbally accomplish the shared act of innovating. Only by studying the routine intra-team interactions of innovative entrepreneurial teams *being* innovative entrepreneurial teams can we uncover the full set of "interactional competencies . . . requisite to participation" (Psathas, 1990, p. 21) in the professions of innovation and innovative entrepreneurship.

Despite the challenges of recording the naturally occurring interactions of innovation teams in action, such recordings are essential to studying the verbal accomplishment of teamwork. The recordings permit researchers to return to the data to examine it directly and repeatedly in the processes of open coding, transcription, and analysis. Field notes and researcher recollections can miss or distort important details from the authentic interactions. The same can be said for invented exchanges or experimentally provoked verbalizations (Heritage, 1984). Consequently, only recorded authentic conversations can serve as the foundation for meaningful inquiries into the language used by teams in action at work.

## A look at methodological traditions

Studies of workplace interaction have their roots in the traditions of ethnomethodology and Conversation Analysis. Springing from Garfinkel's work in the 1960s, ethnomethodology describes the ordinary means by which people co-create and recognize their social settings, acts, and activities. Ethnomethodology treats these settings, acts, and activities as emergent achievements that result from the deliberate and situated contributions of participants.

Verbal conversations are one form of interaction that enables people to co-create and recognize social settings, acts, and activities. In fact, conversations are a vital form, and Conversation Analysis (CA) has emerged within ethnomethodology to attend to them in great detail. Associated closely with the work of Harvey Sacks, Emanuel Schegloff, and Gail Jefferson in the 1970s, CA probes the organizing properties of naturally occurring conversation. Early themes of CA research included the ways that conversational features – such as openings and closings, repairs, and turn-taking – were recognized and achieved by participants. The work asserted that ordinary conversation operated according to social rules – not just proficiency with grammar or vocabulary – that are understood and reinforced by the participants' situated interactional choices. By attending to the observable features of language, researchers can uncover the conversational moves and situated processes of reasoning by which people accomplish collaborative action. In other words, the interactional means by which people understand each other, achieve shared awareness, and accomplish social tasks can be revealed.

Increasingly scholars are analyzing interactional phenomenon in specific activity settings. Research has examined conversations such as medical interviews or police interrogations, for example (Antaki, 2011; Psathas, 1990). As research moves into these applied realms, it can reinforce our understanding of basic interactional phenomena. It also can discover additional ways that these phenomena are accomplished, or it can reveal entirely new characteristics of interactions associated with a particular activity setting. Interactional phenomena that are recognized as part of a specific activity setting can be framed as competencies that constitute adequate participation in that setting. This means that training could be developed to enable new or struggling participants in these settings to improve their ability to contribute productively (Psathas, 1990).

Other scholars have written in compelling detail about the process of using CA to conduct research. Consequently, this book will not focus on how to do CA. However, some specific research that has influenced the work presented in the coming chapters warrants acknowledgement. Scholars have described the means by which participants collaboratively achieve recognizable acts of competence in complex matters such as making a surgical incision (Heritage, 1984), executing a calculation (Anderson, Hughes, & Sharrock, 1989), positioning an underwater probe (Goodwin, 1995), or flying an airplane (Nevile, 2004). These works probe the situated meaning and sequential ordering of utterances used by participants to achieve these complex acts. The works micro-analyze interactions to describe the means by which people enact professional practices.

These influential works also focus on interactions of co-workers engaged in shared tasks and common goals. By examining the interactions of peers at work rather than institutional representatives with clients, they showcase what might be considered "backstage" interactions (Goffman, 1956, 1974). As such, they provide an important foundation upon which the research described in this book relies. They draw from the traditions of CA and ethnomethodology to reveal how people interactionally produce and recognize competent work (Heritage, 1984; Nevile, 2004).

These works, along with others which highlight members of the same team, represent an important departure from the majority of workplace interaction studies. More typical are studies of interactions between professional and non-professional individuals such as interactions between doctors and patients, teachers and students, or lawyers and witnesses. These "frontstage" (Goffman, 1956, 1974) workplace interactions tend to be united by several features: asymmetry of power, transactional episodes, binary outcomes, and known solutions. For example, in doctor/patient interactions, doctors routinely have more medical knowledge and authority than patients. Interactions during an office visit are bounded by a limited time window during which the participants expect to reach a clear diagnosis and definitive outcome. The outcomes tend to have binary elements: the doctor will or will not prescribe antibiotics, for example. And the array of potential treatments exists in advance of the appointment and belongs to a fixed set of possibilities.

The structural features of "frontstage" work are less likely to be present in the interactions of co-workers who are focused on shared workplace goals, including the goals of an early-stage venture. Rather than negotiating asymmetries of power, entrepreneurial team mates might be more likely to grapple with asymmetries of functional knowledge. For example, one team mate might have technical expertise while the other might have marketing expertise. Similarly, innovative entrepreneurial teams may be less likely to have boundaries on the meetings, outcomes, or solutions than "frontstage" workers. Entrepreneurial teams converse over a series of sessions, not within a single 15-minute session as medical appointments do. Moreover the potential outcomes of entrepreneurial interactions are many, sometimes bordering initially on the infinite. Team members interact to define both the problem and the solution simultaneously. What the team members create often is bounded mainly by their abilities and by the market's willingness to validate their emerging product.

## Directional trends

While research continues along the traditional veins of interest, scholars increasingly are considering new topic areas and techniques. As workplaces become more technologically rich, researchers are investigating the impact of technology on communication. Researchers also are exploring the quantitative expression of conversational patterns.

For years, studies into workplace interaction have considered the transmission of knowledge and skills, the achievement of collaboration in the face of conflicting interests, and the challenges of interaction with and through technologies (Arminen, 2005). While telephone interaction proves an exception – CA researchers have investigated the nature of telephone interaction for decades (Hopper, 1992; Hutchby, 2001) – many of these studies have assumed that the participants are co-located and interacting face-to-face. Increasingly, studies have had to address mediated and distributed talk-in-interaction as workplaces have become more technologically complex.

Today's workplace includes a wealth of technologically enabled interaction. The rapid uptake of mobile phones, for example, has enabled researchers to probe additional aspects of distributed voice-only interaction (Hutchby & Barnett, 2005). Simultaneously, popular internet-based technologies that provide videoconferencing have enabled researchers to consider the role of live video in mediated and distributed interaction (Licoppe & Morel, 2012; Mondada, 2007).

Recent decades also have seen the emergence of round-the-clock broadcast talk, another form of workplace interaction that is technologically dependent. Broadcast talk is produced for public consumption yet retains some unscripted features of naturally occurring conversation (Hutchby, 2006). Talk radio and cable television news, for example, have remote and distributed audiences, but the conversational participants who are engaged in a kind of workplace conversation may be co-located or not. Studies of broadcast talk have illuminated the order and logic of these workplace interactions. Formal exchanges of prepared questions from a host that are answered by a guest, and relatively unscripted questions from callers that are mediated by a host and answered by a guest, for example, have added new dimensions to our understanding of institutional turn-taking systems (Heritage & Clayman, 2010; Lundell, 2009; Sacks, Schegloff, & Jefferson, 1974).

In addition to investigating technologically rich workplaces, researchers increasingly are examining interactions quantitatively without betraying the data-driven foundations of CA and ethnomethodology (Arminen, 2005). Traditionally, studies of workplace interaction have excelled at describing the situated phenomena, but they've been limited in their ability to suggest patterns of interaction. Quantifying language moves makes profiles of language patterns sharper and comparisons possible. Quantitative CA can reveal the distribution of interaction patterns across cultures, historical eras, or other categories of communities more crisply than qualitative comparisons can (Arminen, 2009).

The idea of taking a quantitative approach to Conversation Analysis might give pause to some scholars. At the core of their concerns may be an apprehension about context and precedence. For example, if all utterances of "yeah" were counted in an episode of conversation, the tally would have very little value. However, value can come from a phased approach that begins with rich qualitative analysis and segues to a numerical tagging of occurrences of key interactional features that have emerged through the qualitative assessment of the data. Nested approaches to mixing qualitative and quantitative methods can highlight aspects of the data that might warrant deeper (qualitative) investigation (Morse, 2003, p. 192; Tashakkori & Teddie, 2003, p. 230). They are anchored in specific details of interactional data while enabling a wider view of social practice and action.

One early study that points to the potential power of this approach is Clayman and Heritage's 2002 work on the types of journalist questions found in US presidential press conferences (Clayman & Heritage, 2002). Their research utilized both qualitative and quantitative methods to demonstrate how the relative proportions of different types of questions posed to presidents changed over the middle years of the 20th century. Because of their approach, they were able to identify a pattern: journalists' questions became less deferential and more aggressive. Consequently, their work tells us not only about the internal structures of presidential press conferences but also about a societal change in the relationship between the institution of the presidency and the press.

CA, quantitative or not, is well-aligned to support the study of entrepreneurship as practice. The study of practices is a study of interactions and relationships (e.g., between people, settings, and artifacts). Scholars interested in entrepreneurship as practice recognize the connections between macro- and micro-phenomena and attend to interdependencies between activities and contexts (Cicourel & Knorr-Cetina, 1981; Johannisson, 2011; Steyaert, 2007; Watson, 2013). Some are even using CA a part of a toolkit for "zooming in and out" of assemblies of practices (Nicolini, 2009). CA contributes to the "connected situationalism" (Nicolini, 2017) of practice-oriented research by staying true to its "interactional constructivism" roots (i.e., that conversations draw on, create, and alter social relations, and that social relations draw on, create, and alter social institutions) (Levinson, 2005).

By focusing on practices rather than entrepreneurial cognition or environmental characteristics, the scholars advancing the entrepreneurship as practice perspective are investigating the collaborative, real-time work that entrepreneurs do in action. Such research requires methodologies that can reveal the authentic actions used by entrepreneurs at work. While CA is that kind of methodology, more traditional approaches such as interviews or questionnaires are not able to showcase how entrepreneurs (or other teams at the forefront of innovation and discovery) accomplish their shared work in context.

An additional scholarly movement requires a brief mention: the Montreal School of the constitutive role of communication in organizations (CCO). This stream of research traces its origins back to the earlier work of Karl Weick on the communicative nature of organizing and of organizations. Scholars of CCO aim to articulate how situated conversations are rendered into representations and authority structures that shape collective identities and organizational entities (Cooren, Kuhn, Cornelissen, & Clark, 2011). Of great interest to CCO scholars are the processes that transform the intimate understandings achieved by the participants in a given conversation into operating structures, public messages, and other enduring frames, or texts, that are associated with an organization. These strategy-as-practice inquiries have focused mostly on existing organizations rather than entrepreneurial organizations. However, their detailed attention to the interactions of actual teams makes them worth noting in a book about entrepreneurial conversations and practices.

## Embracing these trends

This book accepts and advances these trends. It probes specific activity settings in search of interactional moves that signal competent participation in such work. It is focused on backstage intra-team interactions in technologically rich workplaces. While it always begins with unmotivated looking and observation of the situated logic found in the recorded data, it sometimes uses a blend of qualitative and quantitative approaches to analyze and communicate findings from the data. It strives to build bridges between conversational moves and theories about the practices of innovative entrepreneurial teams. It uses CA to examine how teams verbally *do* several expected practices, to challenge conventional wisdom about some practices, to suggest some potential interventions in entrepreneurial education, and to engage with macro-societal concerns (Antaki, 2011).

A few words should be said about the data, its collection, preparation, and analysis.

Data for this book comes from several sources. Some comes from the workplace conversations of innovative entrepreneurial teams. Other data comes from the workplace interactions of a team that is not engaged in entrepreneurial endeavors but is developing breakthrough technologies. Because innovative entrepreneurial ventures are forged in connection with disruptive products, this non-entrepreneurial team has been included in the section that demonstrates the use of quantitative CA.

One set of data comes from a university-sponsored contest for emerging high-tech, high-growth entrepreneurs. These teams of aspiring innovators were given GoPro cameras to wear during the arc of a six-week contest. They were instructed to use the devices to audio record their naturally occurring conversations throughout the contest. (Video and still images were also captured. However, the usable visual data was limited.) These conversations formed the team meetings during which they collaboratively worked on their emerging products and prepared to demonstrate their prototypes to the contest judges. At the end of the contest, the cameras and data were returned to me. The teams were evaluated by a panel of judges at that point, and winners were chosen. The recorded conversational data included high- and low-performance teams.

Another set of data comes from a team of elite engineers working on a piece of technology for interplanetary exploration. The naturally occurring interactions of this group of experts were captured as part of the creation of a documentary film. While the complete set of footage included team meetings across many months and in many settings, the unedited material selected for this inquiry was captured over the course of one day at one facility. The 60 minutes of footage captures the interactions of the team as they reinvent a core piece of technology essential to a scientific mission into outer space.

Although the data was gathered by a variety of means, a similar analytical approach guided the beginning of each inquiry. I began with a period of unmotivated looking and listening (Psathas, 1990) followed by general note taking about the contours of the conversations. I also removed sections of data from consideration that were garbled or featured non-work topics such as gossip. This was the beginning of an iterative process of description, analysis, and interpretation (Wolcott, 1994).

With the data drawn from the university contest, I focused on the teams that finished at the top and bottom of the rankings. This choice enabled me to "maximize the similarly and differences" of the data in line with Grounded Theory (Creswell, 2003, p. 14). It also prepared for the possibility of a comparative case study; contrasting cases (e.g., a high- and low-performance team) tend to present clear patterns of difference (Eisenhardt & Graebner, 2007, p. 27). Conversational episodes were bracketed by the natural starting and stopping places of the participants.

With the data drawn from the raw footage of the film, the process began with selecting the episodes of conversation. Then I highlighted exchanges which could speak to classic concerns of workplace interaction. The verbal accomplishment of identity, for example, was an early lens through which I viewed the data. Over time, a collection of instances were assembled and a micro-analysis of the sequence order could be undertaken.

Micro-analytical efforts begin with transcription. The transcriptions for the recordings from these teams utilized a modified version of Jeffersonian notation. In order to make the book as accessible as possible, these notational marks are used sparingly in the coming chapters. While some data is inevitably lost by using a lighter form of transcription, this choice will enable readers without expertise in CA to appreciate the excerpts and the findings.

With some sets of data, I mounted a second qualitative analysis with a different aim: I developed a grounded coding scheme to facilitate comparisons between cases. I reviewed each episode utterance by utterance and attached a description of the interactional work being done by the speakers at that instance. Were speakers making a claim, offering support, or telling a joke, for example? Occasionally I would examine these grounded descriptions and attempt to organize them with better and more coherent naming conventions (Miles & Huberman, 1994). Continuing along this path of open coding (Strauss & Corbin, 1990), I regularly compared my grounded codes and categories with relevant concepts and language forms found in the literature (Glaser & Strauss, 2009). The qualitative software Atlas TI was used to do the grounded coding process and a quantitative assessment of the code distribution.

## How this book is organized

Part I of this book is devoted to making sure all readers have a basic understanding of the study of workplace interaction, the contours of the innovative entrepreneurial workplace, and the main themes associated with entrepreneurship research. The next chapter introduces entrepreneurial practices as an interactional matter. It highlights foundational concepts related to ethnomethodology, such as the situated organization of work (Garfinkel, 1948/2006, 2002), and articulates why and how the ethnomethodological approach of CA informs the studies presented in this book. It is followed by a chapter that describes the settings where innovative entrepreneurial work tends to be done, at least in North America and Europe, in terms of practice. Part II of the book considers the verbal means by which innovative entrepreneurial work is accomplished. The chapters describe the interactional machinery behind several practices that are thought to be essential to innovative entrepreneurial work. Part III of the book questions conventional knowledge about the pursuit of innovation. Using CA, the chapters challenge several expected entrepreneurial traits and behaviors with conversational evidence from teams in action. Part IV of the book uses quantitative CA paired with a practice-based view of sensemaking to examine conversational moves and patterns of teams in action. Unlike the other chapters of the book which examine only successful innovative entrepreneurial teams, this chapter looks at an unsuccessful innovative entrepreneurial team and a successful innovation team outside of entrepreneurship. Part V of the book connects the micro-analysis of conversation to enduring puzzles and pressing concerns associated with innovation and entrepreneurship. It uses conversational data to probe issues including the theoretical framing of entrepreneurial stances toward uncertainty and the educational quest to prepare tomorrow's innovators and entrepreneurs.

The book closes with an afterword on one of the most defining needs of the innovation economy: the democratization of innovation. As economic development for communities and financial stability for individuals increasingly are related to the ability to innovate, insights about the practices of high-performance innovative entrepreneurial teams could not be more timely. The concluding pages of the book suggest that understanding and encouraging the conversational competencies of innovative entrepreneurs may be central to the vitality of the economy as a whole. As such, the afterword joins a small body of research that connects the micro-analysis of workplace interaction to macro-societal concerns (Maynard, 1988; Zimmerman, 2005).

Our limited knowledge about entrepreneurial work is defined by "all the missing descriptions of what occupational activities consist of and all the missing analyses of how the practitioners manage the tasks which, for them, are matters of serious and pressing significance" (Heritage, 1984, p. 299). This book attempts to expand our knowledge by micro-analyzing the authentic workplace conversations of teams in action. Understanding the ways that entrepreneurial teams verbally accomplish their work may also be a matter of "serious and pressing significance" for everyone, given that individual and societal flourishing seem to be coupled with acts of innovation and new venture creation.

One important aspect of being a competent innovator and innovative entrepreneur is being accepted by others in the innovation ecosystem. This book demonstrates that achieving this kind of legitimacy is not a matter of adopting buzzwords or acquiring procedural knowledge. Being an innovator or innovative entrepreneur requires the development and display of conversational competencies specific to these professional roles.

# References

Anderson, R. J., Hughes, J. A., & Sharrock, W. (1989). *Working for profit: The social organisation of calculation in an entrepreneurial firm.* Aldershot: Avebury.

Antaki, C. (Ed.). (2011). *Applied conversation analysis: Intervention and change in institutional talk.* New York, NY: Palgrave Macmillon.

Arminen, I. (2005). *Institutional interaction: Studies of talk at work* (Vol. 2). New York, NY: Ashgate Publishing, Ltd.

Arminen, I. (2009). On comparative methodology in studies of social interaction. In M. Haakana, M. Laakso & J. Lindström (Eds.), *Talk in interaction: Comparative dimensions.* Helsinki: Finnish Literature Society.

Azoulay, P., & Shane, S. (2001). Entrepreneurs, contracts, and the failure of young firms. *Management Science, 47*(3).

Baumol, W. J. (1986). Entrepreneurship and a century of growth. *Journal of Business Venturing, 1,* 141–145.

Bhide, A. (2000). *The origin and evolution of new businesses.* New York, NY: Oxford University Press.

Christensen, C. M. (1997). *The innovator's dilemma: When new technologies cause great firms to fail.* Boston, MA: Harvard Business School Press.

Cicourel, A. V., & Knorr-Cetina, K. D. (Eds.). (1981). *Advances in social theory and methodology: Toward an integration of micro-and macro-sociologies.* Boston: Routledge & Kegan Paul.

Clayman, S., & Heritage, J. (2002). *The news interview: Journalists and public figures on the air.* Cambridge: Cambridge University Press.

Cliff, J. E., Jennings, P. D., & Greenwood, R. (2006). New to the game and questioning the rules: The experiences and beliefs of founders who start imitative versus innovative firms. *Journal of Business Venturing, 21*(5), 633–663.

Cooren, F., Kuhn, T., Cornelissen, J. P., & Clark, T. (2011). Communication, organizing and organization: An overview and introduction to the special issue. *Organization Studies, 32*(9), 1149–1170.

Creswell, J. W. (2003). *Research design: Qualitative, quantitative, and mixed methods approaches.* Thousand Oaks, CA: Sage.

Donnellon, A. (1996). *Team talk: The power of language in team dynamics.* Boston, MA: Harvard Business School Press.

Dyer, J. H., Gregersen, H. B., & Christensen, C. (2008). Entrepreneur behaviors, opportunity recognition, and the origins of innovative ventures. *Strategic Entrepreneurship Journal, 2*(4), 317–338.

Eisenhardt, K. M., & Graebner, M. E. (2007). Theory building from cases: Opportunities and challenges. *Academy of Management Journal, 50*(1), 25–32.

Garfinkel, H. (1948 / 2006). *Seeing sociologically: The routine grounds of social action.* Boulder, CO: Paradigm.

Garfinkel, H. (2002). *Ethnomethodology's program: Working out Durkheim's aphorism.* New York, NY: Rowman and Littlefield.

Gibb, A. A. (1996). Entrepreneurship and small business management: Can we afford to neglect them in the twenty-first century business school? *British Journal of Management, 7*(4), 309–324.

Glaser, B. G., & Strauss, A. L. (2009). *The discovery of grounded theory: Strategies for qualitative research.* NJ: Transaction Publishers.

Goffman, E. (1956). *The presentation of self in everyday life.* Edinburgh: University of Edinburgh SSRC.

Goffman, E. (1974). *Frame analysis: An essay on the organization of experience.* Boston, MA: Harvard University Press.

Goodwin, C. (1995). Seeing in depth. *Social Studies of Science, 25*(2), 237–274.

Heritage, J. (1984). *Garfinkel and ethnomethodology.* Cambridge: Polity Press.

Heritage, J., & Clayman, S. (2010). *Talk in action: Interactions, identities, and institutions.*

Hopper, R. (1992). *Telephone conversation.* Indiana University Press.

Hutchby, I. (2001). Technologies, texts and affordances. *Sociology, 35*(2), 441–456.

Hutchby, I. (2006). *Media talk: Conversation analysis and the study of broadcasting.* Maidenhead: Open University Press.

Hutchby, I., & Barnett, S. (2005). Aspects of the sequential organization of mobile phone conversation. *Discourse Studies, 7*(2), 147–171.

Johannisson, B. (2011). Towards a practice theory of entrepreneuring. *Small Business Economics, 36*(2), 135–150.

Lazear, E. P. (2004). Balanced skills and entrepreneurship. *The American Economic Review, 24*(2), 208–211.

Levinson, S. (2005). Living with Manny's dangerous idea. *Discourse Studies, 7*(4–5), 431–453.

Licoppe, C., & Morel, J. (2012). Video-in-interaction: "Talking heads" and the multimodal organization of mobile and skype video calls. *Research on Language and Social Interaction, 45*(4), 399–429.

Lundell, K. (2009). The design and scripting of unscripted talk: Liveness versus control in a TV broadcast interview. *Media, Culture & Society, 31*(2), 271–288.

Maynard, D. (1988). Language, interaction, and social problems. *Social Problems, 35*(4), 311–334.

Miles, M., & Huberman, M. (1994). *Qualitative data analysis: An expanded sourcebook.* Thousand Oaks, CA: Sage.

Mondada, L. (2007). Operating together through videoconference: Members' procedures for accomplishing a common space of action. In S. Hester & D. Francis (Eds.), *Orders of ordinary action* (pp. 51–67). Aldershot: Ashgate.

Morse, J. M. (2003). Principles of mixed methods and multimethod research design. In A. Tashakkori & C. Teddlie (Eds.), *Handbook of mixed methods in social and behavioral research* (pp. 189–208). Sage.

Nevile, M. (2004). *Beyond the black box: Talk-in-interaction in the airline cockpit.* New York, NY: Ashgate Publishing, Ltd.

Nicolini, D. (2009). Zooming in and zooming out: A package of method and theory to study work practices. In S. Ybema, D. Yanow & H. Wels (Eds.), *Organizational ethnography: studying the complexity of everyday life.* Sage.

Nicolini, D. (2017). Is small the only beautiful? In A. Hui, T. Schatzki & E. Shove (Eds.), *The nexus of practices: Connections, constellations, practitioners.* New York, NY: Routledge.

Psathas, G. (1990). *Interaction competence* (Vol. 1). University Press of America.

Reis, E. (2011). *The lean startup.* New York, NY: Crown Business.

Rock, A. (1987, November). Strategy vs. tactics from a venture capitalist. *Harvard Business Review*, 63–67.

Sacks, H., Schegloff, E. A., & Jefferson, G. (1974). A simplest systematics for the organization of turn-taking for conversation. *Language, 50*(4), 696–735.

Shane, S. (2008). *The illusions of entrepreneurship.* New Heaven, CT: Yale Univeristy Press.

Stevenson, H. H. (1983). *Who are the harvard self-employed.* Paper presented at the Frontiers of entrepreneurship research: Proceedings of the annual Babson College Entrepreneurship Research Conference, Wellesley, MA.

Steyaert, C. (2007). Entrepreneuring as a conceptual attractor? A review of process theories in 20 years of entrepreneurship studies. *Entrepreneurship and Regional Development, 19*(6), 453–477.

Strauss, A. L., & Corbin, J. (1990). *Basics of qualitative research: Grounded theory procedures and techniques.* Newbury Park, CA: Sage.

Tashakkori, A., & Teddie, C. (Eds.). (2003). *Handbook of mixed methods in social and behavioral research.* Sage.

Timmons, J. A. (1994). *New venture creation: Entrepreneurship for the 21st Century* (4th ed.). Burr Ridge: Irwin Press.

Watson, T. J. (2013). Entrepreneurship in action: Bringing together the individual, organizational and institutional dimensions of entrepreneurial action. *Entrepreneurship and Regional Development, 25*(5–6), 1–19.

Wolcott, H. F. (1994). *Transforming qualitative data: Description, analysis, and interpretation.* London: Sage.

Zimmerman, D. (2005). Introduction: Conversation analysis and social problems. *Social Problems, 52*(4), 445–448.

# 2

# ENTREPRENEURIAL PRACTICE AS AN INTERACTIONAL CONCERN

What do entrepreneurs do? How do entrepreneurial teams accomplish their shared goals of creating new ventures and validating innovative products? Scholars have traditionally tried to answer these questions by examining the intrapersonal traits of individual founders (such as risk-taking propensity or confidence) or the impersonal elements surrounding the team (such as network diversity or access to resources). Such studies often sought to find fixed features that would differentiate entrepreneurs from non-entrepreneurs.

Increasingly, studies of entrepreneurship have been embracing more dynamic concerns. Some scholars have been exploring theories of effectuation and argue that entrepreneurial teams apply knowledge and control, rather than analysis and prediction, to contend with uncertainties (Sarasvathy, 2001). Effectual views of entrepreneurial organizing and innovating are oriented around the ways in which a founder's logic drives his or her ability to focus on means rather than ends and transform surprises into assets (Wiltbank, Read, Dew, & Sarasvathy, 2009, p. 119).

Other scholars, also interested in issues of agency, have adopted a practice-based view of entrepreneurial work. Research in this vein seeks to understand the ways in which layers of interactions construct and reconstruct companies, products, markets, and the entrepreneurial ecosystem. In other words, this body of research is redefining entrepreneurial work as a set of actions and interactions instead of a type of logic (Johannisson, 2011; Goss et al., 2011; Steyaert, 2007; Watson, 2013). This chapter explores what practice theory is, why practice theory is important to entrepreneurship research, and how practices can be investigated using the ethnomethodological approach of Conversation Analysis.

## Practice basics

Practice theory recognizes the interdependent and context-creating connections between macro- and micro-phenomena in entrepreneurial work (Cicourel &

Knorr-Cetina, 1981). Drawing on the works of Schatzki (2006), Feldman and Orlikowski (2011), Weick et al. (2005), and others, a practice-based view of entrepreneurial work suggests that individuals are both acting in a context and on that context at all times. Because these actions have been established and reinforced over time, they are understood by others. However, actions also are spontaneous and contribute to the co-creation of the current context as it is unfolding. People always are working together to co-create their world "for another first time" (Garfinkel, Lynch, & Livingston, 1981).

Rather than focusing on the internal dimensions or the external circumstances of a person or team, practice theory views work as the result of the dynamic and enduring presence of both. It frames work as situated and socially constructed through an ongoing and interdependent connection between people, environments, activities, and communities (Lave & Wenger, 2003). It probes the connections between organizations, the activities of organizing, and the efforts of the people engaging in the work of organizations and organizing. It also embraces the inherent complexity that is implied by the interdependencies between human and non-human forms of agency (Carlile, Nicolini, Langley, & Tsoukas, 2013; Latour, 2005). Consequently, the study of practices is always an investigation of relationships (e.g., between people, places, objects, and other matters) over time.

The commonplace actions and interactions that enable people to accomplish their work are the building blocks that construct social achievements and organizations (Miettinen, Samra-Fredericks, & Yanow, 2009). Yet a practice approach does more than describe these activities. It views actions and interactions through a performative lens and offers new explanations for what entrepreneurial work is and how entrepreneurial work is accomplished.

Only by actively probing the intimate and idiosyncratic practices of teams at work can scholars develop authentic and comprehensive theories about innovation and entrepreneurship (Anderson & Starnawska, 2008). Although the social world is too complex to ever be fully captured in a single study, meaningful research must embrace the complexity of entrepreneurial work rather than ignore it (Watson, 2013). This, of course, requires theoretical framing and methodological approaches that allow scholars to attend to the details of innovative and entrepreneurial work as it emerges and as it is done by real people in real contexts over time (Johannisson, 2011).

## The move toward practice-based studies

Scholars have long recognized the lack of good theory in the field of entrepreneurship (Zahra, 2007). While the reasons for that are many, chief among them are the artificial focus of the studies, the quantitative orientation of the studies, and the neglected perspective of the entrepreneurs.

Traditionally, the entrepreneurship literature has emphasized static qualities; the intrapersonal traits of the individual entrepreneur rather than the interpersonal (or inter-actor) dynamics, and the characteristics of an entrepreneur's network rather than the relational processes (Johannisson, forthcoming). Even articles attending to a complex construct such as "context" tend to narrow their focus to an isolated factor (Welter, 2011). While such a reductionist approach may make an article easier for readers to grasp, it does not advance our understanding of the actual ways that entrepreneurs accomplish their real work in context. Moreover, it does nothing to close the gap between theory and practice.

Historically, researchers interested in entrepreneurship would conduct quantitative studies. This approach may have been selected to create a legitimate place for entrepreneurship research within the business literature, which is dominated by quantitative studies. However, quantitative methodologies do not lend themselves to capturing the emergent and situated aspects of entrepreneurial work. Such studies lose the actual detail of entrepreneurial work as it happens and say little about the ordinary actions of entrepreneurs (Steyaert & Landstrom, 2011).

Researchers interested in entrepreneurship as practice then turned toward classical qualitative methods such as interviews and observation to try to get closer to the authentic everyday experiences of entrepreneurs. While these efforts are able to highlight the human role(s) and the pervasive uncertainties in entrepreneurial work, they are handicapped by the typical challenges found in qualitative studies: entrepreneurs can misremember their situations in interviews or rationalize their experiences to look more competent, and researchers frame their observations in the interpretive terms of the analyst rather than the terms of the entrepreneur.

Some researchers have advocated an embedded approach to studying the practices of entrepreneurial teams. This kind of "enactive research" requires the analyst to start a venture (Johannisson, 2011). In doing so, s/he can study the ordinary processes and practices as they are experienced, reflect upon the experiences, and report on the experiences through scholarly channels. While this is one way to attend to the dynamic and interdependent aspects of entrepreneurial work in an unmediated way, it is not the only way to uncover the means by which entrepreneurs actually understand their circumstances in real time and collaboratively (re)create them through their situated practical actions. Studies can achieve a holistic sensitivity to the mundane details of entrepreneurial work by drawing on highly detailed forms of empiricism such as those found in the ethnomethodological traditions of Conversation Analysis (CA).

## Heeding the texts and contexts of entrepreneurs

Ethnomethodology is the study of the ordinary means by which people understand, maintain, and evolve social order in their everyday affairs. While not a formal theory of practice, ethnomethodology sets forth a research orientation that attends to the empirical study of practical activities, contexts, and meaning-making (Garfinkel, 1967). It investigates practices as the situated accomplishments of knowledgeable actors in order to produce accounts of the ordinary methods by which these actors (re)produce their context and goals.

With a nod to Garfinkel (Garfinkel, 1967), Nicolini connects studies of practice with four core aspects of ethnomethodological inquiries: accountability, reflexivity, indexicality, and membership (Nicolini, 2012). Accountability encapsulates the concept of the constitutive and reportable nature of everyday activities. All interactions are orderly, and this order is observable in the interactions themselves – both in real time to the participants and later to the analyst. This order also is situated and intelligible to people in a particular context.

Accounts are situated and intelligible, in part, because they are reflexive. In ethnomethodological research, reflexivity is not about the behavior of the analyst. Instead it indicates the process by which participants interpret actions in real time and respond accordingly. Each utterance or gesture will convey meaning in a given context, and people will aim to respond appropriately. Thus actions and interactions reflexively build one on another.

As participants interact, utterances and gestures can only make sense within that context and are therefore indexical. Heritage (Heritage, 2018), for example, writes of the context-dependent nature of "oh". While starting a turn of conversation with "oh" might generally signal a change of state, the specific meaning (is the speaker of "oh" reacting to new information presented by another speaker, is s/he suddenly remembering something important to say, etc.) can be determined only in context.

Membership in ethnomethodology relates to the competent participation in shared activities. It is indicating the language and methods that participants (members) use to adequately function within a particular context.

The observable interactional order that is inherent in an ethnomethodological approach eventually led to the micro-analysis of interaction: to Conversation Analysis (CA). Drawing on the sociological work of Garfinkel, Goffman, Jefferson, Sacks, and Schegloff, CA is a data-driven approach to studying the social world as it is co-constructed in real time and in context by participants (Garfinkel, 1948/2006; Garfinkel & Sacks, 1970; Sacks, Schegloff, & Jefferson, 1974). By micro-analyzing each utterance in a naturally occurring conversational sequence, researchers can recognize the verbal means by which participants come to understand each other and their shared context. The analyst's every assertion is based on the situated meanings constructed by the participants in the course of authentically doing their work. CA work is guided by the essential questions raised by Schegloff – "Whose text? Whose context?" – and the answer must always be the entrepreneur's, not the analyst's (Schegloff, 1997). This ethnomethodologically inspired distance inherent in CA allows researchers to theorize about practice by carefully analyzing the routine ways that practitioners make sense of and advance their work in action.

While it is sometimes confused with other qualitative approaches such as discourse analysis and content analysis, CA does not impose pre-existing categories of interest onto the data. Instead, it seeks to describe the local mechanisms by which participants co-create meaning and accomplish shared goals (Psathas, 1995a). For example, a study might investigate how founders *do* social status within their situated interactions; it would not adopt predefined role structures (male, leader, technologist, etc.) to frame the inquiry or analysis. According to Garfinkel, "the methods essential to work (and organization) will be found in details of attention and mutually oriented methods of work, and ordered properties of mutual action" rather than from externally imposed categories and codes (Rawls, 2008, p. 702).

Because conversation is both context shaping and context renewing (Drew & Heritage, 1992), CA can investigate the situated means by which participants create, maintain, and change shared context. Participants can only understand an utterance based on preceding utterances. In that way, all interactions reveal the situated understandings that allow participants to do their shared work. Simultaneously, every utterance provides the foundation for future meanings and the next utterance. In other words, every utterance maintains, alters, or establishes the context in which the participants are acting.

This double connection between individual utterances and greater context(s) means that CA studies can link the micro-details of interactions with macro contexts of activities, organizations, and wider communities (Drew & Heritage, 1992). Moreover, CA analysts interested in practice recognize that, turn by turn and conversation by conversation, the interactions between participants are organizing their specific context (e.g., new ventures) which in turn influences and is influenced by macro concerns (e.g., accelerator cultures, entrepreneurial identities). They are not arguing that interaction singularly determines every other aspect of social phenomena (Schegloff, 2005), only that the micro-details of founders' conversations provide a valuable window into the means by which the micro and macro elements of entrepreneurial work are linked.

## Conscious participants actively (re)creating context

CA considers the participants in any social activity to be knowledgeable about and aware of their specific environment. Through their interactions they make their understanding recognizable to others through the accountability and indexicality of their contributions to a conversation. Every utterance demonstrates how participants understand other speakers, their roles within the conversation, and their roles beyond the conversation. The moment-by-moment construction of a conversation is observable evidence of each participant's intersubjective understanding of a tasks, identities, and goals. Moreover, this observable evidence is apparent to participants in real time, and understandings between participants are repaired, renewed, and replaced over time through additional interactions.

CA research investigates many interactional elements, including repairs of misunderstandings (Schegloff, Jefferson, & Sacks, 1977), the allocation of turns (Duncan, 1974; Jefferson, 1973; Sacks et al., 1974; Schegloff, 2000), and boundary rituals (Schegloff & Sacks, 1973; Tsui, 1989), among others. Sequence order (Schegloff, 2007), in particular, has emerged as the essential "engine room" of interaction (Heritage, 2005). It is the means by which activities and tasks central to the conversation are managed and the means by which interactional identities (e.g., provider of news, listener, partner in celebration) and general social identities (e.g., entrepreneur, woman, millennial) are established, maintained, and revised (Schegloff, 1992, 2007). In other words, the careful attention to the sequential order of interaction enables researchers to link verbal exchanges with meta-concerns including the organizing of a new venture, the development of a product, or the nature of being a member of a particular profession.

CA allows researchers to transcend the shortcomings typically found in studies of entrepreneurship. Because CA attends to issues of context as they are understood and created by participants, it allows researchers to attend to the authentic practices of entrepreneurs in action. It is a richly detailed form of qualitative research which eliminates the detached findings of quantitative research. Simultaneously it can go beyond the limitations of traditional qualitative methods such as interviews which produce only edited frontstage presentations of select features of work, not the real action that occurs backstage (Alvesson, 2003; P. Atkinson & Silverman, 1997).

In addition, CA attends to context in terms of "texts" – material representations of a team's collective identity and shared intentions that guide the ongoing actions and interactions of a team (Cooren & Taylor, 1997; Taylor & Van Every, 2011). Conversations create texts; conversations are influenced by texts; and the organization emerges and evolves through this cycle of authorship. A text, of course, need not be a written document. It can be a technological prototype, an entrepreneurial team's emerging product. Because the emergence and existence of an innovative entrepreneurial organization is tightly coupled with the creation of its innovative product, the interplay between the invention (the "text") and the venture (the "organization") and the context in which the team operates are all interdependent and dynamic. By adopting a CA approach, researchers are able to investigate these aspects of entrepreneurship as practice. They can, for example, empirically express how an entrepreneurial team talks an innovation and a venture into being (Heritage, 1984).

## Authentic data captured through recordings

CA studies can be done only with recorded data. Because the recordings enable researchers to return to the naturally occurring conversations exactly as they happened, researchers can render more accurate transcriptions and provide better descriptions than they could with field notes alone. Once transcribed, the data is treated with special forms of notation intended to convey as much information as possible about the timing and tonality of the utterances in sequence (Jefferson, 1984).

The means by which recordings are captured is changing. By empowering teams to record themselves, this book acknowledges a major cultural trend: the rise of participatory data capture as evidenced by self-recorded videos and selfie photographs (Burgess & Green, 2013; Senft & Baym, 2015). This approach to data collection is aligned with the mores of contemporary technology use (Senft & Baym, 2015; Turkle, 2011) and embraces popular technologies and applications (Chalfen, 2014). Using self-recording technologies can enable researchers to capture more data and more intimate data than would otherwise be possible. For example, the teams engaged in the contest could meet spontaneously and sometimes at the same time as other teams. Only by enabling the teams to capture their own data was the comparative research accomplished. Similarly, because no researcher is present when the recording takes place, teams might be able to interact more naturally.

Of course, in addition to the potential benefits, embracing self-recording technologies may introduce new complexities into data collection and analysis (Chalfen, 2014). As more data files are captured, additional storage will be required to keep the data. This influx of data may also require new tools for the analysis of qualitative data. Similarly, the newfound intimacy of the collected data may influence the way researchers think about and ensure privacy and anonymity of research subjects.

## New twists in CA

While CA is a qualitative form of investigating practice, it has been combined with quantitative methods to compare conversational moves with demographic attributes and social outcomes. To avoid compromising the situated details of the CA work, the coding necessary for quantification can occur as an independent second-stage analysis of the data (Johnson & Christensen, 2004). CA followed by quantitative coding can enable the identification of features in the data that would remain otherwise opaque, pointing out new terrain worthy of description (Morse, 2003, p. 192; Tashakkori & Teddie, 2003, p. 230). Incorporating quantitative methods as a complementary means of description also makes the qualitative findings more accessible to readers unaccustomed to CA (Creswell, 2003, p. 23), inviting more people with a diversity of understandings into the conversation about the research and its meanings for theory and practice.

The quantitative aspects of a nested research design also helps to guard against missed patterns in the qualitative data. Alternative interpretations or trends within the qualitative data are easy to miss. By looking at the data through a quantitative lens, researchers can reconsider the impressions that had formed from the qualitative engagement with the data. In this way, the coding can inspire a kind of reflection on the qualitative work.

A pioneering use of this approach compared teams that were engaged in an adventure race (a competition that requires teams to navigate an unmarked wilderness course over several days). By blending Conversation Analysis with a grounded coding of utterances, Wilson was able to compare the verbal sensemaking practices of successful and unsuccessful racing teams (Wilson, 2007). The code book in studies such as this tends to incorporate the macro-level sensemaking language cues of information exchange, meaning ascription, and action formulation from the literature (Thomas, Clark, & Gioia, 1993). Descriptive codes built from the grounded analysis of the utterances are associated with these categories.

Even without a nested approach and quantified codes, CA can expose how people, in similar circumstances, tend to accomplish things together. As Sacks has claimed: "detailed study of small phenomena may give an enormous understanding of the way humans do things and the kinds of objects they use to construct and order their affairs" (Sacks, 1984a, p. 299). By focusing on an activity setting that is representative of a kind of work and a naturally occurring interaction that contributes to the achievement of that work, researchers can describe the verbal means and ordered interactions required to do that work. Consequently, these studies present a description of the verbal "machinery" that a particular shared profession's interactions require (Sacks, 1984a) – a description that is both intensely situated and transcendent of a given case (Sacks et al., 1974; Schegloff, 1987). Such studies can challenge and correct assumptions about practice (e.g., Ruusuvuori's [2000] study on interactions in medical consultations); offer additional detail about practice (e.g., Peräkylä's [1995] study on questions in AIDS counseling); and identify additional practices or improve the description of known practices (e.g., Vehviläinen's [2001] study on advice giving in educational counseling).

## Workplace interaction

CA has been used in various professional activity settings to investigate how work is verbally achieved. Studies have been conducted in courtrooms (J. Atkinson & Drew, 1979), medical offices (Heritage & Maynard, 2006), airplane cockpits (Nevile, 2004a; Sexton & Helmreich, 2000), and military settings (Nevile, 2009), among other workplaces where participants are focused on a shared goal relevant to a professional setting (Arminen, 2005). Some studies have been able to empirically connect particular conversational moves with wider social and professional concerns (Ainsworth-Vaughn, 1992; Antaki, 2011; Goodwin & Heritage, 1990; Stokoe, 2006). Using a CA approach, some studies have been able to link conversational moves with outcomes such as landing an airplane (Nevile, 2004b) and receiving a prescription for antibiotics (Stivers, 2007).

Scholars have argued that the study of naturally occurring workplace conversations can reveal the verbal competencies required to participate in particular professions (Psathas, 1990). To paraphrase Psathas, the "interactional competencies" that are essential to performing in a given profession can be discovered and can inform teaching methods and materials designed to prepare individuals who work in or want to work in such professions (Psathas, 1990, p. 21). These critical conversational moves can constitute part of a professional identity – part of what it means to be recognized as a competent doctor, an airline pilot, or at trial lawyer, for example (Drew & Sorjonen, 1997; Heritage, 1984; Nevile, 2004a). These conversational moves reveal how people verbally "do being" a member of a particular group (Sacks, 1984a, 1984b). In some contexts, the assembly of these situated conversational moves forms a unique "fingerprint" for a given profession (Heritage & Clayman, 2010). For example, a conversation in a private room in a medical building is immediately recognizable as a doctor-patient interaction and not a job interview or pharmaceutical sales meeting because of its structural features (Llewellyn & Pence, 2009).

## Importing CA into studies of entrepreneurship

Rarely has CA been used in studies of entrepreneurship. When it is used, it tends to be in studies of pitches (Chalmers & Shaw, 2017), not in intra-team private workplace interactions. However, some researchers have called for a need to gather real-time data for analysis (Davidsson & Wiklund, 2001). Only by studying events as they happen can researchers eliminate concerns such as memory errors and hindsight biases connected with qualitative data based on retrospective accounts. While other approaches also aim to capture the real-time experiences of entrepreneurs in-action (Dew, Read, Sarasvathy, & Wiltbank, 2009; Perry, Gaylen, & Markova, 2012), CA is uniquely connected to the data as it is produced and understood by the participants (ten Have, 2007). Its aim is to go beyond the investigatory reach of other forms of formal analysis and ask "what more" can be discovered about a context by considering the details of its situated interactions (Garfinkel, 2002).

Of course CA, like every other research approach, has its limitations. To conduct CA research, the analyst must have what Garfinkel called "unique adequacy" (Garfinkel & Wieder, 1992). This essentially means that the analyst must have a practitioner's depth of understanding of the tasks and context. In many public settings, such as riding a bus or ordering at a restaurant, most researchers would meet the unique adequacy requirement. However, in specialized workplace settings – such as entrepreneurial work – only analysts who have authentic experience in the same setting can be considered close enough to the context to meet the requirement (Rawls, 2002). In my case, because I have been a founder of high-tech ventures with English-speaking team mates in an American culture, I can claim unique adequacy for such studies. However, I cannot claim unique adequacy for service ventures with Spanish-speaking teams in Cuba. This requirement means that few analysts can embrace ethnomethodology in general and CA in particular to study entrepreneurial practices.

Another limitation is highlighted by Nicolini (2012): the relevance of CA to studies of practice can be hampered by its tight focus on the verbal machinery of interaction. Practices, of course, are constituted through layers of interactions, not just of verbal exchanges between speakers. Because CA studies hone in exclusively on language, they cannot capture the full set of interactional complexities that will be present in a given context. Nevertheless, CA studies can be part of a toolkit for studying practice; they offer a "zoomed in" perspective that can be fortified with a "zoomed out" perspective (Nicolini, 2009).

Despite these limitations, ethnomethodologically informed CA studies, even on their own, provide a rare and empirically rich viewpoint on the practices of entrepreneurial work. Looking at entrepreneurial work through this lens enables scholars to offer more insightful theories about the authentic and routine activities that are essential to the creation of new products and new ventures. It enables them to close the gap between theoretical work and entrepreneurial practice. And it can point the way to new and as of yet unexplored aspects of the relational nature of entrepreneurial work that are worthy of investigation.

While there is much more to say about entrepreneurship as practice, this chapter has presented entrepreneurial work as an activity that is (re)produced interpersonally and communally, as an activity situated in practices that are shared, embodied, and enacted. It has also highlighted the ethnomethodological approach of CA that can enable scholars to attend to the dynamic actions and interactions that enable entrepreneurial teams to accomplish their shared goals (Cicourel & Knorr-Cetina, 1981; Goffman, 1964; Psathas, 1995b).

# References

Ainsworth-Vaughn, N. (1992). Topic transitions in physician-patient interviews: Power, gender, and discourse change. *Language in Society, 21*(3), 409–426.

Alvesson, M. (2003). Beyond neopositivists, romantics, and localists: A reflexive approach to interviews in organizational research. *Academy of Management Review, 28*(1), 13–33.

Anderson, A. R., & Starnawska, M. (2008). Research practices in entrepreneurship problems of definition, description and meaning. *International Journal of Entrepreneurship and Innovation, 9*, 221–230.

Antaki, C. (Ed.). (2011). *Applied conversation analysis: Intervention and change in institutional talk.* New York, NY: Palgrave Macmillon.

Arminen, I. (2005). *Institutional interaction: Studies of talk at work* (Vol. 2). New York, NY: Ashgate Publishing, Ltd.

Atkinson, J., & Drew, P. (1979). *Order in court: The organisation of verbal interaction in judicial settings.* Atlantic Highlands, NJ: Humanities Press.

Atkinson, P., & Silverman, D. (1997). Kundera's immortality: The interview society and the invention of the self. *Qualitative Inquiry, 3*(3), 304–325.

Burgess, J., & Green, J. (2013). *YouTube: Online video and participatory culture.* Malden, MA: Polity Press.

Carlile, P. R., Nicolini, D., Langley, A., & Tsoukas, H. (Eds.). (2013). *How matter matters: Objects, artifacts, and materiality in organization studies.* Oxford: Oxford University Press.

Chalfen, R. (2014). "Your panopticon or mine?" Incorporating wearable technology's Glass and GoPro into visual social science. *Visual Studies, 29*(3), 299–231.

Chalmers, D., & Shaw, E. (2017). The endogenous construction of entrepreneurial contexts: A practice-based perspective. *International Small Business Journal, 19–39*(1), 19–39.

Cicourel, A. V., & Knorr-Cetina, K. D. (Eds.). (1981). *Advances in social theory and methodology: Toward an integration of micro-and macro-sociologies.* Boston: Routledge & Kegan Paul.

Cooren, F., & Taylor, J. R. (1997). Organization as an effect of mediation: Redefining the link between organization and communication. *Communication Theory, 7*(3), 219–260.

Creswell, J. W. (2003). *Research design: Qualitative, quantitative, and mixed methods approaches.* Thousand Oaks, CA: Sage.

Davidsson, P., & Wiklund, J. (2001). Levels of analysis in entrepreneurship research: Current research practice and suggestions for the future. *Entrepreneurship Theory and Practice, 25*(4), 81–99.

Dew, N., Read, S., Sarasvathy, S. D., & Wiltbank, R. (2009). Effectual versus predictive logics in entrepreneurial decision-making: Differences between experts and novices. *Journal of Business Venturing, 24*(4), 287–309.

Drew, P., & Heritage, J. (Eds.). (1992). *Talk at work: Interaction in institutional settings.* Cambridge: Cambridge University Press.

Drew, P., & Sorjonen, M. L. (1997). Institutional dialogue. In T. A. Van Dijk (Ed.), *Discourse as social interaction: Discourse studies: A multidisciplinary introduction* (Vol. 2, pp. 92–118). London: Sage.

Duncan, S. (1974). On the structure of speaker-auditor interaction during speaking turns. *Language in Society, 3*(2), 161–180.

Feldman, M., & Orlikowski, W. (2011). Theorizing practice and practicing theory. *Organization Science*, 22(5), 1240–1253.

Garfinkel, H. (1948 / 2006). *Seeing sociologically: The routine grounds of social action.* Boulder, CO: Paradigm.

Garfinkel, H. (1967). *Studies in ethnomethodology.* Englewood Cliffs, NJ: Prentice-Hall.

Garfinkel, H. (2002). *Ethnomethodology's program: Working out Durkheim's aphorism.* New York, NY: Rowman and Littlefield.

Garfinkel, H., Lynch, M., & Livingston, E. (1981). The work of a discovering science construed with materials from the optically discovered pulsar. *Philosophy of the Social Sciences*, *11*, 131–158.

Garfinkel, H., & Sacks, H. (1970). On formal structures of practical actions. In J. C. McKinney & E. A. Tiryakian (Eds.), *Theoretical sociology: Perspectives and developments* (pp. 337–366). New York, NY: Appleton-Century-Crofts.

Garfinkel, H., & Wieder, D. (1992). Two incommensurable, asymmetrically alternate technologies of social analysis. In G. Watson & R. Seiler (Eds.), *Text in context: Contributions to ethnomethodology.* Newbury Park, CA: Sage.

Goffman, E. (1964). The neglected situation. *American Anthropologist*, *66*(6), 133–136.

Goodwin, C., & Heritage, J. (1990). Conversation analysis. *Annual Review of Anthropology*, *19*, 283–307.

Goss, D., Jones, R., Latham, J., & Betta M. (2011). Power as practice: A micro-sociological analysis of the dynamics of emancipatory entrepreneurship. *Organization Studies*, *32*(2), 211–229.

Heritage, J. (1984). *Garfinkel and ethnomethodology.* Cambridge: Polity Press.

Heritage, J. (2005). Conversation analysis and institutional talk. In K. L. Fitch & R. E. Sanders (Eds.), *Handbook of language and social interaction* (pp. 103–147). Mahwah, NJ: Lawrence Erlbaum Associates.

Heritage, J. (2018). The ubiquity of epistemics: A rebuttal to the "Epistemics of epistemics" group. *Discourse Studies*, *20*(1), 14–56.

Heritage, J., & Clayman, S. (2010). *Talk in action: Interactions, identities, and institutions.* West Sussex, UK: Wiley-Blackwell.

Heritage, J., & Maynard, D. (2006). *Communication in medical care.* New York, NY: Cambridge University Press.

Jefferson, G. (1973). A case of precision timing in ordinary conversation: Overlapped tag-positioned address terms in closing sequences. *Semiotica*, *9*(1), 47–96.

Jefferson, G. (1984). Transcript notation. In J. Heritage (Ed.), *Structures of social interaction.* New York, NY: Cambridge University Press.

Johannisson, B. (2011). Towards a practice theory of entrepreneuring. *Small Business Economics*, *36*(2), 135–150.

Johannisson, B. (forthcoming). Searching for the roots of entrepreneuring as practice – introducing the enactive approach. In W. B. Gartner & B. Teague (Eds.), *Research handbook of entrepreneurial behavior, process, and practice.* Northampton, MA: Edward Elgar.

Johnson, R. B., & Christensen, L. B. (2004). *Educational research: Quantitative, qualitative, and mixed approaches.* Boston, MA: Allyn and Bacon.

Latour, B. (2005). *Reassembling the social: An introduction to actor-network-theory.* Oxford: Oxford University Press.

Lave, J., & Wenger, E. (2003). Practice, person, social world. In H. Daniels (Ed.), *An introduction to Vygotsky* (pp. 149–156). London: Routledge.

Llewellyn, N., & Pence, L. (2009). Practice as a members' phenomenon. *Organization Studies*, *30*(12), 1419–1439.

Miettinen, R., Samra-Fredericks, D., & Yanow, D. (2009). Re-turn to practice: An introductory essay. *Organization Studies, 30*(12), 1309–1327.

Morse, J. M. (2003). Principles of mixed methods and multimethod research design. In A. Tashakkori & C. Teddlie (Eds.), *Handbook of mixed methods in social and behavioral research* (pp. 189–208). Sage.

Nevile, M. (2004a). *Beyond the black box: Talk-in-interaction in the airline cockpit.* New York, NY: Ashgate Publishing, Ltd.

Nevile, M. (2004b). Integrity in the airline cockpit: Embodying claims about progress for the conduct of an approach briefing. *Research on Language & Social Interaction, 37*(4), 447–480.

Nevile, M. (2009). "You are well clear of friendlies": Diagnostic error and cooperative work in an iraq war friendly fire incident. *Computer Supported Cooperative Work, 18*(2–3), 147–173.

Nicolini, D. (2009). Zooming in and out: Studying practices by switching theoretical lenses and trailing connections. *Organization Studies, 30*(12), 1391–1418.

Nicolini, D. (2012). *Practice theory, work, and organization: An introduction.* Oxford: Oxford University Press.

Peräkylä, A. (1995). *AIDS counselling: Institutional interaction and clinical practice.* Cambridge: Cambridge University Press.

Perry, J. T., Gaylen, C., & Markova, G. (2012). Entrepreneurial effectuation: A review and suggestions for future research. *Entrepreneurship Theory and Practice, 36*(4), 837–861.

Psathas, G. (1990). *Interaction competence* (Vol. 1). University Press of America.

Psathas, G. (1995a). *Conversation analysis: The study of talk in interaction.* Thousand Oaks, CA: Sage Publications.

Psathas, G. (1995b). "Talk and Social Structure" and "Studies of Work". *Human Studies, Ethnomethodology: Discussions and Contributions, 18*(2–3), 139–155.

Rawls, A. W. (2002). Editor's introduction. In A. W. Rawls (Ed.), *Ethnomethodology's program: Working out Durkheim's aphorism.* New York: Rowman & Littlefield Publishers.

Rawls, A. W. (2008). Harold Garfinkel, ethnomethodology and workplace studies. *Organization Studies, 29*(5), 701–732.

Ruusuvuori, J. (2000). *Control in the medical consultation: Practices of giving and receiving the reason for the visit in primary health care.* Tampere: Tampere University Press.

Sacks, H. (1984a). Notes on Methodology. In J. M. Atkinsen & J. Heritage (Eds.), Structures of social action: Studies in conversation analysis. Cambridge: Cambrige University Press.

Sacks, H. (1984b). On doing "Being ordinary". In J. M. Atkinsen & J. Heritage (Eds.), Structures of social action: Studies in conversational analysis (pp. 413–429). Cambridge: Cambrige University Press.

Sacks, H., Schegloff, E. A., & Jefferson, G. (1974). A simplest systematics for the organization of turn-taking for conversation. *Language, 50*(4), 696–735.

Sarasvathy, S. D. (2001). Causation and effectuation: Toward a theoretical shift from economic inevitability to entrepreneurial contingency. *Academy of Management Review, 26*(2), 243–263.

Schatzki, T. (2006). On organizations as they happen. *Organization Studies, 27*(12), 1863–1873.

Schegloff, E. A. (1987). Between micro and macro: Contexts and other connections. In J. C. Alexander (Ed.), The micro-macro link (pp. 207–234). CA: University of California Press.

Schegloff, E. A. (1992). Repair after next turn: The last structurally provided defense of intersubjectivity in conversation. *American Journal of Sociology, 97*(5), 1295–1345.

Schegloff, E. A. (1997). Whose text? Whose context? *Discourse & Society, 8*(2), 165–187.

Schegloff, E. A. (2000). Overlapping talk and the organization of turn-taking for conversation. *Language in Society, 29*(1), 1–63.

Schegloff, E. A. (2005). On integrity in inquiry . . . of the investigated, not the investigator. *Discourse Studies, 7*(4–5), 455–480.

Schegloff, E. A. (2007). *Sequence organization in interaction: A primer in conversation analysis* (Vol. 1). Cambridge: Cambridge University Press.

Schegloff, E. A., Jefferson, G., & Sacks, H. (1977). The preference for self-correction in the organisation of repair in conversation. *Language, 53*, 361–382.

Schegloff, E. A., & Sacks, H. (1973). Opening up closings. *Semiotica, 8*(4), 289–327.

Senft, T., & Baym, N. (2015). Selfies introduction: What does the selfie say? Investigating a global phenomenon. *International Journal of Communication, 9*(19), 1588–1606.

Sexton, J. B., & Helmreich, R. L. (2000). Analyzing cockpit communication: The links between language, performance, error, and workload. *Human Performance in Extreme Environments, 5*(1), 63–68.

Steyaert, C. (2007). Of course that is not the whole (toy) story: Entrepreneurship and the cat's cradle. *Journal of Business Venturing, 22*(2): 733–751.

Steyaert, C., & Landstrom, H. (2011). Enacting entrepreneurship research in a pioneering, provocative and participative way: On the work of Bengt Johannisson. *Small Business Economics, 36*(2), 123–134.

Stivers, T. (2007). *Prescribing under pression: Parent-physician conversations and antibiotics.* Oxford: Oxford University Press.

Stokoe, E. (2006). On ethnomethodology, feminism, and the analysis of categorial reference to gender in talk-in-interaction. *The Sociological Review, 54*(3).

Tashakkori, A., & Teddie, C. (Eds.). (2003). *Handbook of mixed methods in social and behavioral research.* Sage.

Taylor, J. R., & Van Every, E. J. (2011). *The situated organization.* New York, NY: Routledge.

ten Have, P. (2007). Doing conversation analysis: A practical guide. Thousand Oaks, CA: Sage.

Thomas, J. B., Clark, S. M., & Gioia, D. A. (1993). Strategic sensemaking and organizational performance: Linkages among scanning, interpretation, action, and outcomes. *The Academy of Management Journal, 36*(2), 239–270.

Tsui, A. B. M. (1989). Beyond the adjacency pair. *Language in Society, 18*(4), 545–564.

Turkle, S. (2011). *Alone together: Why we expect more from technology and less from each other.* New York, NY: Basic Books.

Vehviläinen, S. (2001). Evaluative advice in educational counseling: The use of disagreement in the "stepwise entry" to advice. *Research on Language and Social Interaction, 34*(3), 371–398.

Watson, T. J. (2013). Entrepreneurship in action: Bringing together the individual, organizational and institutional dimensions of entrepreneurial action. *Entrepreneurship and Regional Development, 25*(5–6), 1–19.

Weick, K., Sutcliffe, K., & Obstfeld, D. (2005). Organizing and the process of sensemaking. *Organization Science, 16*(4), 409–421.

Welter, F. (2011). Contextualizing entrepreneurship – conceptual challenges and ways forward. *Entrepreneurship Theory and Practice, 35*(1), 165–184.

Wilson, D. (2007). *Team learning in action* (Doctoral Dissertation), Harvard Graduate School of Education, Cambridge, MA.

Wiltbank, R., Read, S., Dew, N., & Sarasvathy, S. D. (2009). Prediction and control under uncertainty: Outcomes in angel investing. *Journal of Business Venturing, 24*(2), 116–133.

Zahra, S. A. (2007). Contextualizing theory building in entrepreneurship research. *Journal of Business Venturing, 22*, 443–452.

# 3

# THE MATERIALITY OF ACCELERATORS AND INNOVATION SPACES

## Introduction

Because few people have been part of a team devoted to innovating and potentially commercializing a new technology, a portrait of the activity settings dedicated to innovation might be helpful to some readers. Similarly, few scholarly studies of entrepreneurship say much about the settings that surround the entrepreneurs (Zahra, 2007). It is assumed that either everyone can imagine an entrepreneurial workplace or that the physical space is irrelevant to entrepreneurial action. The studies that do mention context tend to include it as a means of contextualizing theory rather than theorizing context (Zahra & Wright, 2011). This chapter presents descriptions of several physical spaces designed to foster innovative entrepreneurial work and anchors them in spatialized theories of practice.

## The rise of accelerators

High-tech, high-growth ventures create nearly half of the new jobs in the United States each year (Decker, Haltiwanger, Jarmin, & Miranda, 2014). Consequently, accelerators, informal learning opportunities to help early-stage entrepreneurial teams, are booming. While only a few accelerators were in operation in 2005, ten years later there were more than 700 in the United States alone (Hathaway, 2016). And the number continues to grow at a rapid pace around the world.

A typical accelerator program begins with a competitive application process aimed to attract promising early-stage teams. Those teams who get accepted into each cohort are given about three months to develop and validate a product and business proposition. During that time participating teams have access to advisors and various events including group dinners, team coaching sessions, Q&A events with luminaries, and other activities to develop the product validation abilities and specialized presentation skills that entrepreneurs need. In general, accelerator programs emphasize learning through interpersonal experiences; fostering conversations between team mates and between teams and more experienced members of the entrepreneurial community.

The frequency and pace of accelerator programs have evolved over the years, but the general approach to cultivating entrepreneurial skills has remained largely the same. The founders of the early accelerators created the informal curricula for their programs based on their own experiences as successful technology entrepreneurs. Sometimes lay theories of entrepreneurship are only descriptions of what worked for a particular team at a particular time and place. However, these ways of knowing also can transcend a single success story and offer a framework that helps others achieve similar goals.

One lay theory that animates accelerator programming is the "lean startup" approach to new venture creation (Reis, 2014). This approach emphasizes the evolution of prototypes and the evaluation of customer data. It encourages entrepreneurs to validate new products with potential customers before investing too much time and effort in their creation. By getting feedback on an emerging product early, an entrepreneur can eliminate unpromising ideas rapidly and devote resources to developing only products that have true market appeal. At the heart of this development process is an iterative cycle: build a prototype, seek and interpret feedback, and apply these insights to the next version of the prototype before seeking feedback again.

The successful completion of this cycle depends on two interrelated activities: the externalization of ideas and the interaction of stakeholders. Teams are expected to share ideas through drawings, partial models, and increasingly articulated prototypes in order to develop and validate a product. This externalization informs a series of experiments that allow prototypes and hypotheses about the market to be tested. These activities necessitate interactions with others. Teams are brought into dialogue with advisors, prospective customers, and potential investors by the drawings and models. Team mates also meet with each other and with advisors to interpret the data from their product experiments.

Externalization and interaction fuel each other because prototypes are artifacts of cognition (Norman, 1991); they are things to think with and talk about. A prototype cultivates a shared understanding of an emerging product. Shared mental models, of course, are important to innovation teams (Grégoire, Corbett, & McMullen, 2011). However, prototypes transform mental models into objects that can be seen, physically experienced, and discussed (Suchman, 1985; Turkle, 1984). They make visible the new insights and interpretations that constitutes the team's progress (Krechevsky, Mardell, Rivard, & Wilson, 2013; Ritchhart & Perkins, 2008). These externalized representations of an emerging product make it possible to share the envisioned products with additional people across the ecosystem and to gather feedback on the viability of the invention (Martin, 2011).

Accelerators support people as they learn to do these activities; as they learn how to *do* entrepreneurial work. They also support people by showing them how to *be* entrepreneurs through a community of practice. Accelerator programs connect aspiring entrepreneurs with members of the entrepreneurial ecosystem. In addition to sharing their knowledge, accomplished members of the community model what it means to be an entrepreneur. Each time they give a presentation to the cohorts, mentor a founding team, and serve on an advisory board, they are demonstrating the behaviors and norms that the community values. The unspoken expectation is that the current cohort of learners will support this community in the future by sharing their time and wisdom with the next generation. As Brad Feld of TechStars, one of the oldest and most successful accelerators, puts it: "give before you get" (Feld, 2012). An emphasis on authentic relationships, not transactional exchanges, is a core value of successful entrepreneurs and essential to a functioning community of practice.

As accelerators have become recognized for their ability to develop innovative entrepreneurs, scholars of entrepreneurship have noticed. Accelerator programs have been described by educational theories of making, problem-based learning, and reflection (Sawyer, 2006; Schwartz, Mennin, & Webb, 2001; Martinez & Stager, 2013). And several key practices of entrepreneurship – play, empathy, experimentation, creativity, and reflection – are becoming a part of the formal and informal entrepreneurship curriculum at universities (Neck, Greene, & Brush, 2014).

This emphasis on practice and informal learning is the latest movement in the history of entrepreneurship education (Neck & Greene, 2011). For many years, observe and absorb was the primary means of teaching entrepreneurship. A teacher in a formal classroom would lecture and occasionally a guest would speak to the class. The transmission method gave way to a planning and pitching method, again based in a formal classroom setting. This second wave emphasized the writing of business plans and the delivery of presentations. In that era, everything from ideation through execution was treated as a linear trajectory. Eventually planning and pitching yielded to more of a practice-based and experiential methodology that valued more informal learning contexts. This contemporary approach encourages learners to identify and develop opportunities for innovations and innovative ventures. It incorporates lean startup, human-based, and design-thinking perspectives on innovation. The adoption of this more active framework for learning has accompanied the influx of university-based accelerators.

While there is much more to say about what people do within accelerator programs, it is also important to remember that accelerators are physical places. They are spaces specifically designed and furnished for learning about the practices associated with innovative entrepreneurial work. These spaces and furnishings do not simply support entrepreneurial practice; they help to constitute it (Hardy & Thomas, 2015). Their shapes and structures organize the actions and interactions of aspiring entrepreneurs – and are also an outcome of those actions and activities (Kornberger & Clegg, 2004).

## Where the magic happens

Pop culture has provided an enduring image about the places where innovators and entrepreneurs work. Favorite memes include the lone inventor working in a garage and the dog-friendly office where people play ping-pong and wear roller blades. However, the real workplaces where innovators and entrepreneurs actually work tend to be more functional than funky. Based on a recent review of the top ten university-based entrepreneurial activity centers in the United States (Gabbet & Bowden, 2016), four features of these spaces dedicated to supporting innovative entrepreneurial work and learning stand out.

They are bright spaces. Most of the top accelerators are painted bright white; bright yellow is a common accent color. Some spaces – such as those hosted by Stanford University and the University of Texas (Austin) – are bathed in natural light from an abundance of windows. Others, including the spaces at Cornell, Harvard, and Yale universities, illuminate with bright artificial lighting.

They are practical, not precious, spaces. While well-appointed, the top accelerator spaces are not fancy. They are designed to be used, and the furnishings are functional and durable. That said, they are well cared for. People are expected to use their individual spaces as well as the communal areas respectfully. Some spaces, such as the temporary MIT Beehive, post rules on the wall to remind people to clean up after themselves and to alert staff about needed supplies.

They are flexible spaces. Open and modular design is the norm. Movable furniture helps spaces transform from team-based meeting places to large group presentation spaces or any other necessary configuration. Versatile objects are intended to be repurposed; a large cube can serve as a desk, a seat, or a conference table, for example. Electrical outlets are found throughout the space.

They are mostly low-tech spaces. Signal strength for Wi-Fi and mobile phones is strong, and shared printers are accessible. Otherwise, the spaces tend to offer an abundance of whiteboards. Newer, fancier technologies, such as 3D printers, are sometimes provided, but old-fashioned workbenches with hammers and glue are more common. Participants are expected to have their own digital devices and software.

Y Combinator, one of the first accelerators, incorporates these features in its space. It is an open workplace with movable furnishings. Whiteboards are abundant, as are benches and work tables. Everything looks durable and well-maintained. Access to the network and the power supply is easy no matter where you are in the space. While a smaller space is just off the main work area to allow for interviews and other more private conversations, the main action is meant to occur in the open space.

Similarly, the Harvard i-Lab, one of the newer accelerators, also embodies these traits in the materiality of its space. The facility includes an area intended to function as a classroom, a few dozen rooms intended to function as meeting areas, a workshop for building prototypes, and a large open community area. The contours of the space are defined by unadorned concrete floors and exposed ceilings, ventilation, and wiring. Walls are coated with a special paint to allow any surface to function as a whiteboard. Actual whiteboards also are available along with folding tables on wheels and electrical connections on pulleys in the ceiling to allow teams to easily reconfigure the space to meet particular needs. As its founding director stated at the time of its opening, the space and its furnishings were selected to foster "structured spontaneity" ("Hi" to the Harvard Innovation Lab, 2011).

In short, while the physical spaces designed to function as accelerators are comfortable and informal, they are not recreational or accidental. They are serious places where innovators and aspiring entrepreneurs come to work and learn. The design of accelerators reveals what educators and practitioners think about entrepreneurial work. But how do the spaces and furnishings of accelerators play a role in the core activities – in the experiments and interactions – of accelerator participants?

## Matter matters

Many scholars have made the claim that material objects and physical settings play a performative role in social affairs (such as accelerator programs) (Carlile, Nicolini, Langley, & Tsoukas, 2013; Latour, 2005; Orlikowski, 2007). This body of research into socio-material culture has demonstrated how places and objects influence the creation and maintenance of social worlds. While entrepreneurship scholars and practitioners might be accustomed to thinking about objects as either situated resources to be used by humans (e.g., whiteboards) or as practical accomplishments that are created by humans (e.g., prototypes), this third way considers objects as an equal agent in the enactment of social goals (Latour, 2005). Practice theory highlights the embeddedness and interrelatedness of actors, objects, and contexts as essential features of work (Geiger, 2009; Reckwitz, 2002).

Seen through this lens, accelerators are not only places or programs; they are networks of heterogeneous actors that are mutually constituted through interactions and relationships (Fenwick, Edwards, & Sawchuk, 2011). This network view suggests that the all of the actors – the spaces, practices, people, and objects – are interdependent upon each other in the present and can reach across space, time, and form (McGregor, 2004). In other words, by participating in an accelerator, an aspiring entrepreneur is interacting with and contributing to the extensive community of people, practices, objects, and texts that have come to be known as entrepreneurship.

If accelerators are continually created and (re)created through social and material processes then even the most basic objects – for example, whiteboards – are playing a role in entrepreneurial work. Seen from a socio-material perspective, a whiteboard possesses properties of power and can influence the work of an entrepreneurial team in several ways.

Whiteboards can inspire involvement. When multiple team members collaborate at the whiteboard, the whiteboard is increasing the agency of each member who picks up a pen. It is also democratizing participation by making it possible for multiple team mates to contribute, possibly at the same time.

Whiteboards can serve as a facilitator. When one person at a time is entitled to go to the board, the whiteboard (and the act of approaching it) bestows the role of presenter on that person.

Whiteboards can serve as an amplification device. When used as a backdrop for a presenter, it can present lists or drawings that help the person articulate his/her points.

Whiteboards can promote iteration. They can do this rapidly when marks on the board are changed in the context of a single conversation. They also can do this gradually: the writing on boards can be photographed for future consideration and reference.

Whiteboards can contribute in these and other ways over the course of an accelerator program. While it is easy to imagine a team using a whiteboard early in the program – sketching out their initial ideas – whiteboards also matter to the teams near the end of the program. According to the partners at Y Combinator, whiteboards are instrumental as teams get ready to explain their young companies to the press and to investors (Y Combinator LLC, 2016):

> When each startup is ready to launch, they stand in front of a whiteboard with a YC partner and figure out what the basic pitch should be. The founders usually photograph this and write up an initial draft that we help revise. On the day they launch, we turn that into an email to whatever publication they've chosen. . . . The whiteboard pitch is useful for more than just launching. It becomes the basis of how the company will describe itself, particularly to investors. In fact it usually helps the founders themselves both clarify and agree with one another about the vision for the company.[1]

Y Combinator and other accelerators also gather teams and partners around the whiteboard as demo day approaches. Demo day is the finale that concludes most accelerator programs. It is the event in which the teams pitch their ventures and demonstrate their products to investors and other influential people in the ecosystem. As teams at Y Combinator prepare for this event they again engage the whiteboard (Y Combinator LLC, 2016):

> Usually we begin with a whiteboard conversation like the one before launching, during which we figure out the most important points to convey. Then the startup makes a presentation based on that, we (and whatever other founders are around) watch it, and then they fix what's broken and try again. These sessions make the presentations markedly better than they'd otherwise have been. Startups who come to YC a lot the week before Demo Day always have better presentations than the ones who for whatever reason don't, even if their companies aren't actually as good.[2]

In both of these accounts the whiteboards are encouraging collaboration and interpersonal interaction. They also are fostering iteration in real time and over time.

## Cohorts of illegal architects

Whiteboards are often, but not always, fixed elements. Scholars of socio-materiality would assert that whiteboards exert a kind of magnetism by bringing people to the part of a room where the whiteboard is located. Other furnishings typically selected for use in accelerators are not fixed. The rolling tables, lightweight benches, and other objects are meant to be moved frequently. However, they too exert power in the space and influence the interactions.

Given that entrepreneurs must learn to hold things in a provisional state to grapple with the uncertainties they face, they simultaneously must recognize things as they are and envision things as they could be. The accelerator and its movable furnishings encourage founding teams to become "illegal architects" who use and rearrange space to fit their needs in a given situation (Hill, 1998; Kornberger & Clegg, 2004).

When seeking a material expression of a provisional state, we need look no further than chairs: they are recognizable as complete and also as capable of many other configurations at the same time. Chairs might be the most often moved object in any space. Each time a chair is used it is likely to be moved, at least slightly. Sometimes chairs are arranged in a semi-circle for presentations or group games. Sometimes they are clustered or stacked to get them out of the way. Sometimes they serve as a makeshift easel or coat holder. In other words, chairs, like the other moveable furnishings in accelerators, are consistently available but always possess an emergent character.

The moveable nature of chairs and other furnishings also accents the agency of participants in the accelerator. Participants can reconfigure the objects in the space, and they reassign the objects (and the inhabited space) to serve their goals. That said, participants do not act as unencumbered selves. They are part of a cohort, and as such their agency is tempered by the shared context.

The shared nature of the space and the furnishings remind participants that they are part of an interconnected network, not rulers of all they see. The communal aspects of the material surroundings assert a humbling force. They also underscore goal of the accelerator to develop high-impact ventures. By sharing the material components of the accelerator the participants encounter one of the tenets of high-impact entrepreneurship: entrepreneurs can be royal or rich (not both) (Wasserman, 2006). A "royal" entrepreneur might control all resources, but s/he won't necessarily have many resources. A "rich" entrepreneur, however, is able to share resources (and ownership). By taking a smaller slice of a much bigger pie, a rich entrepreneur is able to create a high-impact venture. Accelerators, of course, want to support rich, not royal, entrepreneurs, and they do that, in part, by establishing a context of shared resources.

## What are the differences between the types of spaces?

- Incubators: these workspaces are designed to be used by very early-stage teams. Consequently they tend to provide some structures intended to support the operations of a small, incomplete, and inexperienced team. Incubators might offer a leased office with an entry and phone system shared by many small teams, for example. The incubator may provide these services in exchange for a monthly fee or a minor equity stake in the young company.

- Accelerators: these spaces focus on emerging ventures with the potential for rapid growth and good financial returns. Accelerators tend to select teams through a competition. While in residence, the teams get physical space for working and guidance from advisors and/or investors. These support services last for a limited period of time. At the conclusion of the residency period the advisors and investors may or may not opt to continue their involvement with the emerging venture. Accelerators may or may not require an equity stake.
- Co-working spaces (and innovation districts): these workplaces and meeting spaces are available at affordable rates through short-term contracts. Office spaces tend to be open plan and informal with the intent of stimulating networking opportunities and a sense of community. They are populated by sole proprietors, incomplete teams, and some early-stage ventures. Sometimes they are organized around themes such as social responsibility or green technology.
- Maker spaces: these spaces provide affordable shared access to tools and technologies that might be too expensive for one team to buy independently. The spaces tend to be optimized around the use of tools – from welding supplies to 3D printers. Access to the spaces may be gated by membership in a university community or by paying an affordable rate for short-term participation. The spaces attract individual tinkerers as well as teams.

## Double benefits

The resources that enable accelerators to operate also contribute to the iterative development of the accelerators themselves. For example, in the Y Combinator context, participants are expected and encouraged to meet with mentors and advisors over the three months of their engagement. There is no limit on the number of meetings participants can schedule, and meetings are booked using basic scheduling software. However, the software's utility does not end there. It also serves as a resource for improving the practices of the accelerator. The directors of the accelerator can use the software to determine if teams are getting enough of their attention. If the requests for meetings exceed the offered time slots, the directors respond by offering more potential meeting slots during the week. The software also reveals teams that might not be reaching out enough and allows the directors to suggest a meeting.

This social practice of using scheduling software as a means to reserve meeting times and to revisit structures and relationships is an illustration of double-loop learning (Argyris, 1976). The directors are able to respond to the emergent needs of the participants based on the data presented by the software. As such, the scheduling software is enabling the routine work of the accelerator and improving the practice of the accelerator at the same time. While the lean startup approach advocated by the accelerator curriculum encourages a single iterative loop in the development of a team's product, this use of the scheduling software enables productive change on many levels for the entire accelerator.

The use of scheduling software in these ways also is evidence of the accelerator as a network of people, places, resources, and practices that are mutually constituted through interactions and relationships (McGregor, 2004). The participants use the software to schedule an advisory session that will occur within the physical space. The meeting will help the participants master the practices of innovative entrepreneurship through the interactions with the advisors. The queue of requests for meetings allows the directors to adapt their practice and make more time slots available to participants when needed. The queue also helps the directors identify participants that might not be maximizing their opportunities to learn from in-person interactions.

All of these elements of the accelerator and its operations are interdependent. They also are accomplished outside of the bounds of a particular moment. The scheduling software, for example, is a result of a long series of developmental conversations and ideas including many possibilities that were abandoned before current version of the software took shape. The software is experienced as a whole, despite the many interactions and variations that came before. The accelerator comprises many of these assemblies: previous programming formats, the experiences of the directors when they were nascent entrepreneurs, and every other aspect of the accelerator. Moreover, each of these elements and the accelerator as a whole are all still in a process of creating and recreating the connections that are recognized as an accelerator. While they are viewed as symmetrical, intertwined, or entangled, these assemblies and connections between human and non-human actors and across time are recognized as vital to practice (Latour, 1987; Pickering, 1995; Suchman, 2007).

## From entrepreneur to entrepreneurial actor

By recognizing the interdependent network of all of the actors – the spaces, objects, and people – the term entrepreneur becomes less accurate than "entrepreneurial actor" (Watson, 2013b). This shift in terminology impacts the idea of entrepreneurial identity. An entrepreneurial actor who is part of a larger network of actors seems far less heroic than the visionary entrepreneur studied in traditional streams of research (Anderson & Warren, 2011). The new framing and naming also highlights the situated nature of entrepreneurial efforts; a given individual may act entrepreneurially in one situation but not another (Ruef, 2010).

Seeing the people engaged in entrepreneurial work as entrepreneurial actors reminds researchers to focus on action, on the practices that constitute entrepreneurial work. This shift highlights the routine activities that individuals do while accomplishing entrepreneurial work. Many scholars have cited the need to uncover what entrepreneurs actually do in order to build theory and to teach people how to have successful entrepreneurial careers. However, the majority of published studies continue to put the individual in the foreground with little concern for the interdependent network of other human and non-human actors.

As the practice-turn shapes more entrepreneurial research, additional studies about established entrepreneurial constructs may attend to socio-material concerns. For example, while effectuation suggests that entrepreneurs are able to leverage surprises, the emphasis placed on the cognition of the entrepreneur limits our understanding of the situated experience of leveraging surprises. Practice-oriented studies can uncover the interactions with technologies and objects that help entrepreneurial teams make sense of surprises. They can demonstrate the role that a workplace contributes to a team's ability to synthesize shocks and reimagine new possibilities. In short, a shift to practice-oriented studies can prompt new research questions and offer new insights about individual entrepreneurial actors and about their social, material, and spatial contexts (Watson, 2013a).

## Accelerators as machines for entrepreneurial creation

People and practices are shaped by the places in which they happen (McGregor, 2004). And, in a self-reinforcing pattern, spaces are constructed anew and continually redesigned from within to support specific people and enable specific practices. Over time, the shifts in the ways that cohorts' experiences are materialized in practice – from the creation of prototypes to the use of scheduling software – are producing different learning structures, different accelerators, and different entrepreneurs. Together these performative changes are redesigning the nature of entrepreneurial learning, entrepreneurial work, and entrepreneurial workplaces.

The accelerator, like every entrepreneurial workplace, is a dynamic context – a complex activity setting (Goffman, 1956) – and not an inert container. As founding teams interact with each other, they co-create an attention zone which influences their interpretations and actions. Their interactions with the surrounding physical space and furnishing influence the teams' interpretations and actions. The generative nature of the accelerator space organizes the work of the participating teams; shaping their communications, movements, and ideas. Accelerators are the combination of the ongoing relationships between people, spaces, and objects. The intersections of these relational forces are where unpredictable outcomes emerge – including breakthrough products and breakout ventures (Hillier, 1996).

Recognizing that space and materiality play a role in the social construction of accelerators is valuable because it underscores the idea that entrepreneurship is enacted in and through situated practice. Nearly 100 years ago Le Corbusier asserted that the structure of a house influenced the routines and rituals – the practices – of daily life (Corbusier, 1923). Just as a house, school, or church brings to mind certain ways of interacting, ways of structuring activities, and ways of interfacing with the wider world, an accelerator is a socially constructed space which organizes practices that constitute entrepreneurial work. Simultaneously, an accelerator is continually (re)created by the acts of aspiring entrepreneurs and members of the entrepreneurial ecosystem. In this ongoing social process of creation and renewal, accelerators and the definition of entrepreneurial work continue to evolve while stimulating the development of innovative products and new ventures.

## Looking forward

Contexts for innovative entrepreneurial work involve more than the physical places where people create new products and ventures, and much of this book attends to the means by which innovators and entrepreneurs understand, respond to, and (re)construct context. However, it is worth looking at the physical spaces that have been developed to house aspiring innovative entrepreneurs as they work and learn. While this chapter has highlighted some of the socio-material aspects of accelerators, many more could be explored, including virtual learning opportunities affiliated with accelerators, the methods for archiving prototypes, and the role of photographs in the innovative entrepreneurial process.

Regardless of the specific focus, a socio-material view of accelerators suggests that the spaces themselves are not neutral containers for entrepreneurial learning. They have been constructed with ideas of entrepreneurial work in mind, and they encourage embodied expressions of entrepreneurial agency and dynamism. Spaces, objects, people, and practices are mutually constituted through interactions and relationships (Nespor, 2003) and these connections persist through time and varied forms (McGregor, 2004). As practice theory identifies more details about what entrepreneurs actually do, such findings can inform the next generation of informal contexts for entrepreneurial learning.

## Notes

1  © 2018 Y Combinator, LLC.
2  © 2018 Y Combinator, LLC.

## References

Anderson, A. R., & Warren, L. (2011). The entrepreneur as hero and jester: Enacting the entrepreneurial discourse. *International Small Business Journal, 29*(6), 589–609.

Argyris, C. (1976). Single-loop and double-loop models in research on decision making. *Administrative Science Quarterly, 21*(3), 363–375.

Carlile, P. R., Nicolini, D., Langley, A., & Tsoukas, H. (Eds.). (2013). *How matter matters: Objects, artifacts, and materiality in organization studies.* Oxford: Oxford University Press.

Corbusier, L. (1923). *Toward a new architecture.* Oxford: Architectural Press.

Decker, R., Haltiwanger, J., Jarmin, R., & Miranda, J. (2014). The role of entrepreneurship in US job creation and economic dynamism. *Journal of Economic Perspectives, 28*(3), 3–24.

Feld, B. (2012). *Startup communities.* Hoboken, NJ: Wiley.

Fenwick, T., Edwards, R., & Sawchuk, P. (2011). *Emerging approaches to educational research: Tracing the socio-material*. New York, NY: Routledge.

Gabbet, J., & Bowden, A. (2016). The top 50 universities producing vc-backed entrepreneurs. In G. Black (Ed.), *Pitchbook*. Seattle, WA: PitchBook Venture Capital.

Geiger, D. (2009). Revisiting the concept of practice: Toward an argumentative understanding of practicing. *Management Learning, 40*(2), 129–144.

Goffman, E. (1956). *The presentation of self in everyday life*. Edinburgh: University of Edinburgh SSRC.

Grégoire, D. A., Corbett, A. C., & McMullen, J. S. (2011). The cognitive perspective in entrepreneurship: An agenda for future research. *Journal of Management Studies, 48*(6).

Hardy, C., & Thomas, R. (2015). Discourse in a material world. *Journal of Management Studies, 52*(5), 680–696.

Hathaway, I. (2016). What startup accelerators really do. *Harvard Business Review*.

"Hi" to the Harvard Innovation Lab. (2011). *Harvard Magazine*. Retrieved from https://harvardmagazine.com/2011/11/harvard-innovation-lab-opens

Hill, J. (1998). *The illegal architect*. London: Black Dog.

Hillier, B. (1996). *Space is the machine: A configurational theory of architecture*. Cambridge: Cambridge University Press.

Kornberger, M., & Clegg, S. (2004). Bringing space back in: Organizing the generative building. *Organization Studies, 25*(7), 1095–1114.

Krechevsky, M., Mardell, B., Rivard, M., & Wilson, D. (2013). *Visible learners: Promoting reggio-inspired approaches in all schools*. San Francisco, CA: Jossey-Bass.

Latour, B. (1987). *Science in action*. Boston, MA: Harvard University Press.

Latour, B. (2005). *Reassembling the social: An introduction to actor-network-theory*. Oxford: Oxford University Press.

Martin, R. (2011). The innovation catalysts. *Harvard Business Review* (June).

Martinez, S., & Stager, G. (2013). *Invent to learn: Making, tinkering, and engineering in the classroom*. Torrance, CA: Constructing Modern Knowledge Press.

McGregor, J. (2004). Spatiality and the place of the material in schools. *Pedagogy Culture and Society, 12*(3), 347–372.

Neck, H. M., & Greene, P. G. (2011). Entrepreneurship education: Known worlds and new frontiers. *Journal of Small Business Management, 49*(1), 55–70.

Neck, H., Greene, P., & Brush, C. (2014). *Teaching Entrepreneurship*. Northampton, MA: Edward Elgar.

Nespor, J. (2003). Undergraduate curricula as networks and trajectories. In R. Edwards & R. Usher (Eds.), *Space, curriculum and learning*. Greenwich: IAP.

Norman, D. (1991). Cognitive artifacts. In J. M. Carroll (Ed.), *Designing interaction: Psychology at the human-computer interface* (pp. 17–38). New York, NY: Cambridge University Press.

Orlikowski, W. J. (2007). Sociomaterial practices: Exploring technology at work. *Organization Studies, 28*(9), 1435–1448.

Pickering, A. (1995). *The mangle of practice: Time, agency and science*. Chicago, IL: University of Chicago Press.

Reckwitz, A. (2002). Toward a theory of social practices: A development in culturalist theorizing. *European Journal of Social Theory, 5*(2), 243–263.

Reis, E. (2014). *The lean startup*, Retrieved from http://theleanstartup.com/

Ritchhart, R., & Perkins, D. N. (2008). Making thinking visible. *Educational Leadership, 65*(5), 57–61.

Ruef, M. (2010). *The entrepreneurially group: Social identities, relations and collective action*. Princeton, NJ: Princeton University Press.

Sawyer, R. (Ed.) (2006). *The Cambridge handbook of the learning sciences.* NY: Cambridge University Press.

Schwartz, P., Mennin, S., & Webb, G. (2001). *Problem-based learning.* London: Kogan Page.

Suchman, L. (1985). Plans and situated actions. Palo Alto, CA: XEROX.

Suchman, L. (2007). *Human-machine reconfigurations: Plans and situated actions* (2nd ed.). Cambridge: Cambridge University Press.

Turkle, S. (1984). *The second self.* New York, NY: Simon and Schuster.

Wasserman, N. (2006). Rich versus king: Strategic choice and the entrepreneur. [Best Paper]. *Academy of Management Proceedings, 2006*(1), 001–006.

Watson, T. J. (2013a). Entrepreneurial action and the Euro-American social science tradition: pragmatism, realism and looking beyond "The entrepreneur". *Entrepreneurship & Regional Development, 25*(1–2), 16–33.

Watson, T. J. (2013b). Entrepreneurship in action: Bringing together the individual, organizational and institutional dimensions of entrepreneurial action. *Entrepreneurship and Regional Development, 25*(5–6), 1–19.

Y Combinator LLC. (November 2016). "What happens at Y combinator", Retrieved from www.ycombinator.com/atyc/

Zahra, S. A. (2007). Contextualizing theory building in entrepreneurship research. *Journal of Business Venturing, 22*, 443–452.

Zahra, S. A., & Wright, M. (2011). Entrepreneurship's next act. *Academy of Management Perspectives, 25*(4), 67–83.

# PART II

# Verbally accomplishing innovative entrepreneurial work

Given that all professional work is verbal work, this part considers the role of language in the accomplishment of work at the forefront of new technologies and new ventures. A close examination of the workplace conversations of several teams in action reveals a set of language patterns that accompanies the innovative entrepreneurial process. Part II describes in detail the conversational moves used by successful teams enacting the design-thinking principles echoed in the lean startup process: doing play, doing reflection, and doing empathy.

# 4

# DOING PLAY

## Introduction

Entrepreneurship seems like fun. Even without the stereotypical bean bag chairs in the office, entrepreneurship is associated with creative empowerment; with a professional life that is self-directed and self-actualized. It promises a career that incorporates acts of serious play as founders explore the possibilities for imperfect objects and the spaces in-between accepted ideas (Hjorth, 2004).

This kind of play is relational (Shotter, 1993). It recognizes (and resets) boundaries and requires interaction between people, ideas, and objects. Play helps individuals form and evolve individual and collective identities. Through acts of play, people develop emotional, cognitive, social, and ethical abilities that inform their actions in other contexts (Statler, Roos, & Victor, 2009). And by playing together, people establish a shared sense of community and form a shared identity as part of a community or organization (Henricks, 2015; Sutton-Smith, 1997).

In addition to contributing to the development of shared identity and belonging between members of a group, playful talk also enables people to evolve and assert individual identities. Playful talk allows people to position themselves within a group in ways that emphasize particular competencies or roles without disrupting social bonds (Sullivan & Wilson, 2015). Play and playful talk also provide opportunities for people to temporarily try new roles that can expand an individual's sense of self.

Engaging in play is inherently satisfying (Schell, 2014). The pleasure one gets from manipulating an idea or object encourages voluntary and spontaneous participation (Ellis, 1973; Terr, 1999). The intrinsic reward and self-selected engagement of play differentiates it from the expected structures and rules of work. However, acts of play are not without their own structures and rules.

For example, while working in New York City, a colleague referred to our morning coffee place as "Snacks Fifth Avenue". His word play was not random. To create his pun, he needed to know the rules of rhyming in English, the rules of word replacement in puns, and the cultural category of shopping venues. While his pun may not have been very funny, it did adhere to these rules and succeeded as a pun in a way that "Coffee Random Street" would not have.

The rules of play go beyond the linguistic features of puns; they include a sustained appreciation for other people in the conversation. Heedful interrelating has been linked to acts of play, and to team success (Campbell, 2014; Dougherty & Takacs, 2004). Heedful interactions are careful, thoughtful, and contextualized, not mindless or habitual. They also prioritize the needs of the group over those of the self. As team mates relate heedfully, they are primed to respond creatively to uncertainties and unexpected circumstances (Weick & Roberts, 1993). In other words, heedful interactions support playfulness and the rules of play encourage heedfulness (Dougherty & Takacs, 2004).

Playful interactions have a specific sequential order. Scholars have argued that humor is an adjacency pair; a playful utterance prompts an acknowledging response (Hay, 2001). The response may be in the form of laughter or another non-verbal gesture, or it may be a series of utterances that develop the levity over several turns of conversation (Attardo, Pickering, & Baker, 2011). Gestures and facial expressions as well as tone, pitch, speed, and volume of speaking may all play a role in a speaker's ability to signal and a responder's ability to understand playful utterances (Pickering et al., 2009).

Scholars have cited the need to study entrepreneurial play, its relational nature, and its structures (Hjorth, 2004). Some studies have used the lens of improvisation to look at the creative and spontaneous aspects of entrepreneurship (Austin, Devin, & Sullivan, 2011; Baker, Miner, & Eesley, 2003). These investigations have explored how play enables creativity by encouraging the sustained manipulation of models and relaxing expectations of predetermined results (Schrage, 1999). However, these studies miss the situated means by which teams express and experience playfulness in ordinary workplaces (Hjorth, 2004). Only by adopting a methodological approach that attends to the situated, relational, and emergent nature of play in entrepreneurial work can we reveal the interactional mechanics of play.

This chapter examines the interactional details of entrepreneurial teams using play while accomplishing their work. It reveals the interactional rules that signal and support play between team mates. It also highlights the interactional means by which teams accomplish heedfulness and identities while playfully enacting their work as innovators.

## The background of play at work

Empirical research has linked humor in the workplace with rapport between team mates and with group morale (Clouse & Spurgeon, 1995; Romero & Cruthirds, 2006). Plus, challenges of workers, such as boredom, frustration, and stress, can be eased by playfulness at work (Duncan & Feisal, 1989; Pryor, Singleton, Taneja, & Humphreys, 2010). And, of course, humor and play have a positive impact on team creativity and productivity (Duncan & Feisal, 1989; Holmes, 2007).

A growing body of research is defining humor and play specifically in terms of communication. Recent studies have asserted that playful talk is communication that is perceived as amusing and results in a positive experience for the individuals and groups who are involved (Romero & Cruthirds, 2006). As such, play is understood to be a context-dependent co-constructed social phenomenon, not just a personality trait (i.e., a funny person).

While humor can have a dark side, playful talk is an affiliative act. Humor can be used in self-disparaging or interpersonally aggressive ways that diminish the self or others (Martin, Puhlik-Doris, Larsen, Gray, & Weir, 2003). These functions of humor when expressed in the workplace do not contribute to a positive organization. However, affiliative humor that is affirming to the self and others does enhance co-worker relationships, team cohesion, and organizational success (Dutton, 2003; Martin et al., 2003). This affiliative type of humor is at the heart of play and playful talk.

## Micro-analysis of playful talk in action

Conversation Analysis, with its focus on the sequence and order of naturally occurring workplace interactions, can advance our understanding of the playful dimensions of entrepreneurial work. It can demonstrate how entrepreneurial teams play in action.

The following excerpts come from the recorded conversations of several early-stage innovative entrepreneurial teams. Each team had two members, and none of the founders had a significant background doing entrepreneurial work. After the period of data collection, each team went on to raise venture capital, hire employees, and launch a successful product.

Three fields of play are highlighted in the following excerpts: the playful manipulation of material artifacts through words (two examples), the playful manipulation of social expectations through words, and the playful accomplishment of identity through words. While these are not exhaustive of the types of play that teams can enact, they are observed multiple times in the data. They show some ways, albeit not all of the ways, that entrepreneurial teams accomplish play through orderly, situated interaction.

## Playing with objects

While the first excerpt may not seem overly playful at first glance, it does capture a team engaged in the imagined manipulation of the internal technology for their prototype. It does not include overt humor, but it does show the team mates playing with the components as if they were fitting a jigsaw puzzle piece. In the current configuration, the prototype is oddly shaped, and the team would like to redesign its internal layout to fit within a less complicated enclosure. They discuss a variety of possible configurations for the necessary components, and through their conversation they are able to reimagine a new design and organize their materials.

### Excerpt 4.1 Heedful reimagining of the prototype's configuration

| Line | Speaker | Utterance |
| --- | --- | --- |
| 1 | S1 | So well next question is where do we want to put the (.) SD card. Is where it is still a good place for it↑ |
| 2 | S2 | I actually think that this is like (.) if you just cut this off↑ |
| 3 | S1 | that is (.) the right |
| 4 | S2 | It's kind of the right orientation for everything |
| 5 | S1 | [okay] |
| 6 | S2 | [cause] then the xp can (.) go <u>there</u> and the sd card's on top° |
| 7 | S1 | yep so you said maybe half an inch (.) allow or maybe more like an inch |
| 8 | S2 | yeah |
| 9 | S1 | (12) 'k and can you send me the valve and (.) or <u>pump</u> and valve |
| 10 | S2 | (20) I'll just put it on dropbox↑ |
| 11 | S1 | Sure |
| 12 | S2 | (13) okay so there's (7) all that stuff is now on dropbox. It's under technical (.) pump and valves |

In line 1, Speaker 1 seeks the opinion of her partner about the position of the SD card. She does not assert an idea about its placement; she requests his feedback on the usefulness of the SD cards current placement. Speaker 2 suggests a new shape for the board that will necessitate a new and better position for the SD card. His contribution of this new idea is framed in a provisional way. His use of the phrase "I think" positions his vision as a suggestion that is open to feedback from Speaker 1.

Although Speaker 1 accepts this new solution (line 5), Speaker 2 adds a richer explanation about the benefits of this new configuration (line 6). Again, Speaker 1 expresses agreement and comprehension of the suggestion (line 7) and seeks to add specificity to the proposed change in shape for the board. This request for more detail uses the word "maybe" which echoes the provisionality expressed by Speaker 2. This wording also expresses Speaker 1's desire to ensure she has grasped Speaker 2's vision. Once Speaker 2 confirms the new shape (line 6), Speaker 1 asks for access to all of the written information about the components (line 9). In line 10 Speaker 2 checks his comprehension of her request by asking if it is okay to upload the written information to their shared account in the cloud. After Speaker 1 agrees (line 11), Speaker 2 closes the topic by indicating the information has been uploaded. He also adds the exact location of the information to make it easy for Speaker 1 to find.

Excerpt 4.2 captures a team mate offering a facetious solution to a configuration problem. The tonality of Speaker 1's suggested course of action and Speaker 2's response suggest that they both understand that the idea of hitting the prototype with a hammer is not a serious proposal. Their intonation and light laughter (lines 1–3) reveals that the idea of brute force to solve their problem is tempting but not wise or worth trying.

### Excerpt 4.2 *Facetious suggestion in the redesign of a prototype*

| Line | Speaker | Utterance |
| --- | --- | --- |
| 1 | S1 | 'Cause could we (.) put them all in first and like give them some persuasion with a little hammer? (laughter) |
| 2 | S2 | (laugher) I suppose we could yeah (.) I would be a little bit (.) concerned about trying to ream out the hole because (.) the connections to the ground and the (.) um five hold plain |
| 3 | S1 | Yeah |
| 4 | S2 | is <u>internal</u> |
| 5 | S1 | Okay |
| 6 | S2 | So basically like there's a copper plane ↑ |
| 7 | S1 | Mmhm |
| 8 | S2 | and then (.) they drill and then it's plated |
| 9 | S1 | Okay |
| 10 | S2 | And that plating is what connects this hold to the copper plane |
| 11 | S1 | Okay then I wouldn't want to do that. Nevermind. But then we could also make these a little smaller |
| 12 | S2 | Yeah yeah that <u>that's</u> probably a better (.) |
| 13 | S1 | A better approach |
| 14 | S2 | better approach |

Speaker 2 thinks aloud about the reasons why forcing the components would cause additional problems (lines 2, 4). This accounting of the configuration serves to ensure that both partners are aware of the same features on the board. Speaker 1 follows his reasoning and expresses alignment (lines 3, 5, 7, 9) before formally retracting her wishful utterance. She then (line 11) expresses a new idea based on his review of the elements. Speaker 2 expresses agreement that her insight would improve the design of their board (12, 14).

## Playing with social expectations

Entrepreneurial teams also use words to play with conventions about social situations. In the initial excerpt from this set, the team is planning to demonstrate their prototype at a public showcase for innovations. As they imagine their booth at the event, they decide that they will have a signup sheet for people who would like to be on mailing list about their venture's progress. Then they playfully imagine a magic pen that only works if the person using it has money to invest.

## Excerpt 4.3  Wishing for a magic pen

| Line | Speaker | Utterance |
| --- | --- | --- |
| 1 | S1 | um (2) we need it to be like magic ink |
| 2 | S2 | mm |
| 3 | S1 | and if you don't put (.) investor as why you're interested (.) >it just erases your name< ° |
| 4 | S2 | ((laughter)) |
| 5 | S1 | ((laughter)) |
| 6 | S2 | that would be a really fun pitch to make for that product |
| 7 | S1 | yeah |
| 8 | S2 | ((laughter)) |
| 9 | S1 | this pen only works if you have money |
| 10 | S2 | ((laughter)) |
| 11 | S1 | it can sense |
| 12 | S2 | that's awesome |
| 13 | S1 | alright um (2) we need that= we <need> the cardstock, so okay let's let's envision the table |

When Speaker 1 first expresses the idea of a pen with magic ink (line 1), he signals the playfulness of the suggestion through a higher tone of voice than normal. Speaker 2 plays along by offering an "mmm" which conveys a mock seriousness and an awareness that Speaker 1 has more to say on the matter. Speaker 1 builds on his ridiculous invention (line 3) by extending the magic powers of the pen to include the ability to erase the names of people who are not investors. Their complementary laughter indicates a shared understanding of the imagined invention, a shared recognition of the absurdity of the idea, and a shared awareness of the need to attract and impress potential investors. The silly detour is ended by the speaker who started it (line 13) as he redirects the conversation back to the actual tasks they must accomplish.

## Playing with identity

In Excerpt 4.4, the team mates are talking about the need to include a packet of desiccant in a chamber of their product to protect it from moisture and humidity.

## Excerpt 4.4  Contextualizing silica gel

| Line | Speaker | Utterance |
| --- | --- | --- |
| 1 | S1 | but anyway what I think they are is silica gel |
| 2 | S2 | (2) mmhm |
| 3 | S1 | which is (.) what – |
| 4 | S2 | it's like what's in the (.) when you buy electronics and stuff right |
| 5 | S1 | I was gonna say <u>shoes</u> But sure (laugh) |
| 6 | S2 | oh yeah yeah shoes too yeah yeah (.) same story (laugh) |
| 7 | S1 | um but which is what I would have asked for anyways (.) um |
| 8 | S2 | Okay |
| 9 | S1 | so I think we can (.) go ahead and use them |

After Speaker 1 brings up the idea of silica gel, she starts to clarify what silica gel is to ensure that her partner knows what she means (line 3). He has comprehended her meaning and demonstrates his understanding by interjecting his knowledge of silica gel, "it's like what's in the box when you buy electronics" (line 4). Speaker 1, in a higher pitch than usual, says that she was going to reference "shoes" rather than electronics (line 5). Her pitch also suggests a self-directed laugh: she primarily associates silica gel with shoes, a product with a feminine connotation, rather than electronics, even though she is a PhD student in mechanical engineering in an elite university. Speaker 2 acknowledges her humor by sharing in the laugh. He also confirms that her impulse is right; shoes include silica gel, too (line 6).

## The practice of playful interactions

Together these excerpts provide a window into the playful workplace interactions of innovative entrepreneurial teams. Whether the teams are playing with products or with social expectations, the team mates are immediate in their responsiveness to prompts for play. A sequence order of utterances guides the expressions and experiences of play. The conversational data also shows that the team mates use playful discourse to enact individual and shared identities. And it reveals how heedfulness is verbally accomplished in situated moment by moment interactions.

Each excerpt highlights a unique aspect of play in the entrepreneurial workplace. Excerpt 4.1 is not marked by laughter or other features of spirited play, but the conversational data captures a fundamental aspect of play in the workplace: the sustained imaginary manipulation of a product's configuration. Excerpt 4.2 also shows a team playing with possible ways to improve a prototype, but in this case, the observable data includes an exchange that is overtly playful. Excerpts 4.3 and 4.4 look beyond the product development orientation of entrepreneurial work and hone in on the social elements. Excerpt 4.3 captures a team engaging in an extended conversation about a fantasy product. And Excerpt 4.4 shows a team doing individual identity through humor. While group identity and heedfulness are not the focal point of any excerpt, they are observable in the interactions of every excerpt.

At first glance, it may be difficult to see a unifying sequence order in the four very different excerpts. These are naturally occurring "backstage" conversations, and as such they will not be as overtly ordered as a 911 call in which one person has a script and the range of outcomes is somewhat predetermined. The first observable feature of the order of playful interaction is the responsiveness of the second speaker. In each excerpt the prompt for play is understood and responded to immediately in the next turn. Moreover, the response is not only immediate, it is fitted. If a laugh is in the prompt then a laugh is in the response. If a provisional framing is used in the prompt then a provisional framing is in the response. This is observed even in the case which requires a topical redirection. In Excerpt 4.2, Speaker 1's facetious suggestion of a hammer tap receives a response that echoes the small laugh and proceeds to consider the implications of using a hammer.

Another structural element that is observable in the data is the opening and closing of playful exchanges. In all of the excerpts the speaker who starts the levity also signals the end of the levity. This self-closing maneuver is similar to the structure found in storytelling. A speaker signals the start of the story and is granted an extended set of turns to complete it by listeners (Goodwin & Heritage, 1990). Excerpt 4.3 in particular casts playful talk as an act of storytelling, but all of the excerpts allow the person who initiates the departure to playful talk to signal the return to ordinary talk.

Looking across all of these excerpts, the interactional order suggests that accepting invitations to play is preferred in entrepreneurial workplace interaction. The concept of preference characterizes the recurrent features of turn and sequence, not the personal desires of the speakers (Heritage, 1989). Preferred responses tend to happen without delay, as observed in the data. In this case, a "dispreferred" response to a prompt for play would be either to reject it by ignoring it or to overtly redirect the conversation back to the topic of serious workplace concerns. Research into preference organization has demonstrated that many prompts, including those for invitations and proposals, rarely receive dispreferred responses (Davidson, 1984).

These features of the interactional structure of play benefit from and contribute to heedfulness. A speaker's willingness to attune to and defer to his/her team mate is an example of heedful interaction. In the data, individuals who received a prompt for play acted heedfully by accepting the first speaker's influence on the topic and tone of interaction. Sometimes overt affirmation is given, as in the case of Excerpt 4.3 in lines 6 and 12, but every excerpt includes a willingness for the speakers to yield to the prompt for play. These attentive dynamics that emphasize the cultivation of a bond are hallmarks of heedfulness (Dougherty & Takacs, 2004).

It is worth pausing to consider the role of laughter in these exchanges. Laughter occurs in several instances across the excerpts. Studies of laughter have shown that it functions as a kind of adjacency pair. One speaker invites laughter, and the other acknowledges the invitation and its acceptance through laughter in response (Psathas, 1979). Laughter is particular to the interpersonal context in which it arises (Goodwin & Heritage, 1990). Consequently, it does not necessarily mean that something is funny. Instead it signals a state of attunement between the speakers.

This kind of shared laughter is an interactional marker and maker of collective identity. Conversations are essential to the co-construction of collective identity (Hardy, Lawrence, & Grant, 2005). The topics or purposes of the conversations do not necessarily matter to the creation and establishment of a shared identity, only the shared engagement and experience (Collins, 1981). A team's sense of belonging can impact how they respond to each other and to circumstances. Simultaneously how team mates interact with each other can increase or inhibit their shared identity. It is through shared experiences that are made explicit through verbal interactions that people arrive at shared meanings and collective identity (Weick, Sutcliffe, & Obstfeld, 2005).

Laughing at the self is another interactional means by which identity is accomplished. In Excerpt 4.4, Speaker 1 playfully interjects the fact that she associates silica gel packets with new shoes before new technology. She sees the humor in the stereotypes that link women with shoes and men with technology. Her impulse to share that humorous insight does not advance the team's decision to include silica gel with their product. However, it does highlight the contours of her individual identity as a female engineer. Her playful observation allows her to claim the feminine side of her identity, and for both team mates to bring the whole person to work.

## Emphasizing the interactional foundations of play

Playfulness at work is a socially constructed phenomenon that is spontaneous and surprising – and bound by interactional order and patterns. Based on this micro-analysis of the workplace conversations of entrepreneurial teams in action it is possible to see how – in specific interactional ways – play in entrepreneurial work is accomplished. Play is initiated and shaped within a specific organization of turns. Patterns for opening and closing episodes of play, for example, can be observed in the data. And through the co-construction of these sequential productions of playful talk, team mates can enact heedfulness and express identities.

CA offers a powerful approach to understanding entrepreneurial play: it enables the investigation of play as a moment-by-moment construction that includes how play is recognized and (re)created by team mates. CA allows researchers to examine the situated conversational cues that prompt team mates to engage in a playful exchange and the sequential trajectories which follow. Because CA shows how a team mate's utterance influences what happens in the next turn, it highlights the interactional structures that enable teams to play in the context of their work. It makes explicit how the practice of play in an entrepreneurial workplace operates, and how that architecture of interaction supports and is supported by heedfulness. It also reveals how collective and individual identities are engaged through the order of playful interaction.

While this chapter looked at excerpts from several teams engaging in several occasions of playful interaction, it did not attempt to address all of the possible variations of play in the entrepreneurial workplace. For example, all of the excerpts were from two-person teams working in the same office. How might larger teams organize the sequence order of playful talk? And how might geographically distributed teams working over a videoconferencing platform organize and verbally accomplish play? Similarly, this chapter looked at only the audible verbal exchanges between team mates, but gestures also influence workplace interaction. Future studies could take up these and other aspects of playful talk that would add interactional detail to the organizational and psychological research that links play to entrepreneurship.

CA investigations into entrepreneurial work shift the emphasis from social skills of entrepreneurs (Baron & Tang, 2009; Lamine, Mian, & Fayolle, 2014) to the socially constructed foundations of entrepreneurial identities, products, and organizations (Chalmers & Shaw, 2017; Downing, 2005; Fletcher, 2006). The observable details of entrepreneurial conversations can reveal the sequential organization of the playful interactions associated with innovative entrepreneurial work. This chapter provided a glimpse into the verbal means by which innovative entrepreneurial teams engage in the practice of play.

## References

Attardo, S., Pickering, L., & Baker, A. (2011). Prosodic and multimodal markers of humor in conversation. *Pragmatics & Cognition, 19*(2), 224–247.

Austin, R. D., Devin, L., & Sullivan, E. E. (2011). Accidental innovation: Supporting valuable unpredictability in the creative process. *Organization Science, 23*(5), 1505–1522.

Baker, T., Miner, A. S., & Eesley, D. T. (2003). Improvising firms: Bricolage, account giving and improvisational competencies in the founding process. *Research Policy, 32,* 255–276.

Baron, R. A., & Tang, J. (2009). Entrepreneurs' social skills and new venture performance: Mediating mechanisms and cultural generality. *Journal of Management, 35*(2), 282–306.

Campbell, B. (2014). *Entrepreneurship as a conversational accomplishment: An inductive analysis of the verbal sensemaking behaviors of early-stage innovative entrepreneurial teams* (PhD), University of Exeter, Exeter, England.

Chalmers, D., & Shaw, E. (2017). The endogenous construction of entrepreneurial contexts: A practice-based perspective. *International Small Business Journal, 35*(1), 19–39.

Clouse, R., & Spurgeon, K. (1995). Corporate analysis of humor. *Psychology: A Journal of Human Behavior, 32*(3/4), 1–24.

Collins, R. (1981). On the microfoundations of macrosociology. *American Journal of Sociology, 86,* 984–1013.

Davidson, J. (1984). Subsequent versions of invitations, offers, requests and proposals dealing with potential or actual rejection. In J. M. Atkinsen & J. Heritage (Eds.), *Structures of social action: Studies in conversation analysis* (pp. 102–128). Cambridge: Cambridge University Press.

Dougherty, D., & Takacs, C. H. (2004). Team play: Heedful interrelating as the boundary for innovation. *Long Range Planning, 37*(6), 569–590.

Downing, S. (2005). The social construction of entrepreneurship: Narrative and dramatic processes in the coproduction of organizations and identities. *Entrepreneurship Theory and Practice, 29*(2), 185–204.

Duncan, W., & Feisal, J. (1989). No laughing matter: Patterns of humor in the workplace. *Organizational Dynamics, 17*(4), 18–30.

Dutton, J. E. (2003). *Energize your workplace: How to create and sustain high-quality connections at work.* San Francisco, CA: John Wiley and Sons.

Ellis, M. (1973). *Why people play.* Englewood Cliffs, NJ: Prentice-Hall.

Fletcher, D. E. (2006). Entrepreneurial processes and the social construction of opportunity. *Entrepreneurship and Regional Development, 18*(5), 412–440.

Goodwin, C., & Heritage, J. (1990). Conversation analysis. *Annual Review of Anthropology, 19,* 283–307.

Hardy, C., Lawrence, T. B., & Grant, D. (2005). Discourse and collaboration: The role of conversations and collective identity. *The Academy of Management Review, 30*(1), 58–77.

Hay, J. (2001). The pragmatics of humor support. *Humor, 14*(1), 55–82.

Henricks, T. (2015). Play as self-realization toward a general theory of play. *American Journal of Play, 6,* 190–213.

Heritage, J. (1989). Current developments in conversation analysis. In D. Roger & P. Bull (Eds.), *Conversation: An interdisciplinary perspective* (pp. 21–47). Philadelphia, PA: Mulitlingual Matters.

Hjorth, D. (2004). Creating space for play/invention – concepts of space and organizational entrepreneurship. *Entrepreneurship & Regional Development, 16*(5), 413–432.

Holmes, J. (2007). Making humour work: creativity on the job. *Applied Linguistics, 28*(4), 518–537.

Lamine, W., Mian, S., & Fayolle, A. (2014). How do social skills enable nascent entrepreneurs to enact perseverance strategies in the face of challenges? A comparative case study of success and failure. *International Journal of Entrepreneurial Behavior and Research, 20*(6), 517–541.

Martin, R., Puhlik-Doris, P., Larsen, G., Gray, J., & Weir, K. (2003). Individual differences in uses of humor and their relation to psychological well-being: Development of the humor styles questionnaire. *Journal of Research in Personality, 37*(1), 48–75.

Pickering, L., Corduas, M., Eisterhold, J., Seifried, B., Eggleston, A., & Attardo, S. (2009). Prosodic markers of saliency in humorous narratives. *Discourse Processes, 46*(6), 517–540.

Pryor, M., Singleton, L., Taneja, S., & Humphreys, J. (2010). Workplace fun and its correlates: A conceptual inquiry. *International Journal of Management, 27*(2), 294–302.

Psathas, G. (Ed.). (1979). *Everyday language: Studies in ethnomethodology.* New York, NY: Irvington.

Romero, E., & Cruthirds, K. (2006). The use of humor in the workplace. *Academy of Management Perspectives, 20*(2), 58–69.

Schell, J. (2014). *The art of game design: A book of lenses.* Burlington, MA: Elsevier.

Schrage, M. (1999). *Serious play: How the world's best companies simulate to innovate.* Cambridge, MA: Harvard Business Review Press.

Shotter, J. (1993). *Cultural politics of everyday life.* Toronto: University of Toronto Press.

Statler, M., Roos, J., & Victor, B. (2009). Ain't misbehavin': Taking play seriously in organizations. *Journal of Change Management, 9*(1), 87–107.

Sullivan, F., & Wilson, N. (2015). Playful talk: Negotiating opportunities to learn in collaborative groups. *Journal of the Learning Sciences, 24*(1), 5–52.

Sutton-Smith, B. (1997). *The ambiguity of play.* Boston, MA: Harvard University Press.

Terr, L. (1999). *Beyond love and work: Why adults need to play.* New York, NY: Scribner.

Weick, K. E., & Roberts, K. H. (1993). Collective mind in organizations: Heedful interrelating on flight decks. *Administrative Science Quarterly, 38*(3), 357–381.

Weick, K. E., Sutcliffe, K. M., & Obstfeld, D. (2005). Organizing and the process of sensemaking. *Organization Science, 16*(4), 409–421.

# 5

# DOING REFLECTION

## Introduction

New venture formation is an act of organizing and therefore has roots in social processes and interpersonal interactions (Gartner, 2016; Katz, 1993), including reflective dialogues (Schön, 1983; Weick, Sutcliffe, & Obstfeld, 2005). However, because entrepreneurial work tends to be viewed as action oriented rather than reflective (Bird, 1988; Bird & Schjoedt, 2009), much remains to be understood about the reflective practices of early-stage entrepreneurial teams.

Reflective practice is both an individual and shared activity (Schön, 1992). Individuals can have an introspective dialogue, or team mates can engage in a collaborative dialogue. At either level, reflective practitioners consider the content of work (what are we doing?), the process of work (how are we doing it?), and the premise of work (why are we doing it in this way, and why are we doing it at all?) (Mezirow, 2000). Engaging in these acts of reflection is thought to result in enhanced creativity that may lead to entrepreneurial capabilities such as the generation of new ideas, strategies, and solutions (Hargadon & Bechky, 2006; Valkenburg & Dorst, 1998, p. 251). Reflection also may help entrepreneurs manage stress, learn, and innovate (Cope & Watts, 2000; Jacobs & Heracleous, 2005; Tikkamäki, Heikkilä, & Ainasoja, 2016).

By engaging in reflection and action, an individual or team brings to fruition new ideas, actions, and material innovations (Valkenburg & Dorst, 1998, p. 251). However, the fruits of reflective practice are not necessarily predicated by a team knowing more – the team members may or may not have sought or integrated new information. Rather reflective practice leads to a team knowing differently – they develop new interpretations that lead to advances in their work (Kegan, 2000). Of course, there is a role in the entrepreneurial innovation process for conversations that can be advanced by the introduction of new information; for discussions about what Heifetz would call *technical* challenges that can be overcome by new, better, or different information. However, entrepreneurial teams may be facing not only or not even mostly technical challenges; they may be facing *adaptive* challenges that require them to know differently (Heifetz, 1994).

As they engage in the reflective dialogues, entrepreneurial innovation teams may become able to "look at" what they previously had been able to only "look through" (Kegan & Lahey, 2010, p. 438). For example, a team might realize that an assumption they had been holding – about the product's features, about the way they've been developing the product, or about the motivations for their actions to date – is faulty. Through reflection they become able to detach a former assumption from their work whereas previously the assumption had defined their work. They become able to alter the theory-in-use that orients their work (Argyris, 1976).

While the term "reflective" might suggest that these dialogues are retrospective conversations about experiences long past, that may not be the case (Raelin, 2001, p. 19). In addition to reflection on-action after the fact, reflection also can be anticipatory; enabling active thought about possible alternatives and the likely result of actions. In this mode teams can learn "from the future as it emerges" (Scharmer, 2007). Reflection also can occur in real time with thought and action happening as an event unfolds (Van Manen, 2006, p. 87). In other words, people can think about the consequences of actions before they take them, and they can think about actions while they are doing them (Schön, 1983).

Reflection in-action is an interpretive, meaning-making activity (Jacobs & Heracleous, 2005). It enables people to question their assumptions and to (re)interpret the meaning(s) of events (that may be in the present, past, or future) (Maitlis, 2005). As such, reflection in-action requires participants to hold multiple possibilities or perspectives in mind simultaneously (Schön, 1987). This is true for the introspective reflections of an individual as well as the interpersonal reflective dialogues of a team (Schön, 1988). Entrepreneurial team mates, for example, need to hold their own visions in mind along with the feedback from advisors, prospective customers, and co-workers as part of their reflective practice.

Despite its potential importance to innovative entrepreneurial ventures, reflection has not been studied sufficiently, and additional research into the foundational facets associated with reflective dialogue within entrepreneurial work is needed (Jacobs & Heracleous, 2005). This chapter uses Conversation Analysis (CA) to investigate the structural organization of reflection in-action for successful innovative entrepreneurial teams.

## Understanding the organizational structure of interactions

In addition to sequence order – the turn-by-turn structural markers that guide conversations – interactions are accomplished through an overall structure. A basic example of structural organization can be recognized in informal telephone conversations which all tend to start and finish in the same way; with "hello" and "bye". Other recognizable structures organize in-person interactions in various workplaces. In medical appointments, for example, doctor-patient conversations progress through several routine structural phases of activity. They initially establish the reason for the appointment (e.g., a sore throat), an elaboration of symptoms, a diagnosis, and a prescribed treatment (Robinson, 2003). A sequenced order of turns is embedded in each of these phases which, as a whole, constitute an overall structural organization for the medical visit.

Retrospective reflection on-action has received this kind of structural analysis in several workplace settings. In medical education, scholars have revealed that senior doctors and residents organize their reflection on-action by indexing a particular event, expanding upon a reason for sharing that event, highlighting the learning issue presented by this event, and anchoring the uptake of new knowledge gained through this reflection on-action (Veen & Croix, 2017). And in architectural education settings, scholars have examined the structural organization of design critiques. In these semi-public reviews, educators and experts give feedback on student designs by indexing the object for review, imaginatively expanding the object, and helping students learn to represent their design work for others (Fleming, 1998).

To establish an overall structural organization for an interaction in a particular setting, several types of evidence must be observed in the naturally occurring workplace conversations. First, the activities leading to a social outcome must be routinely observed in the interactions. Evidence that the structural features are normatively ordered (e.g., Heritage, 1984) also must be observed. In other words, each structural activity must be oriented to the accomplishment of the project as a whole. Thus, the utterances are relevant to the current activity as well as the immediate next activities associated with the construction of the larger social action (Bavelas, 1991; Drew & Heritage, 1992; Heritage, 2005).

This chapter examines the reflective dialogues of several innovative entrepreneurial teams in action. After reviewing the interactional features observed in the data, it proposes an overall structure of interaction that organizes the reflection in-action between team mates. It then highlights the implications of a structural organization for reflection in-action from a theoretical and educational perspective.

## Looking at the data

The data comes from several early-stage innovative entrepreneurial teams competing in a lean startup contest. After the contest, these teams each go on to raise money, build an organization, and launch market-changing products. The teams are male-female dyads, and everyone has very limited experience with entrepreneurship. Representative episodes have been selected from the hours of recorded data to describe core interactional structures that enable reflection in-action.

A logical place to start an analysis of structural organization is at the beginning of an episode of reflection in-action. How do team mates initiate an instance of reflection in-action? And given the rich body of work on openings and closings, it also makes sense to examine how team mates conclude an instance of reflection in-action.

Excerpt 5.1 offers some details of openings and closings. In it, the team is talking about written comments that the judges gave them after the first round of evaluation. The feedback form, given to all the teams, was intended to help the teams as if the judges were advisors.

## Excerpt 5.1 Reflecting on what and why

| Line | Speaker | Utterance |
|------|---------|-----------|
| 1 | S1 | What did you think of the comments of the judges by the way? Oh you did open one Okay . . . no this one's not open either . . . well I might; I can't find the one you opened |
| 2 | S2 | okay yeah just open that one |
| 3 | S1 | they're not in here at least; maybe it's elsewhere |
| 4 | S2 | I thought their comments were interesting I mean (.) it wasn't (.) it's kind of like everything's great but your market is not venture backable |
| 5 | S1 | yeah I don't actually remember what they said. I skimmed it and it basically got that impression that there were no red flags = |
| 6 | S2 | tight |
| 7 | S1 | = but they just didn't think it was V. C. type company |
| 8 | S2 | right . . . which is like what's the point |
| 9 | S1 | mmhm . . . this was not a vc competition, so they said. well actually now we know it was |

Although there is minor distraction in between the question and the response, Speaker 1 asks her team mate about his take on the judge's comments (line 1), and Speaker 2 gives his interpretation of their reactions (line 4). As he summarizes: "it's kind of like everything's great but your market is not venture backable". Speaker 1 concurs with his assessment (lines 5, 7). Her understanding was that the judges thought the product creation process was progressing well enough, but the prospects for funding the venture were slim. Speaker 2 agrees with her summary and shares with her the meaning he takes from the comments, "like what's the point" (line 8). Speaker 1 has come to the same conclusion; the comments have changed her understanding of the contest (line 9). While she initially thought the competition was solely about product development – because lean startup contests hinge on the validation of prototypes – she now recognizes that the reason for validating products in a lean startup framework is to raise venture capital.

The reflection in-action begins with a question; a question seeking an opinion or perspective. The question indexes a shared artifact that is relevant to the team's greater goal of participating in and ascending within the contest. After both speakers have shared perspectives and a unified view is achieved, the reflection in-action concludes. The concluding encapsulation connects the focus of the reflective dialogue (the comments) with the team's normative goal (doing well in the contest).

While the first team was engaged in reflection in-action on a recently received set of comments, the second team is engaged in an instance of anticipatory reflection in-action. In Excerpt 5.2, the team mates are discussing a demonstration of their prototype that they are preparing to give to judges (and prospective funders). The excerpt also serves as an additional case for the structural features of opening and closing a reflective dialogue in-action.

## Excerpt 5.2 *Reflecting on what we are doing and why beforehand*

| Line | Speaker | Utterance |
|---|---|---|
| 1 | S1 | what are our goals for the demo↓ I think there's 2 goals (3) um (2) >that I can think of < that we can strive for. one is <u>impressing</u> the judges = maybe there's 3 goals- impressing the judges (.) beforehand (hhh) |
| 2 | S2 | <u>Oooo</u> |
| 3 | S1 | try and (.) get them to like us |
| 4 | S2 | ok (.) cause we'll have an opportunity to meet them |
| 5 | S1 | I think they'll come all around |
| 6 | S2 | right? |
| 7 | S1 | yeah |
| 8 | S2 | ok |
| 9 | S1 | the other one is to impress as many people as we can <u>beforehand</u> |
| 10 | S2 | ok |
| 11 | S1 | to try and go for audience <u>participation</u> |
| 12 | S2 | that's great |
| 13 | S1 | which I think is our better bet, |
| 14 | S2 | that's great |
| 15 | S1 | or 3 just (.) if someone appears to be investor like (.) try and impress them |
| 16 | S2 | judges to win (.) people there for audience choice |
| 17 | S1 | yeah |
| 18 | S2 | and investors for money (.) yeah |

Like the first, this episode begins with a question. Speaker 1 makes what appears to be an open-ended appeal for suggestions. However, he limits the question by immediately offering several answers. His question indexes the "demo" which is scheduled for the next day (line 1). Participating in the demo show is essential to being in the contest, and doing well in the demo show is critical to winning the contest. As Speaker 1 expands his ideas about the goals for the demo, Speaker 2 indicates that she is attending to his suggestions (lines 2, 4, 6, 8, 10, 12). She then summarizes the goals (lines 16, 18). Once the team mates achieve a unified view, the reflection in-action concludes by linking the focus of the reflective dialogue (the demo) with the team's normative goal (succeeding in the contest).

Together these two episodes demonstrate that reflection in-action can emphasize events that have already happened as well as those that have yet to happen. They also suggest possible features of the structural organization of reflection in-action. Questions can open episodes of reflection in-action, and an articulation of the shared view that has emerged through the reflection can close them. The topic of the questions, however, is not random: the topic is oriented toward a matter of vital importance to the normative goals of the team's work. They refer to a meaningful element in the team's shared experience and treat that element as something worth reconsidering from additional vantage points. These markers – referring to something consequential and seeking alternative perspectives – are what makes the question an opening to reflection in-action.

Another episode of naturally occurring workplace conversation between members of an innovative entrepreneurial team highlight this observation. In Excerpt 5.3, the team mates are discussing their "numbers" – their financial projections for the venture, including their sales forecasts. Both of these related number sets are part of the pitch that the team must give the next day in the contest finale. As such, they are critical to the normative goals of the team.

## Excerpt 5.3 Reflecting on projections

| Line | Speaker | Utterance |
|---|---|---|
| 1 | S1 | I think also in terms of our numbers (.) we should probably revisit them (2) and I'm learning a lot more about how to evaluate (.)uh(.) the value of something in this class I'm taking |
| 2 | S2 | okay |
| 3 | S1 | and you asked me earlier to show you (.) the slides from that class which I will do |
| 4 | S2 | yeah |
| 5 | S1 | = and its really really helpful but just (.) not only um (.) not only like (.) an evaluation of of the idea or an early-stage company = |
| 6 | S2 | mmhm |
| 7 | S1 | = >but< also we're learning about options value too and sensitivity analysis ↑ |
| 8 | S2 | okay |
| 9 | S1 | and and in doing a little more of a robust analysis of (.) um (.) given some of our assumptions ↑ like = |
| 10 | S2 | yeah |
| 11 | S1 | = what and building in some likelihoods ↑ |
| 12 | S2 | okay |
| 13 | S1 | and then doing anal analysis of basically like what's the (.) probability of this likelihood and how is |
| 14 | S2 | [yeah] |
| 15 | S1 | [that] effecting the overall (garble) |
| 16 | S2 | yeah I'm game = |
| 17 | S1 | okay |
| 18 | S2 | = cause we've <never> become 100% certain of our numbers |
| 19 | S1 | right and we won't be [like] |
| 20 | S2 | [no] |
| 21 | S1 | that's the biggest lesson from this class that there's so much that (.) there's su such a guess work but I think adding on this sensitivity analysis will help |
| 22 | S2 | yeah |
| 23 | S1 | Uh |
| 24 | S2 | we should start (.) start fresh = |
| 25 | S1 | yeah |
| 26 | S2 | = try and ignore what we know right now = |

| 27 | S1 | yeah |
|----|----|----|
| 28 | S2 | = and then = |
| 29 | S1 | I totally agree |
| 30 | S2 | yeah okay |
| 31 | S1 | yeah |
| 32 | S2 | that's good |
| 33 | S1 | we don't have to do that by tomorrow though |
| 34 | S2 | ((*laughter*)) no ° |
| 35 | S1 | ((*laughter*)) |
| 36 | S2 | we don't wanna do that by tomorrow |
| 37 | S1 | yeah (hhh) |
| 38 | S2 | show up tomorrow and be like yeah we realized last night >It's not gonna work<° ((*laughter*)) |
| 39 | S1 | ((*laughter*)) unfurl the flag ↑ [yeah] |
| 40 | S2 | [uh] |
| 41 | S1 | (2) one thing that one of the early round judges gave in the feedback was that they don't think (.) that we're going to sell that many |
| 42 | S2 | yeah |
| 43 | S1 | um and ↑ (3) |
| 44 | S2 | there's always that = |
| 45 | S1 | >right< there's always that there's always that risk (.) um (.2) but (.5) it I think it totally depends on our marketing and = |
| 46 | S2 | yeah |
| 47 | S1 | = and and and our go to market strategy, but (.) I just I have a hard time seeing that given like all the like anecdotal and ↑(2) data we have to confirm the market |
| 48 | S2 | yeah I I agree um (3) but we'll >worry about that later< right |
| 49 | S1 | yeah agreed. Ok, |

The opening of this reflective episode is indicated by Speaker 1 bringing up their "numbers", their financial projections (line 1). She overtly suggests that they "revisit" the numbers. This starts the reflective episode by indexing a relevant topic and deeming it worthy of reflective attention – even without a question prompt.

Speaker 1 then refers to the class she is taking and her team mate's earlier request to be kept informed about it. This indexical reference to a shared experience from their recent past serves to fortify the call for reflection – again without a question prompt. Speaker 2 signals attention and comprehension (lines 2, 4, 6, 8, 10, 12) without overlapping her utterances until line 14.

At this point Speaker 1 concludes her thought (line 15), and Speaker 2 adds a complementary perspective (line 16). Speaker 1 revives her thought and continues to build on Speaker 2's comment (lines 19, 21). After indicating his agreement and waiting for Speaker 1 to signal she has concluded her thought, Speaker 2 proposes a course of action for reflecting on their work; suggesting that they "start fresh" and attempt to ignore what they think they currently know (lines 24, 26). In this utterance, Speaker 2 is offering a perspective not on the content of their reflections but on the process of doing reflection. He is proposing a course of action to guide future reflective dialogue.

The speakers concur that his proposal makes sense (lines 29–32). Speaker 1 suggests that they can suspend any action on this topic and return to it when they are less pressed for time (line 33). The team mates then engage in a playful exchange as they imagine a ridiculous turn of events during tomorrow's finale (lines 34–39).

After a brief pause, Speaker 1 returns to a serious tone and reorients the team's attention to reflections about their conversation with one of the contest judges (line 41). This is another opening for reflection, again without a question prompt. Sacks referred to this kind of utterance as "musing out loud" (Sacks, 1992, p. 405). Presenting a topic to elicit interest without asking a specific question signals that the speaker is inwardly considering this topic. By sharing this musing aloud, Speaker 1 indirectly invites the other person to share a perspective on the topic.

The pause at the beginning of the musing (line 41) also indicates that Speaker 1 has not come to closure on the topic. While the shared levity might have served as a way to unify perspective and close the reflection, the pause suggests that Speaker 1 must disrupt that flow. It is well documented that latencies preface utterances that include some discomfort (Bavelas, 1991), including the discomfort of steering the conversation back to a topic rather than allowing it to conclude.

Speaker 2 offers his confirmation of her recollection and recognition of their shared uncertainty (lines 42, 44). Speaker 1 shares her struggle to reconcile divergent feedback and data (lines 45, 47). Speaker 1 affirms her assessment and struggle while also redirecting the team's attention to the task at hand (line 48). Speaker 2 offers her willingness to suspend the conversation about the (re)interpretation of data (line 49).

At this point in the exchange, Speaker 2 confirms Speaker 1's initial idea by building upon it while also indicating that there are other concerns to incorporate; they also must orient to pressures of the contest and the requirements of the judging on the next day. This sequence demonstrates how both team mates are accountable for completing their shared work. It is a way of treating Speaker 1's idea as the starting point for defining their work and envisioning a course of action. However, it is Speaker 2 who tempers those suggestions by orienting to the constraints of the contest. While Speaker 1 is advancing matters of what they need to do, Speaker 2 is enveloping those tasks in the goals of the contest. Speaker 2's utterance shapes the immediate conversation; the last word in the conversational flow. This interactional position suggests situated roles of someone who is attending to the mechanics of building a product and venture and someone who is adjusting what can be done to fit the limitations of their available time.

The final two utterances of the episode (lines 48, 49) reunites the team mates' perspectives on all of the matters – the divergent feedback, the urgency to complete preparations for the presentation, and the suspension of some conversations. They synthesize the team mates' perspectives on the content, premise, and process of their shared work (Mezirow, 2003). By reaching this unified understanding, the utterances indicate that the reflection in-action has been interactionally accomplished and the episode of reflection can be closed.

## Proposing a model of reflection in-action

In formal activity settings such as courtrooms, the structural organization of interactions are predetermined by the institutional context (Maynard, 1984). In more informal settings, structural organization can emerge in the moment based on the goals relevant to that context. The selected episodes show how entrepreneurial team mates can transform their specific concerns into manageable events through reflection. More importantly, they show the verbal means by which the team mates structurally organize that reflection; how they raise and attend to the problems that require reflective attention (Drew & Heritage, 1992).

While the selected episodes are not exhaustive of every possible means by which innovative entrepreneurial teams can do reflection in-action, they do present several recurring aspects that suggest a model of structural organization for reflection in-action in an early entrepreneurial context. All of the episodes begin by referring to a topic that is recognizable as relevant to that team's shared work. This opening may be accomplished with or without a question prompt and serves to introduce the topic for reflection. The topic becomes an object of reflection as the speakers treat it as a matter worthy of (re)consideration. This may be achieved by directly or indirectly inviting perspectives on the topic. The matter is then internalized. As the speakers share and clarify their perspectives they collaboratively (re)construct the topic based on their individual representations of it. The closure of the reflection in-action may follow these utterances, or there may be additional turns devoted to creating a plan (e.g., for postponing the reflective dialogue or taking other action first). The closure of the reflection in-action is accomplished by (re)uniting perspectives on the topic and possibly on the content, premise, and process of the reflection. It may also include an articulation of the impact the refection has had on their shared normative goals.

All of the episodes progress from a verbal "mapping" of the team's current concerns (Vehvilainen, 2001) toward an articulation of a newly affirmed shared understanding of the topic of concern as it contributes to their organizational goals. Moving from opening an episode of reflection in-action to closing it requires each speaker to verbally attend to the issue their partner has brought up, the connections between that issue and possible actions that the team could take, and the bonds between that issue and the team's external obligations. The team mates demonstrate their orientation toward these three modes of reflection through each turn of talk and through the overall structural organization of the reflective episode. Closing an episode of reflection in-action also involves completing several prerequisite activities including eliciting, sharing, and unifying perspectives. The team mates are accountable for progressing through these activities by anchoring each transitional point in their own turn of talk.

Of course, these excerpts may not represent every way that every team could do reflection in every circumstance. Even these teams would enact future reflective dialogues for "another next first time" potentially resulting in a different verbal process and outcome (Garfinkel, 2002; Taylor & Van Every, 2011). Nevertheless, the methodological approach of CA enables the identification of the conversational machinery necessary to socially construct shared work. Based on the episodes presented in this chapter, the structural organization of reflection in-action in the service of early-stage entrepreneurial work includes at least four ordered segments: open with referral to issue, make issue reflectable, collect and internalize perspectives, and (re)unite perspectives.

By reviewing the observable language found in the naturally occurring workplace interactions of several innovative entrepreneurial teams, this chapter has been able to identify a model for the overall structural organization associated with reflection in-action. It also suggests several paths forward for future research.

This micro-analysis of the workplace interactions of teams advances scholarly understanding of entrepreneurial reflective practice. Specifically it demonstrates that teams reflect not only after the fact on their work but also in-action. Moreover, it suggests a model of the structural organization of reflection in-action based on empirical evidence.

There is much more, of course, to learn about reflection in entrepreneurial work. Future research needs to examine additional workplace interactions of innovative entrepreneurial teams engaging in reflection in-action. Such inquiries will be able to affirm, edit, or enhance the model for reflection in-action that has been proposed in this chapter. Although the teams featured in these episodes were able to complete reflection in-action, other teams (and these teams in other instances) may not be able to move from openings to closures so effectively. Future research can explore the verbal means by which entrepreneurial teams have difficulty reunifying perspectives and effectively closing the reflective dialogue. Being able to articulate one's own perspective, inquire about others' perspectives and experiences, and maintain an inquisitive stance can help people productively engage in reflective dialogue (Raelin, 2001, p. 24). How these attributes are observable in the language present in the different segments of reflection in-action is another area for future consideration.

## References

Argyris, C. (1976). Single-loop and double-loop models in research on decision making. *Administrative Science Quarterly, 21*(3), 363–375.

Bavelas, J. (1991). Some problems with linking goals to discourse. In K. Tracy (Ed.), *Understanding face-to-face interaction: Issues linking goals and discourse* (pp. 119–130). Hillsdale, NJ: Lawrence Erlbaum Associates.

Bird, B. (1988). Implementing entrepreneurial ideas: The case for intention. *Academy of Management Review, 13*(3), 442–453.

Bird, B., & Schjoedt, L. (2009). Entrepreneurial behavior: Its nature, scope, recent research, and agenda for future research. In M. B. Carsrud (Ed.), *Understanding the entrepreneurial mind international studies in entrepreneurship* (Vol. 24, pp. 327–358). New York, NY: Springer Science & Business Media, LLC.

Cope, J., & Watts, G. (2000). Learning by doing: An exploration of experience, critical incidents and reflection in entrepreneurial learning. *International Journal of Entrepreneurial Behaviour and Research, 6*(3), 104–124.

Drew, P., & Heritage, J. (Eds.). (1992). *Talk at work: Interaction in institutional settings*. Cambridge: Cambridge University Press.

Fleming, D. (1998). Design talk: Constructing the object in studio conversations. *Design Issues, 14*(2), 41–62.

Garfinkel, H. (2002). *Ethnomethodology's program: Working out Durkheim's aphorism*. New York, NY: Rowman and Littlefield.

Gartner, W. B. (2016). *Entrepreneurship as organizing*. Northampton, MA: Edward Elgar Publishing.

Hargadon, A. B., & Bechky, B. A. (2006). When collections of creatives become creative collectives: A field study of problem solving at work. *Organization Science, 17*(4), 484–500.

Heifetz, R. (1994). *Leadership without easy answers*. Cambridge, MA: Harvard University Press.

Heritage, J. (1984). *Garfinkel and Ethnomethodology*. Cambridge, UK: Polity Press.

Heritage, J. (2005). Conversation analysis and institutional talk. In K. L. Fitch & R. E. Sanders (Eds.), *Handbook of language and social interaction* (pp. 103–147). Mahwah, NJ: Lawrence Erlbaum Associates.

Jacobs, C. D., & Heracleous, L. T. (2005). Answers for questions to come: Reflective dialogue as an enabler of strategic innovation. *Journal of Organizational Change Management, 18*(4), 338–352.

Katz, J. A. (1993). The dynamics of organizational emergence: A contemporary group formation perspective. *Entrepreneurship Theory and Practice, 17*(2), 97–102.

Kegan, R. (2000). What "form" transforms? A constructive-developmental approach to transformative learning. In J. Mezirow (Ed.), *Learning as transformation: Critical perspectives on a theory in progress* (pp. 35–70). San Francisco, CA: Jossey-Bass.

Kegan, R., & Lahey, L. (2010). From subject to object: A constructive-developmental approach to reflective practice. In N. Lyons (Ed.), *Handbook of reflection and reflective inquiry: Mapping a way of knowing for professional reflective inquiry* (pp. 433–449). New York, NY: Springer.

Maitlis, S. (2005). The social processes of organizational sense making. *Academy of Management Journal, 48*(1), 21–49.

Maynard, D. (1984). *Inside plea bargaining: The language of negotiation*. New York, NY: Plenum.

Mezirow, J. (2000). Learning to think like an adult: Core concepts of transformation theory. In J. Mezirow (Ed.), *Learning as transformation: Critical perspectives on at theory in progress* (pp. 3–33). San Francisco, CA: Jossey-Bass.

Mezirow, J. (2003). Transformative learning as discourse. *Journal of Transformative Education, 1*(1), 58–63.

Raelin, J. (2001). Public reflection as the basis of learning. *Management Learning, 32*(1), 11–30.

Robinson, J. (2003). An interactional structure of medical activities during acute visits and its implications for patients' participation. *Health Communication, 15*(1), 27–59.

Sacks, H. (1992). *Lectures on conversation* (Vol. 1 (Fall 1964-Spring 1968)). Oxford Blackwell.

Scharmer, C. O. (2007). *Theory U. Leading from the future as it emerges. The social technology of presencing*. Cambridge, MA: Society for Organizational Learning.

Schön, D. A. (1983). *The reflective practitioner: How professionals think in action*. New York, NY: Basic Books.

Schön, D. A. (1987). *Educating the reflective practitioner*. San Francisco, CA: Jossey-Bass.

Schön, D. A. (1988). Designing: Rules, types and words. *Design Studies, 9*(3), 181–190.

Schön, D. A. (1992). Designing as a reflective conversation with the materials of a design situation. *Knowledge-Based Systems, 5*(1), 3–14.

Taylor, J. R., & Van Every, E. J. (2011). *The situated organization*. New York, NY: Routledge.

Tikkamäki, K., Heikkilä, P., & Ainasoja, M. (2016). Positive stress and reflective practice among entrepreneurs. *Journal of Entrepreneurship, Management and Innovation, 12*(1), 35–56.

Valkenburg, R., & Dorst, K. (1998). The reflective practice of design teams. *Design Studies, 19*(3), 249–271.

Van Manen, M. (2006). Reflexivity and the pedagogical moment: The practical-ethical nature of pedagogical thinking and acting. In I. Westbury & G. Milburn (Eds.), *Rethinking schooling: Twenty-five years of the journal of curriculum studies*. New York, NY: Routledge.

Veen, M., & Croix, A. (2017). The swamplands of reflection: Using conversation analysis to reveal the architecture of group reflection sessions. *Medical Education, 51*(3), 324–336.

Vehvilainen, S. (2001). Evaluative dvice in educational counseling: The use of disagreement in the "Stepwise Entry" to advice'. *Research on Language and Social Interaction, 34*(3), 371–398.

Weick, K. E., Sutcliffe, K. M., & Obstfeld, D. (2005). Organizing and the process of sensemaking. *Organization Science, 16*(4).

# 6

# DOING EMPATHY

## The most valuable thing

Ever since design-thinking became an articulated approach to innovation and entrepreneurship, empathy has been in demand (Dandavate, Sanders, & Stuart, 1996; Koskinen, Battarbee, & Mattelmaki, 2003; Mattelmäki, Vaajakallio, & Koskinen, 2014). It has even been called "the most valuable thing" taught at Harvard Business School (Allworth, 2012). However, recent research suggests that our ability to experience and express empathy is on the decline (Konrath, O'Brien, & Hsing, 2010; Turkle, 2015; Ward, Cody, Schaal, & Hojat, 2012). Although many accounts have been published and workshops conducted on the value of empathy in the innovation process, few studies have focused on intra-team empathy – and fewer have described how it is accomplished through the workplace conversations of teams in action.

## Defining empathy

Empathy has become a popular term used by business leaders, scholars, and the media. While this widespread use suggests that an inquiry into the inner workings of empathy is warranted, it also means the definitions of empathy are many (Davis, 1980; Eisenberg & Miller, 1987). Traditionally, empathy has been considered either a cognitive reaction or an emotional response. In the former case, empathy tends to mean the capacity to recognize another person's perspective (Ickes, 1997). In the latter, empathy is the embodied sensation of matching and internalizing another person's feelings (Feshbach & Roe, 1968). Together these descriptions suggest that rational and emotional definitions of empathy might exist on a polarized continuum (New & Kimbell, 2013). More recently, empathy has become associated with concerned motivation: the ability to understand another person's experience and attune to their feelings while demonstrating appropriate concern or engaging in prosocial action (Cikara, Bruneau, & Saxe, 2011; Goleman, 2007).

This kind of empathy may be most valuable in the early stages of innovation, a complicated phase in the development of a new product or service (Postma, Zwartkruis-Pelgrim, Daemen, & Du, 2012). At this time innovators must synthesize data from different users or prospective customers. They must find an intersection between the abilities of the team and the wishes of the market (Baker & Nelson, 2005; Sarasvathy, 2001). And they must engage in an iterative process of observation, discussion, and action while they seek to define the problem and an array of possible solutions simultaneously (Dong, Lepri, Kim, Pianesi, & Pentland, 2012; Fleming, 1998; Oak, 2011). During these early-stage challenges, empathy can serve as a compass. It allows innovators to build an authentic understanding of the needs of prospective customers which can inform the contours of a new product (Wright & McCarthy, 2005). This grounded sense of the prospective customer's experience – this "feel" for the other person's reality – can productively guide the innovation process (Fulton Suri, 2003; Postma, Lauche, & Stappers, 2009).

While many scholars and practitioners have invested in understanding the role of empathy between innovators and potential customers, few efforts have been made to understand the role of empathy between members of the same team (Stephens & Carmeli, 2016). In other intra-team contexts, empathy has been shown to reduce intrapersonal conflict while increasing productivity and feelings of group cohesion (Ayoko, Callan, & Hartel, 2008).

## Expressing empathy

In addition to being a feeling, thought, and kind of motivation, empathy is a socially constructed act that is created and recognized through conversation. Empathy can be conveyed by non-verbal aspects of communication such as eye contact, body orientation, and closeness (Haase & Tepper, 1972). Of course, what we say and how we say it also matters. When a person responds to another with words that are genuine and reflexive, empathy is expressed through the validation and verification of the other's experience (Morse, Bottorff, Anderson, O'Brien, & Solberg, 2006). Empathy also is expressed through communications that aim to solve problems rather than assign blame and through communication skills such as active listening and playing back details for clarification (Coulehan et al., 2001; Gittell, Seidner, & Wimbush, 2010).

Studies conducted in medical settings have offered several insights on the interactional accomplishment of empathy. One means of conveying empathy is through utterances that overtly communicate comprehension of the other person's concern. A therapist, for example, might demonstrate an awareness of the patient's perspective by repeating, confirming, or elaborating on a patient's expressed problem (Wynn & Wynn, 2006). Another means is through utterances that suggest affiliation and alignment (Stivers, Mondada, & Steensig, 2011). A therapist could express this kind of alignment by reassuring the patient that anyone would have done the same thing or felt the same way.

Several communicative responses that can support the interactional accomplishment of empathy have been defined (Heritage, 2011): response cries convey empathetic understanding through prosody; subjunctive assessments affirm the first speaker's feelings through expressions of solidarity; and observational responses offer a detached concern. Other responses, such as sharing parallel stories or asking ancillary questions, may work against the creation of an empathic bond (Heritage, 2011). Additional research has described the structural features that accompany and conclude empathic exchanges (Jefferson, 1988). After a speaker has explained the troubled situation and has received a response that registers as sufficiently empathetic, the speaker can advance the topic. This does not mean move to a new topic; just pivot to reveal more intimate details of the troubling matter. As an exchange focused on troubles comes to its end, speakers offer an optimistic perspective that casts the discussed difficulty in the most positive way possible. Then, speakers may mark the closure of the episode by introducing an unrelated, uncomplicated topic.

The conversational achievement of empathy may require different interactional sequences in different contexts. For example, advice from a medical professional that follows a patient's disclosure of a problem is treated as a supportive gesture by the patient (Jefferson & Lee, 1992). However, advice from a friend in response to a peer's disclosure of problem in everyday conversation may be treated as unhelpful and intrusive. In other words, the sequences that convey empathy may rely on the particular expectations of specific contexts (Drew & Heritage, 1992).

This chapter focuses on the interactional accomplishment of empathy in innovative entrepreneurial workplaces; professional contexts that feature interactions between peers on the same team.

## Micro-analysis of empathy in action

The following excerpts come from the recorded conversations of early-stage innovative entrepreneurial teams. They self-recorded their naturally occurring workplace interactions. The teams are all mixed gender dyads. In some cases they both have technical expertise and are complete beginners on business matters; in others one team mate is technology oriented and the other is business oriented. All dyads are still learning the fundamentals of entrepreneurship. And all of the teams go on to develop successful companies.

The analysis of the recorded data began with the identification of episodes focused on troubles (i.e., problems, challenges, and concerns). Sequences with one team mate indicating a troublesome matter and another team mate responding were identified as empathy-oriented episodes. Episodes were analyzed in detail, using Conversation Analysis, to investigate the structure and order of turns that were required to address the difficulty. Representative excerpts have been selected to reveal several ways in which successful innovative entrepreneurial teams engage in practices of empathy.

In Excerpt 6.1, Speaker 1 proposes the development of an end user profile to help define the features of their product (line 3). However, Speaker 2 is not familiar with that term (line 4).

## *Excerpt 6.1 Empathizing with disclosures of lack of knowledge*

| Line | Speaker | Utterance |
|------|---------|-----------|
| 1 | S1 | oh (.) one thing that I think would be helpful for us though is just |
| 2 | S2 | Yeah |
| 3 | S1 | as an exercise is building our <end user profiles>↑ |
| 4 | S2 | (2) what does that mean |
| 5 | S1 | uh it means building a profile of (.) the target use case↑ |
| 6 | S2 | okay↑ |
| 7 | S1 | and that's across like (.) >so we're very broadly saying the diabetic consumer< but is it the diabetic consumer who= what= what does that demographic look like (.) is it a <u>mom</u> (.) is it a <u>child</u> (.) do they eat out often (.) how often |
| 8 | S2 | [okay] |
| 9 | S1 | [do] they eat out (.) What's their (.) like income level (.) just <u>really</u> diving into that |
| 10 | S2 | what what's the term again↑ End use↑ |
| 11 | S1 | end us= build an end user profile↑ |
| 12 | S2 | Okay |
| 13 | S1 | or MORE than (.) the profile persona for >the beach head market< maybe (3) yeah this is= |
| 14 | S2 | okay |
| 15 | S1 | like going back to the class slides, i'm >gonna just< <u>read through</u> some of the things and let me know (.) if anything triggers something else that we should focus on |

Speaker 1 responds matter-of-factly with a definition of an end user profile (line 5). She elaborates on this definition with various examples to ensure her basic definition makes sense (lines 7, 9). Speaker 2 contributes tokens of attention to indicate that he is intently listening while she speaks (lines 6, 8). Speaker 2 asks Speaker 1 to repeat the term again and partially articulates it (line 10). Speaker 1 restates the term, "end user profile" (line 11). Speaker 2 indicates that he is making an effort to remember that term and concept (line 12). Speaker 1 tweaks her definition (line 13) and opens a new line of conversation (line 15). By suggesting that they read through some slides from the entrepreneurship class as a means of selecting the next topic, she is empowering Speaker 2 to participate in the selection of the next topic. She is also signaling that they should make sure they both are using the same terms and envision the same course of action for their innovation process.

Excerpt 6.2 is exceptionally long according to the standards of Conversation Analysis. However, the naturally occurring break in the conversation includes all of these turns. It is what Sacks would have called a "big package" that has many turns and an order that is complex (Jefferson, 1988).

Speaker 2 had been part of a different early-stage team. Some months earlier she decided to leave that team and start the venture that she and Speaker 1 are now developing. Speaker 1 knows that it was not an easy decision for Speaker 2 to make.

He also knows that the other venture is becoming increasingly viable. Speaker 1 wants to know why Speaker 2 decided to leave the other team (line 1).

## Excerpt 6.2 *Empathizing with a significant decision from the recent past*

| Line | Speaker | Utterance |
|------|---------|-----------|
| 1 | S1 | you just didn't wanna do it↑ |
| 2 | S2 | um (3) the problem with them is (.) it's (.) \<another> (3) it's just another a network issue |
| 3 | S1 | Yeah |
| 4 | S2 | in order for it to be really powerful <u>everyone</u> has to adopt |
| 5 | S1 | Yeah |
| 6 | S2 | and I (.) |
| 7 | S1 | like all of em |
| 8 | S2 | What↑ |
| 9 | S1 | like <u>all</u> of them |
| 10 | S2 | like <u>all</u> of them, right ↑ and I I didn't see it being as \<compelling to> (2) for the switching costs like to to outweigh the switching costs of someone to just log in= he= what he tried to do and >I feel like he succeed in a sense< was make filling out the profile information really <u>fun</u> like |
| 11 | S1 | Okay |
| 12 | S2 | and like kind of integrated ↑ um (3) but (2) I mean [zcom] is in this space (.) in a sense \<and> |
| 13 | S1 | Yeah |
| 14 | S2 | there's a ><u>ton</u> of other niche sites that are in this space< |
| 15 | S1 | yeah they've just gotta do something but one thing better than everyone else and get bought by one of the big ones↓ |
| 16 | S2 | Right |
| 17 | S1 | makes sense |
| 18 | S2 | right yeah |
| 19 | S1 | Um |
| 20 | S2 | yeah and ken= the other thing that is challenging is ken (2) ken is >challenging to work with<° |
| 21 | S1 | Yeah |
| 22 | S2 | \<he is> like he= I <u>love</u> him but he= once he gets an idea= like so we worked with two people from the other university↑ |
| 23 | S1 | Yeah |
| 24 | S2 | um and he was just= it was really hard for him to (.) balance ideas and >he got< really <u>frustrated</u> |
| 25 | S1 | Yeah |
| 26 | S2 | and it was a really intense class cause we had to build this whole business um plan |
| 27 | S1 | yeah |
| 28 | S2 | for <u>this</u> ↑ |
| 29 | S1 | Mmhm |
| 30 | S2 | basically um and it had a different name when we did it |
| 31 | S1 | Okay |

| 32 | S2 | he renamed it (.) but it was the same idea. Anyhow I I don't think I could work with ken |
| 33 | S1 | (.) I understand (.) um |
| 34 | S2 | but he's done it and and I mean this is <u>all</u> him |
| 35 | S1 | yeah |
| 36 | S2 | and he's worked <u>so</u> hard on it |
| 37 | S1 | well good↑ |
| 38 | S2 | but I I don't= I think there's a lot of people who (.) don't believe in it (.) too, like don't get it |
| 39 | S1 | yeah (.) aaahh I can see both sides ° |
| 40 | S2 | kay |
| 41 | S1 | (3) aaa alright um so yeah you're uh looking to numbers and then we're gonna do the market profile |

Speaker 2 shares her perspective on the problems with the concept behind the other venture (lines 2–14). Speaker 1 offers tokens of agreement and acknowledgement while she explains her views (lines 3, 6). In lines 7 and 9 Speaker 1 offers affirmation by repeating Speaker 2's claim that a large number of users are needed in order for the other venture to succeed. Speaker 2 continues to share her concerns about the other venture's position in the market (lines 10–14). Speaker 1 offers qualified agreement (line 15). He can see that the space is crowded. However, he can also appreciate the other venture's strategy as reported by Speaker 2; a venture that does one thing exceptionally well could be acquired.

After status checks (16, 18) and an affirmation from Speaker 1 (line17), Speaker 1 pauses with an "um" (line 19), uncertain if Speaker 2 has completed her story. Then Speaker 2 shares another reason for her departure (line 20): she did not enjoy working with Ken, the other venture's lead entrepreneur. As she shares her conflicted feelings about working with Ken (lines 20–38), Speaker 1 indicates that he is following her account by offering tokens of agreement and acknowledgement (lines 21–31). He also offers overt affiliation with "I understand" (line 33) and assessment with "well good" (line 35). In line 37, Speaker 1 hesitates before offering his statement that validates her conflicted views. Speaker 2 signals that she knows he has heard her by saying "kay" (line 40). Speaker 1 again hesitates before facilitating the conversation onto a different topic (line 41).

The next excerpt begins with one team mate struggling to get a sticky label off of a device.

### Excerpt 6.3 Empathizing with a minor material problem in the moment

| Line | Speaker | Utterance |
| --- | --- | --- |
| 1 | S1 | ((*Picking at a sticky label on a device*)) |
| 2 | S2 | Not coming off ↑((*laugh*)) |
| 3 | S1 | I can't get that off there ((*laugh laying down the device and letting go*)) |
| 4 | S2 | You need fingernails ((*Pulling it toward her and scraping the label*)) |
| 5 | S1 | Yeah |

| 6 | S2 | ((*Letting go of the device with the label removed*)) |
| 7 | S1 | Well I really like this <u>box</u> |
| 8 | S2 | You like the box↑ |
| 9 | S1 | I do |

As Speaker 1 tries to remove the sticker, Speaker 2 notices his trouble and asks about it (line 2). Speaker 1 confesses that he cannot remove the label and puts down the device (line 3). Speaker 2 suggests a solution which she can accomplish on behalf of the team (line 4). As she picks at the label, Speaker 1 agrees that he needs help and that her suggestion will work (line 5). After Speaker 2 completes the removal of the sticky label and puts down the device, Speaker 1 opens up a new topic of conversation (line 7) with a discourse marker, "well".

## Discussion

These three excerpts illustrate three very different cases of empathy in innovative entrepreneurial workplaces. The topic organization and responsive techniques that they capture reveal several ways that teams can verbally accomplish empathy. Excerpt 6.1 is set apart from the others by issues of face (Goffman, 1967). This dynamic influences the topic order, response mechanisms, and closure techniques that animate the trouble-telling exchanges. Excerpt 6.2 is a long-form story that has emotional impact for the teller. Excerpt 6.3 is a pre-emptive act of empathy toward a partner who is having a minor problem in that moment. The excerpts demonstrate the range of interactional mechanisms that construct empathy in an entrepreneurial context.

People are aware of the social dynamics related to self-image and self-esteem, and they take efforts to save their own and others' face (Goffman, 1955). Consequently, people may avoid asking for help or seeking feedback because these actions may lead to embarrassment and threats to face (Lee, 1997). When speakers do reveal vulnerabilities, other participants in the conversation tend to enact specific conversational moves to protect the speaker from threats to face (Goffman, 1955, 1967). Evidence of this delicacy can be observed in the Excerpt 6.1. Speaker 2 reveals a lack of knowledge when he asks Speaker 1 to define the term, "end user profile". Speaker 1 pauses briefly with "uh" before offering a matter-of-fact definition of the term. The marker "uh" indicates that she recognizes that Speaker 1's disclosure could make him feel vulnerable and that her response needs to be adapted to manage that risk. She goes on to give a rich explanation of the meaning of the term that is relevant to their market segment to ensure comprehension. Even as Speaker 2 asks a second time for the exact turn of phrase, Speaker 1 responds clearly and patiently.

In Excerpt 6.1, Speaker 1 had to reveal his lack of knowledge about end user profiles in order to participate productively in the team's work. However, in the second episode Speaker 1 opens up an unnecessary topic by directly asking Speaker 2 why she chose to leave a different team. Speaker 1 may not have known in advance that Speaker 2's story would be sensitive, but their interactions demonstrate several structural features of empathetic exchanges. Throughout Speaker 2's story, Speaker 1 offers many response tokens – "yeah" and "mmhm" – that overlap the story without interrupting it. These small verbalizations are economical and effective displays of empathy (Kitzinger & Kitzinger, 2007). Speaker 1 also offers assessments such as "makes sense" which indicate his ongoing interest in her story as well as his empathy for her experience (Goodwin, 1986; Goodwin & Goodwin, 1992).

Speaker 1's utterance of "makes sense" communicates affiliation so effectively that it stimulates a pivot in the storytelling; the topic shifts to a more sensitive matter or to what Jefferson would call an "affiliation response" (Jefferson, 1988). In the first part of her story, Speaker 2 was sharing her evaluation of the other venture's potential. However, after she hears "makes sense" from Speaker 1, she discloses a more personal reason for leaving the other team: she did not like working with Ken. The sequence of turns that establishes the affiliation response changes the relational distance between the two participants. Speaker 2's utterances reveal more emotionally charged details of the story. Speaker 1 continues to express empathy with four response tokens of "yeah" in close succession.

Another pivot occurs when Speaker 1 expresses that he has attuned to the rational and emotional reasons for her decision. After he says, "I understand", Speaker 2 begins to recalibrate the relational distance between the two speakers and return to a normal stance. Her utterances start to signal what Jefferson would call a "close implicature" (Jefferson, 1988). Instead of expressing the dissonance that caused her to leave the other venture, she begins to talk diplomatically about Ken and his achievements. Speaker 1 mirrors this emotional return to normal. As Speaker 2 praises Ken for his hard work, Speaker 1 matches her assessment with "well good". And as Speaker 2 adds another criticism of the other venture, Speaker 1 hesitates but ultimately matches her wavering stance by saying the he can "see both sides".

At the close of the conversations captured in both Excerpts 6.1 and 6.2, the speakers both engage in a "conversation restart" (Jefferson, 1988). They find a way to conclude the sensitive topics and return to routine conversation. In both cases, the person who has been in the role of expressing empathy is the one who moves the conversation to a different topic. As an exchange focused on troubles comes to its end, the empathizing people introduce an uncomplicated topic distinct from the troubles and related to routine work.

Excerpt 6.3 represents a very different exchange. It captures a pre-emptive noticing of a minor trouble in real time. As Speaker 1 grapples with a sticker on one of the components of their device, Speaker 2 indicates that she notices his challenge. This is a subjunctive assessment that affirms Speaker 1's experience and creates a sense of solidarity. After Speaker 1 confesses that he "can't get that off there" Speaker 2 suggests that it requires "fingernails" – which she has and he does not. In other more serious situations, pointing out something essential that a person lacks would not be interpreted as empathetic. However, in this case, the lack of fingernails is not a threat to Speaker 1's identity or competence. This allows Speaker 2 to highlight her fingernails as a unique contribution to their shared work without raising issues of face.

After Speaker 2 successfully removes the sticker, Speaker 1 signals the end of the empathetic exchange. This is different from the dynamics captured in Excerpts 6.1 and 6.2. In the first two excerpts which were more complex interpersonal episodes, the person who offered the empathy was the person who made the conversational move to return to a workplace topic unrelated to vulnerability or need. However, in Excerpt 6.3, the person who has received the assistance initiates the return to a routine topic.

## From emotion and cognition to social construction

Together these excerpts reveal the interactional mechanisms by which innovative entrepreneurial teams verbally accomplish empathy. The observable language in the data indicates that teams conversational moves incorporate the expected language patterns and follow the expected topical organization. The data also show that different interactional rules may apply based on the level of vulnerability – of face – that a particular situation involves.

The team mates offer a range of utterances to convey empathy. Reaction tokens such as "yeah" are contributed frequently to show attentiveness. Assessments and agreement are given to demonstrate affiliation (Nofsinger, 1991). Repeated statements indicate an acceptance of the terms presented by the person talking about the trouble. All of these responses used by the team mates correspond to conversational moves associated with creating "empathic union" in other contexts (Anssi & Sorjonen, 2012).

Similarly, the team mates mostly organize the conversational episodes in ways that the literature on "troubles-telling" would expect (Jefferson, 1988). The superficial aspects of a troubling matter are shared by a speaker until her team mate is able to convey a significant level of affiliation. At that point, the more personal and sensitive dimensions of the speaker's issue is shared. Another pivot occurs after the team mate again is able to offer an effective statement of attunement. At that instant the team mates begin to return to more routine and less sensitive ways of interacting in the workplace. The speaker signals this return by framing the situation in less personal and more detached terms.

Not all of the teams, however, exit the empathy-oriented episodes in the same way. Two of the episodes conclude with the team mate who had been expressing empathy in the exchange overtly changing the topic. However, in Excerpt 6.3, the team mate who had received empathy is the one to overtly direct the conversation onto a new topic. The situated differences that give rise to these two different ways of enacting closure are not well documented in the literature. One interpretation that has emerged from this data involves issues of face. In circumstances with limited vulnerability or threat to face, the interactional process for exiting a conversation requiring empathy may be relaxed. Alternatively, the closure rules may favor the empowerment of the recipient of an empathetic response.

This chapter's main contribution is twofold. It has considered empathy in the innovation process as a socially constructed act. It also has considered empathy not as a customer-focused practice, but as an intra-team accomplishment. While the three excerpts in this chapter have been able to highlight several relevant conversational moves, there are many other aspects of conversation that could be studied. Studies of empathy in casual conversation have focused on prosody, gesture, and physical distance (Stivers et al., 2011). These and other interactional dimensions could be imported into studies of empathy in innovative entrepreneurial teams.

Because innovative entrepreneurial teams function in a context of uncertainty and risk, it is no wonder that they have stories of distress and trouble to tell (Baum, Frese, Baron, & Katz, 2007). And given the intensity with which teams work on their ventures, it stands to reason that rich interpersonal bonds between team mates would evolve (Francis & Sandberg, 2000). The CA approach used in this chapter shows how team mates request, give, and receive empathy through their naturally occurring workplace conversations.

## References

Allworth, J. (2012). Empathy: The most valuable thing they teach at HBS from https://hbr.org/2012/05/empathy-the-most-valuable-thing-they-t#

Anssi, P., & Sorjonen, M. L. (Eds.). (2012). *Emotion in interaction*. Oxford: Oxford University Press.

Ayoko, O., Callan, V., & Hartel, C. (2008). The influence of team emotional intelligence climate on conflict and team members' reactions to conflict. *Small Group Research, 39*(2), 121–149.

Baker, T., & Nelson, R. (2005). Creating something from nothing: Resource construction through entrepreneurial bricolage. *Administrative Science Quarterly, 50*(3), 329–366.

Baum, J. R., Frese, M., Baron, R. A., & Katz, J. A. (2007). Entrepreneurship as an area of psychology study: An introduction. *The Psychology of Entrepreneurship, 1*(18).

Cikara, M., Bruneau, E., & Saxe, R. (2011). Us and them: Intergroup failures of empathy. *Current Directions in Psychological Science, 20*(3), 149–153.

Coulehan, J., Platt, F., Egener, B., Frankel, R., Lin, C., Lown, B., & Salazar, W. (2001). "Let me see if i have this right . . .": words that help build empathy. *Annals of Internal Medicine, 135*(3), 221–227.

Dandavate, U., Sanders, E., & Stuart, S. (1996, October). *Emotions matter: User empathy in the product development process*. Paper presented at the proceedings of the human factors and ergonomics society annual meeting.

Davis, M. (1980). A multidimensional approach to individual differences in empathy. *JSAS Catalog of Selected Documents in Psychology* (10), 85.

Dong, W., Lepri, B., Kim, T., Pianesi, F., & Pentland, A. (2012). *Modeling Conversational Dynamics and Performance in a Social Dilemma Task*. Paper presented at the 5th international symposium on communications, control, and signal processing, Rome, Italy.

Drew, P., & Heritage, J. (Eds.). (1992). *Talk at work: Interaction in institutional settings*. Cambridge: Cambridge University Press.

Eisenberg, N., & Miller, P. A. (1987). The relation of empathy to prosocial and related behaviors. *Psychological Bulletin, 101*(1), 91.

Feshbach, N. D., & Roe, K. (1968). Empathy in six and seven-yearolds. *Child Development, 39*(1), 133–145.

Fleming, D. (1998). Design talk: Constructing the object in studio conversations. *Design Issues, 14*(2), 41–62.

Francis, D., & Sandberg, W. (2000). Friendship within entrepreneurial teams and its association with team and venture performance. *Entrepreneurship Theory and Practice, 25*(2), 5–26.

Fulton Suri, J. (2003). Empathic design: Informed and inspired by other people's experience. In I. Koskinen, K. Battarbee & T. Mattelmaki (Eds.), *Empathic design, user experience in product design* (pp. 51–57). Helsinki, Finland: IT Press.

Gittell, J., Seidner, R., & Wimbush, J. (2010). A relational model of how highperformance work systems work. *Organizational Science, 21*, 490–506.

Goffman, E. (1955). On face-work: An analysis of ritual elements in social interaction. *Psychiatry, 18*(3), 213–231.

Goffman, E. (1967). *Interaction ritual: Essays in face to face behavior.* New York: Anchor Books.

Goleman, D. (2007). Three kinds of empathy: Cognitive, emotional, compassionate from http://danielgoleman.info/2007/06/12/three-kinds-of-empathy-cognitive-emotional-compassionate/

Goodwin, C. (1986). Between and within: Alternative sequential treatments of continuers and assessments. *Human Studies, 9*(2–3), 205–217.

Goodwin, C., & Goodwin, M. H. (1992). Assessments and the construction of context. *Rethinking context: Language as an interactive phenomenon* (pp. 147–190). Cambridge: Cambridge University Press.

Haase, R., & Tepper, D. (1972). Nonverbal components of empathic communication. *Journal of Counseling Psychology, 19*(5), 417–424.

Heritage, J. (2011). Territories of knowledge, territories of experience: Empathic moments in interaction. In T. Stivers, L. Mondada & J. Steensig (Eds.), *The morality of knowledge in conversation* (pp. 159–183). Cambridge: Cambridge University Press.

Ickes, W. J. (1997). *Empathic accuracy.* New York, NY: Guilford Press.

Jefferson, G. (1988). On the sequential organization of troubles talk in ordinary conversation. *Social Problems, 35*(4), 418–442.

Jefferson, G., & Lee, J. (1992). The rejection of advice: Managing the problematic convergence of a "Troubles-telling" and a "Service Encounter". In P. Drew & J. Heritage (Eds.), *Talk at work: Interaction in institutional settings* (pp. 521–548). Cambridge: Cambridge University Press.

Kitzinger, C., & Kitzinger, S. (2007). Birth trauma: Talking with women and the value of conversation analysis. *British Journal of Midwifery, 15*(5), 256–264.

Konrath, S. H., O'Brien, E. H., & Hsing, C. (2010). Changes in dispositional empathy in American college students over time: A meta-analysis. *Personality and Social Psychology Review. 15*(2), 180–198.

Koskinen, I., Battarbee, K., & Mattelmaki, T. (Eds.). (2003). *Empathic design, user experience in product design.* Helsinki, Finland: IT Press.

Lee, F. (1997). When the going gets tough, do the tough ask for help? Help seeking and power moti-vation in organizations. *Organizational Behavior and Human Decision Processes, 72*, 336–363.

Mattelmäki, T., Vaajakallio, K., & Koskinen, I. (2014). What happened to empathic design? *Design Issues, 30*(1), 67–77.

Morse, J. M., Bottorff, J., Anderson, G., O'Brien, B., & Solberg, S. (2006). Beyond empathy: Expanding expressions of caring. *Journal of Advanced Nursing, 53*(1), 75–87.

New, S., & Kimbell, L. (2013). *Chimps, designers, consultants and empathy: A "Theory of Mind" for service design.* Paper presented at the 2nd Cambridge Academic Design Management Conference, Cambridge UK.

Nofsinger, R. (1991). *Everyday conversation.* Newbury Park, CA: Sage.

Oak, A. (2011). What can talk tell us about design? Analyzing conversation to understand practice. *Design Studies, 32*(3), 211–234.

Postma, C., Lauche, K., & Stappers, P. J. (2009). *Trialogues: A framework for bridging the gap between people research and design.* Paper presented at the Proceedings of the 4th International Conference on Designing Pleasurable Products and Interfaces, DPPI'09, Compiegne.

Postma, C., Zwartkruis-Pelgrim, E., Daemen, E., & Du, J. (2012). Challenges of doing empathic design: Experiences from industry. *International Journal of Design, 6*(1), 59–70.

Sarasvathy, S. D. (2001). Causation and effectuation: Toward a theoretical shift from economic inevitability to entrepreneurial contingency. *Academy of Management Review, 26*(2), 243–263.

Stephens, J., & Carmeli, A. (2016). The positive effect of expressing negative emotions on knowledge creation capability and performance of project teams. *International Journal of Project Management, 34*(5), 862–873.

Stivers, T., Mondada, L., & Steensig, J. (2011). Knowledge, morality and affiliation in social interaction. In J. Steensig & L. Mondada (Eds.), *The morality of knowledge in conversation* (pp. 3–24). Cambridge: Cambridge University Press.

Turkle, S. (2015). *Reclaiming conversation: The power of talk in a digital age.* New York, NY: Penguin Press.

Ward, J., Cody, J., Schaal, M., & Hojat, M. (2012). The empathy enigma: An empirical study of decline in empathy among undergraduate nursing students. *Journal of Professional Nursing, 28*(1), 34–40.

Wright, P., & McCarthy, J. (2005). The value of the novel in designing for experience. In A. Pirhonen, R. C., P. Saariluoma & H. Isom (Eds.), *Future interaction design* (pp. 9–30). London, UK: Springer-Verlag.

Wynn, R., & Wynn, M. (2006). Empathy as an interactionally achieved phenomenon in psychotherapy: Characteristics of some conversational resources. *Journal of Pragmatics, 38*(9), 1385–1397.

# PART III

# Uncovering myths and misperceptions

Much of what scholars and practitioners know about innovative entrepreneurship comes from observations of pitches or from interviews with founders. Part III challenges conventional wisdom about innovative entrepreneurship by analyzing the naturally occurring conversations of teams doing routine work in real time.

# 7

# EVERYONE KNOWS SUCCESSFUL ENTREPRENEURS ARE FAST AND BOLD

## Introduction

In a widely reported interview in 2010, entrepreneur Mark Zuckerberg talked about the origins and orientation of Facebook (Blodget, 2010). According to his recollection, the earliest conversations that prompted the founding of the social media venture were not about the mechanics of entrepreneurship or the technology of the internet. Instead he and his friends "spent a lot of time of talking about what [they] thought were the big issues with the world". And while they were discussing big issues such as autonomy and privacy in an age of information technology, Zuckerberg "just built this little thing" – a website to enable Harvard students to share information about themselves within the university community. As the site became popular with students, Zuckerberg started to think an organization might need to form in order to develop the technology and support the potential users from other universities. However, the organization and the website were secondary to the main goal of making "the world more open and connected". The combination of nimble innovation and bold goals became the ethos of the company. As he put it, everyone at Facebook is encouraged to "move fast, be bold". Or as the company's mantra once stated: "Move fast and break things".

Fast action and bold moves are synonymous with the innovative entrepreneurial approach; so the conventional wisdom goes. The news media and popular culture both celebrate the entrepreneur as a nimble and ambitious leader. And the entrepreneurship literature tends to agree.

Speed in terms of decision making and product development is thought to confer special value for innovative entrepreneurs because of the intense uncertainty that frames their work. A venture's competitive advantage can be quickly lost in dynamic circumstances with interdependent links to technological, market, and additional unknowns. Consequently, innovative entrepreneurs need to make quick and continuous adjustments to their strategy and product offerings to stay ahead of this erosion (Baum, 2009). Rapid experimentation and fast decision making both have been linked with better levels of entrepreneurial success (Baum & Bird, 2010; Baum & Wally, 2003).

Boldness and ambition also are associated with the entrepreneurial character (Anderson & Warren, 2011; Nicholson & Anderson, 2005). Again, because of the uncertainties associated with innovative entrepreneurship, people who succeed need more than a good idea and technological skills. They need to be willing and able to take the initiative and bare the risks that accompany the act of innovating (McMullen & Shepherd, 2006). This boldness is thought to help entrepreneurs launch ventures despite the odds of failure and to persist despite the challenges that continually arise (Busenitz & Barney, 1997; Hayward, Forster, Sarasvathy, & Fredrickson, 2010; Markman, Baron, & Balkin, 2005; Zhou, Hills, & Seibert, 2005).

Boldness in entrepreneurship also can refer to the radical creativity associated with breakthrough thinking (Kirzner, 2009). The Schumpeterian view pairs boldness with creativity. The idea of creative destruction connects disruptive innovation with venture ascendency. Scholars in the Austrian school of thought also see boldness as necessary to successful entrepreneurship. Theories of entrepreneurship as a coordinative act suggest that only bold entrepreneurs can reveal and repair market imbalances that have already occurred but upon which most people feel secure. In both scholarly traditions, entrepreneurs are capable of identifying and making moves that look visionary to others.

And lastly, one other connotation of boldness in entrepreneurship can be found in the concept of individualism. The idea of the entrepreneur as unencumbered self has persisted for decades in both pop culture and scholarly research (Nicholson & Anderson, 2005; Toffler, 1985). Even research into entrepreneurial networks and contexts for entrepreneurial learning often emphasize the techno-liberal attitude of self-interest (Ascigil & Magner, 2013; Jones, Semel, & Le, 2015). Traits of individualistic people include low levels of cooperative behavior and altruistic action toward team mates (Moorman & Blakely, 1995; Wagner, 1995). A growing body of research also suggests that more individualistic people tend to favor the use of first person singular pronouns (e.g., I, me, my) that emphasize uniqueness over first person plural pronouns (e.g., we, us) that signal solidarity (Brown & Gilman, 1960; Twenge, Campbell, & Gentile, 2013).

Given that conventional wisdom and scholarly research are in concert, it would be easy to assume that speed and boldness are consistent hallmarks of entrepreneurial behavior. However, conventional wisdom tends to rely on the narrative accounts of successful entrepreneurs who are looking back on their achievements. Similarly, much of the existing research has focused on retrospective interviews with innovative entrepreneurs. In either arena, the founders are remembering their work. Consequently, while they are honestly recounting their experience, they may not be relaying the actual details of the work as it occurred. Their recollections might not accurately describe their situated actions.

Another stream of research has focused on the analysis of entrepreneurial pitches to investors. In these studies, the founders are observed in real time. However, pitches are performances. As such they may not be representative of the ways that successful founders do the day-to-day work of creating new products and new ventures in private with team mates. The pitches – and their evidence of quick wits and persuasive claims – may not approximate the kind of behaviors and interactions that define the routine work of innovative entrepreneurial teams.

Despite the widely accepted view that successful innovative entrepreneurs are fast and bold, we must look at the naturally occurring workplace interactions of innovative entrepreneurial teams before we can assert that these dispositions play a role in the accomplishment of their actual work. Only by examining the conversations of a successful innovative entrepreneurial team in action can we determine the presence or impact of speed and boldness in routine innovative entrepreneurial work.

## Micro-analysis of decision making in action

The following excerpts come from the recorded conversations of an early-stage innovative entrepreneurial team working on their venture in their private workspace. The team is a dyad – one man with technical know-how and one woman with business prowess. Both are relatively inexperienced with new venture creation. At the time of the recording he was a recent recipient of a graduate degree and she was a student in an MBA program. Shortly after the recorded conversational data was captured, the team went on to obtain a winning position in a university-sponsored lean startup competition. Then, over the next 3 years, the team raised more than $10 million in venture capital, hired more than 20 workers, and launched a market-changing product. By any standard measure of entrepreneurship, their fledgling venture has become a successful young company.

It is worth noting that this team excels at pitching. In fact, they won an Audience Choice award for one of their pitches at a demo show. I witnessed that pitch and could recognize the quick wit and confidence that animated their performance. Twice during that pitch, the audience erupted into warm laughter, applause, and cheers for this team in response to their clever exchanges with the judges. In the first instance, the technical team member answered a question with a potentially troubling detail about the prototype's stability only to have his team mate playfully interject: "That's the technical answer. The marketing response is that we're looking into it". Seconds later, when a judge suggested that the team might not need the full funding as indicated in its projections, the marketing team member responded impishly, "How much would you like to give us?" just before their time expired. These exchanges suggest the team's ability to quickly and confidently address unexpected challenges.

Because rapid decision making is associated in the literature and in pop culture with successful outcomes for innovative entrepreneurial teams, the analysis began with the identification of instances of decision making in the team's recorded data. Decision points are driven by tactical or strategic concerns. Tactical decisions are framed by matters that are likely to have a limited impact on the venture. Strategic decisions involve choices that are likely to impact the team's perceived legitimacy or long-term structure. In both cases, several variables are present in the data.

The instances of decision making are examined for the turns required before, or if, a choice is made. The interactional significance of pronoun choice also is considered in each conversational episode. Together, these probes investigate the ways in which a successful innovative entrepreneurial team is, or is not, fast and bold in the enactment of routine work.

### Tactical: deciding order among parts

Most teams need to build slide decks in order to participate in fundraising activities. In Excerpt 7.1, the team is deciding how to structure the parts of a presentation. While developing a slide deck for the demo show, they are considering various places to insert a slide about intellectual property (IP) among a progression of existing slides on market, timing, and competition.

### Excerpt 7.1  Where do you want to put IP?

| Line | Speaker | Utterance |
| --- | --- | --- |
| 1 | S1 | uh (.) where do you want to put IP in↑ (.) market timing (.) after the market ↑ before the market ↑ |
| 2 | S2 | I think after market before timing ↓ |
| 3 | S1 | after <u>competition</u> ↑before competition ↓ |
| 4 | S2 | <u>after</u> competition ↓ |
| 5 | S1 | all right |

The team names the options and quickly selects a place for the slide on IP. There is zero deliberation about the merits of the different possibilities; zero hesitation. Speaker 1 asks a question. Speaker 2 offers a reaction. Speaker 1 signals agreement, either by moving on to the next question or by articulating "all right".

Using singular pronouns, both team mates acknowledge their questions and opinions as their own. As Speaker 1 refers to his team mate as "you" (line 1) and Speaker 2 replies with "I think" (line 2), they are evoking their individual identities explicitly. While shared identity as a team is not stated aloud, it may be implied through the silent acceptance of the sought-after opinions.

### From tactical to strategic: a simple choice inspires a calculated one

In Excerpt 7.2, the team initially is considering whether or not to make a document about their fundraising pitch available to everyone at a demo show. They make their decision about this possibility quickly and without deep discussion. However, the rejection of one option leads to an idea with strategic implications:

the possibility of collecting names and contact information from interested attend-ees who might include prospective customers and investors.

## Excerpt 7.2  *What if we print up a sheet for signup or something?*

| Line | Speaker | Utterance |
|------|---------|-----------|
| 1 | S1 | should we have an investor pitch↑ that we're (.) willing to let <u>anyone</u> take↑ |
| 2 | S2 | Hmm |
| 3 | S1 | (3) or should we not ↓ <have something> anyone can take |
| 4 | S2 | I think we <u>should not</u> (.) we |
| 5 | S1 | Okay |
| 6 | S2 | should just say like if you're interested to go the website |
| 7 | S1 | Okay |
| 8 | S2 | and um |
| 9 | S1 | and leave us your contact information |
| 10 | S2 | and leave us= yeah= and let us know |
| 11 | S1 | okay (.) what if we print up a sheet (.) for signup or something ↓ |
| 12 | S2 | mmm print out a sheet |
| 13 | S1 | so like you can write your name |
| 14 | S2 | Yeah |
| 15 | S1 | or something |
| 16 | S2 | <u>Yeah</u> |
| 17 | S1 | do you think anyone will↑ |
| 19 | S2 | we might as well <u>have</u> it ↑ |
| 20 | S1 | Okay |
| 21 | S2 | if you're like interested in developments and |
| 22 | S1 | we don't have to <u>put it out</u>= just be like you can write your <u>name down</u> here like |
| 23 | S2 | yeah no or we could <u>have it out</u> and just say if you're interested in further developments and want to stay= want to be on our newsletter |
| 24 | S1 | Yeah |
| 25 | S2 | Yeah |
| 26 | S1 | all right |
| 27 | S2 | their email address |
| 28 | S1 | that sounds good |
| 29 | S2 | Okay |
| 30 | S1 | we need that |

The team mates are able to swiftly raise and reject the option of making a printed version of their investor pitch available at the show. Then they come upon a new idea – creating a document with strategic merit (line 11).

While Speaker 2 expresses her reaction in the first person singular (line 4) to the tactical question asked of her, the team uses mostly plural pronouns when talking about the strategic choice to develop a signup sheet for the venture. They tend to refer to themselves in the plural as they define the fields for the signup sheet, make jokes about a magic pen, and proclaim the need to buy cardstock in order to make the sheet.

The second person pronoun "you" has multiple meanings throughout the episode. At times it refers to the imagined attendees of the demo show (lines 6 and 13). However, in other utterances, the speakers evoke their individual identities by referring to their team mate as "you". For example, when Speaker 1 asks her team mate, "do you think anyone will?" (line 17), she is seeking his opinion as differentiated from her own. He evokes the plural identity of the team in his reply, "we might as well have it" (line 19), and underscores their solidarity by immediately referring to the imaginary others as "you" again (line 21). Speaker 1 echoes the use of "we" to indicate the team and "you" to indicate the others in her follow-on idea, "we don't have to put it out just be like you can write your name down" (line 22). Speaker 2 continues to evoke the shared identity of the team with the use of "our" in contrast with the use of "you" for unknown others (line 23).

Beginning in line 27, the anonymous others are indicated by the pronoun "their". This shift suggests that the team mates have stopped imagining single representatives and have started planning for a group of unknown others. The episode concludes with Speaker 1 evoking the shared identity of the team by using "we" when affirming their decision to make signup sheet (line 30).

### Strategic: integrating feedback and envisioning the market

One of the main tasks of innovative entrepreneurial teams is to integrate feedback from knowledgeable others. The information they receive from advisors and investors as well as from prospective customers can shape a new venture's business model and product. In Excerpt 7.3, the team confronts contrasting evidence about the viability of their venture. They opt to postpone a conversation – and any decisions – about how to interpret that discordant data.

### Excerpt 7.3 We'll worry about that later

| Line | Speaker | Utterance |
| --- | --- | --- |
| 1 | S1 | (2) one thing that one of the early round judges gave in the feedback was that they don't think (.) that we're going to sell that many |
| 2 | S2 | Yeah |
| 3 | S1 | um and ↑ (3) |
| 4 | S2 | there's always that = |
| 5 | S1 | >right< there's always that there's always that risk (.) um (.2) but (.5) it I think it totally depends on our marketing and = |
| 6 | S2 | Yeah |
| 7 | S1 | = and and and our go to market strategy, but (.) I just I have a hard time seeing that given like all the like anecdotal and ↑(2) data we have to confirm the market |
| 8 | S2 | yeah I I agree um (3) but we'll >worry about that later< right |
| 9 | S1 | yeah agreed. Ok, |

The team is beginning to grapple with a discrepancy between their advisor's feedback and their own instincts and observations. Rather than accept or reject the feedback instantly, they opt to pause; to suspend any decisions until the matter can be discussed at length. While it only takes a few turns to decide to postpone the discussion, the discussion is given that future time slot, in part, because the team mates anticipate a lengthy exchange on the topic.

Speaker 1 initiates the conversation with the pronoun "we", suggesting that the topic is crucial for them as a team (line 1). She also differentiates the team from others by referring to advisors and investors as, "they". Speaker 1 then uses the singular first person to indicate that she individually has noted a gap between interpretations that might be hers alone and the data that the team has collectively gathered (lines 5, 7). Both team mates consistently use plural pronouns when referring to their shared objective of new venture success (lines 7, 8). The plural is used by Speaker 2 in line 8 in a way that conveys solidarity; Speaker 1 has articulated the discrepancy and the two of them will figure out how to interpret it together. Speaker 2, also, evokes his individual identity at the start of line 8. By saying, "I agree" he evokes his individual identity and offers validation and support for his team mate.

### Strategic: reflective critique and situated humility

Most innovative entrepreneurial teams need to write business plans, even brief ones, to engage in the fundraising process. These artifacts also help to document the progress of the team and inform new people who join the team. Typically a business plan articulates the vision for the venture as well as the means by which this team will execute the vision. The content includes a range of topics that include technical descriptions of product offerings, a financial plan with projections, a market analysis, and an organizational plan that emphasizes the competitive advantages of the founding team.

As this team prepares to transform their outline for a business plan into a fully detailed plan, they must decide how to craft it (and the strategy it communicates) for maximum impact.

### Excerpt 7.4  The main help I'll give you is to question your assumptions

| Line | Speaker | Utterance |
|------|---------|-----------|
| 1 | S2 | what else is important in the next (.) couple days um (11) because I think that's probably more important= you should do that first and then we'll (.) revisit our numbers |
| 2 | S1 | Yes |
| 3 | S2 | yeah we should do that first |
| 4 | S1 | Yeah |
| 5 | S2 | um (3) I mean there are only= the main help there I'll give you is to question your assumptions |
| 6 | S1 | no I think that's that would be <u>really</u> helpful |
| 7 | S2 | Uh |

| 8 | S1 | (7) so (.) breaking down= yeah how to ta= so this I think are really good things that that we should= that we should think (.) and (.) and <u>draft</u> |
| 9 | S2 | Yeah |
| 10 | S1 | <u>not</u> before tomorrow clearly ↑ |
| 11 | S2 | no we= we won't work on this until= |
| 12 | S1 | no yeah but I think um (4) I think <u>maybe</u> a way >that we can both work on it together< is <u>obviously</u> our backgrounds and skill sets lend to different areas more naturally ↑ |
| 13 | S2 | Yeah |
| 14 | S1 | but I would <u>love</u> to >go through all of those< sections with you and we can just say like what we're thinking each of us and as a preliminary like jotting down some notes, um and then we can maybe section it off and each take <u>go deeper</u> on the sections that we're a little more appropriately suited |
| 15 | S2 | I think that's a good idea |
| 16 | S1 | Uhuh |
| 17 | S2 | um (2) maybe at the end of the week↑ |
| 18 | S1 | Yeah |
| 19 | S2 | all right |
| 20 | S1 | Yeah |
| 21 | S2 | cause we you're busy tomorrow and then (.) we only have a few more hours tonight |
| 22 | S1 | Yeah |
| 23 | S2 | all right |

Speaker 2 proposes a course of action that allows the most pressing tasks to be addressed first (line 1). The team mates are quick to decide that the review of the numbers and other matters will take more time than they have before the demo show. It takes no negotiation to move from the proposal of talking about those topics "at the end of the week" (line 17), to the agreement (line 18), and the joint confirmation (lines 19 and 20).

Speaker 2 also demonstrates humility by acknowledging his contribution to some of the work may be limited to questioning assumptions. He evokes his individual identity through the use of singular pronouns, but he positions his individual contribution in terms of its value to his team mate and their shared goals: "the main help there I'll give you is to question your assumptions" (line 5). In her response, Speaker 1 also evokes individual identity to express appreciation for his offer: "I think that's that would be really helpful" (line 6). By blending individual and collective identities repeatedly, both team mates indicate respect for the other's skills and organize their shared work to capture the unique talents each brings to the venture. As Speaker 1 states, "I think maybe a way that we can both work on it together is obviously our backgrounds and skill sets lend to different areas" (line 12).

## Aware of the limitations of the self and the team

Together these excerpts paint a portrait of this team's routine work interactions, including their tendencies to be fast and bold – or not. The team mates are swift in their ability to dispense with decisions of little consequence. The conversational data shows that zero clarification or negotiation is needed in order for the team to select the position of a slide in a deck, for example. They also are quick to decide that decisions of greater complexity must be postponed. Again, few turns are required in order for them to decide to suspend a conversation about their financial projections until a later date when they can portion off time to consider the topic appropriately.

By suspending those more difficult conversations, however, the team is not making rapid decisions on important matters. The act of suspension itself slows any decision making. Moreover, their choice to schedule a future time to share data, discuss it, and form an opinion suggests that they expect their decisions may only emerge after a lengthy set of exchanges. Rather than optimizing for speed, the team seems to be aware of the need to proceed with caution on a strategic matter that may require more information or re-interpretation.

The excerpts also reveal the identities of the team mates through their use of pronouns. Pronouns signaling individualism are used sparingly. When "I" and "you" are used to indicate the team members, they are used heedfully. Their use signals a respectful differentiation of responsibility or capability, not a direction or command from one overtly bold team mate to another. Utterances, sometimes shift between "I", "you", and "we" as in Excerpt 7.4, line 14 ("I would love to go through all of those sections with you and we can just say like what we're thinking each of us and as a preliminary like jotting down some notes and then we can maybe section it off and each take go deeper on the sections that we're a little more appropriately suited"). In these instances, the speaker moves in and out of her individual and shared identity, emphasizing what each team mate can contribute to their collaborative endeavor. The use of the plural in this way suggests that the team mates are not engaged in the parallel pursuit of individual quests but that they are working together toward shared goals. Such usage suggests that the shared identity is at least equal to if not stronger than their individual identities.

In Excerpts 7.2 and 7.3, the speakers use the plural pronoun "we" when articulating decisions. These instances have strategic implications for the venture, and the speaker evokes the team's shared identity when proclaiming choices have occurred. This use of the plural may serve to confirm the speaker's understanding of the agreement and to strengthen the shared commitment.

The examination of pronoun usage also makes available an additional point: the team mates are defining the team and their role within it through and in the conversation. In other words, the team itself is conversationally and situationally accomplished and affirmed (Antaki & Widdicombe, 1998; Jenkins, 2014; Nevile, 2004).

Both of the observations – the contextual circumstances for rapid decision making and the collaborative orientation toward the team and its work – resemble traits associated with resilient teams. In his 1993 work about firefighters, Weick argued that attitudes of wisdom and doubt and tendencies toward heedful interrelating would benefit teams facing dynamic and uncertain situations (Weick, 1993). By recognizing the complexity of some topics and choosing to postpone decisions until deeper discussion could occur, the team demonstrates a productive blend of "wisdom and doubt". They reveal additional dimensions of this trait by acknowledging the limitations of their individual talents. And their willingness to highlight their partner's strengths and to prioritize the needs of the team are both examples of heedfulness.

Together these traits of wisdom and doubt and heedfulness convey a sense of "situated humility" (Barton & Sutcliffe, 2010). The team members seem to be able to evaluate the challenges facing them with clarity. They also seem to be able to assess their own strengths and weaknesses in conjunction with that specific set of circumstances. As such, they are neither completely confident – as some of the entrepreneurship literature might posit – nor are they entirely humble. They are able to cultivate a situated humility which guides their tempo and checks their temerity.

## Toward a more nuanced conception of speed and boldness

The impressions that have emerged from the close consideration of the team's decision making conversations do not easily align with the fast and bold behaviors typically associated with innovative entrepreneurs. Instead the data suggests that these team mates are willing and able to make swift decisions when the stakes are low – and just as willing and able to slow the pace of decision making when the decisions are expected to matter. The data also suggests that these team mates are more collaborative than they are individualistic. They are conscious of the productive power of their unique contributions and frame their work in a way that fortifies their solidarity as a team.

Of course, these impressions come from a single team's interactions. As such they must be considered with a grain of salt. However, unexpected insights about contexts and cultures can arise from the study of intimate details found in naturally occurring interactions in a particular case (Sacks, 1984). The examination of this particular team's decision making conversations suggests that fast and bold might not be the only, or the optimal, dispositions of successful innovative entrepreneurial teams in general.

Uncovering the means by which this team verbally addressed tactical and strategic decisions prompts two pressing questions. First is a question about the kinds of dispositions which might foster successful innovative entrepreneurship. If an orientation toward fast and bold behavior is advantageous in some instances (such as pitching and tactical decision making) and an inclination toward collaboration and cautious commitments in others (such as teamwork and strategic decision making), what other situated dispositions might need to be acknowledged? The second is a question about teaching and learning opportunities for aspiring innovative entrepreneurs. How can optimal, and sometimes situated, dispositions be taught and encouraged?

One way to identify a fuller range of dispositions which foster innovative entrepreneurial work is to study more teams in action. By analyzing the detailed means by which teams accomplish their routine work, scholars will be able to separate the expected attitudes and actions from the authentic ones. Such future studies may be of exceptional value in the quest to identify situated dispositions in particular.

Teaching dispositions, situated or not, is its own challenge. Scholars of education have suggested that teaching *for* dispositions may be advantageous (Perkins & Tishman, 2006). In other words, facilitators of educational experiences for aspiring innovators and entrepreneurs might encourage learners to assess the need (or not) for rapid decision making in a particular instance rather than telling them when to act fast or be cautious. Or facilitators might encourage learners to assess the situational need (or not) to voice individual views rather than telling them when to speak up and when to yield. The materials for and methods of entrepreneurial education continue to be evaluated and revised (Neck, Greene, & Brush, 2014). Perhaps part of this evolution could include attention to the development of dispositions.

Of course, not all learning opportunities for aspiring innovative entrepreneurs are based on formal coursework. Informal educational platforms reach a large population of aspiring entrepreneurs and emphasize the fast and bold ideals, if only through the term "accelerator". Facilitators of accelerators may want to talk explicitly with learners about the stereotypes associated with entrepreneurship. Alternatively, facilitators may consider revising the names and images associated with their learning platforms; potential learners may not see themselves in the fast and bold framing and opt out of opportunities that could help them build critical skills.

While fast action and bold moves are part of the innovative entrepreneurial approach, they may not represent the behaviors of a successful team in all contexts. Quick wits, rapid decision making, and confidence can serve a team well in pitching for venture capital or in making tactical decisions, for example. However, a disposition that favors cautious commitments and collaboration may be more advantageous when grappling with the challenges of teamwork and strategic decision making.

The idea of "move fast, be bold" still seems to animate how many people think about innovative entrepreneurship. However, a cue from Facebook, which continues to drive the innovation of social media ventures, suggests a growing awareness of the limitations of that perspective. In 2014, Mark Zuckerberg publicly proclaimed a revision to the company's mantra. As the company wanted to emphasize the importance of the co-creation process between teams within the company it replaced "move fast and break things" with "move fast with stable infrastructure" (Statt, 2014). While no known data exists that would let researchers examine the intra-team conversations at Facebook in its earliest days, perhaps they have been making cautious internal commitments and collaborating all along.

## References

Anderson, A. R., & Warren, L. (2011). The entrepreneur as hero and jester: Enacting the entrepreneurial discourse. *International Small Business Journal, 29*(6), 589–609.

Antaki, C., & Widdicombe, S. (Eds.). (1998). *Identities in talk.* Thousand Oaks, CA: Sage.

Ascigil, S. F., & Magner, N. R. (2013). Is individualism a predictor of social capital in business incubators? *Journal of Management Policy and Practice, 14*(5), 113.

Barton, M. A., & Sutcliffe, K. M. (2010). Learning when to stop momentum. *MIT Sloan Management Review, 51*(3), 69–76.

Baum, J. R. (2009). Gain entrepreneurship success through swiftness and experimentation In E. A. Locke (Ed.), *Handbook of priniciples of organizational behavior* (pp. 559–578). UK: Wiley.

Baum, J. R., & Bird, B. (2010). The successful intelligence of high growth entrepreneurs: Links to new venture growth. *Organization Science, 21*(2), 397–412.

Baum, J. R., & Wally, S. (2003). Strategic decision speed and firm performance. *Strategic Management Journal, 24*(11), 1107–1129.

Blodget, H. (2010). Mark Zuckerberg, Moving Fast And Breaking Things. *Business Insider.*

Brown, R., & Gilman, A. (1960). The pronouns of power and solidarity. In T. Sebeok (Ed.), *Style in language* (pp. 253–276). Cambridge, MA: MIT Press.

Busenitz, L. W., & Barney, J. B. (1997). Differences between entrepreneurs and managers in large organizations: Biases and heuristics in strategic decision-making. *Journal of Business Venturing, 12*(1), 9–30.

Hayward, M. L. A., Forster, W., Sarasvathy, S. D., & Fredrickson, B. (2010). Beyond hubris: How highly confident entrepreneurs rebound to venture again. *Journal of Business Venturing, 25*(6), 569–578.

Jenkins, R. (2014). *Social identity.* New York, NY: Routledge.

Jones, G. M., Semel, B., & Le, A. (2015). "There's no rules. It's hackathon": Negotiating commitment in a context of volatile sociality. *Journal of Linguistic Anthropology, 25*(3), 322–345.

Kirzner, I. M. (2009). The alert and creative entrepreneur: A clarification. *Small Business Economics, 32*(2), 145–152.

Markman, G. D., Baron, R. A., & Balkin, D. B. (2005). Are perseverance and self-efficacy costless? Assessing entrepreneurs' regretful thinking. *Journal of Organizational Behavior, 26*(1), 1–19.

McMullen, J. S., & Shepherd, D. A. (2006). Entrepreneurial action and the role of uncertainty in the theory of the entrepreneur. *The Academy of Management Review, 31*(1), 132–152.

Moorman, R. H., & Blakely, G. L. (1995). Individualism-collectivism as an individual difference predictor of organizational citizenship behavior. *Journal of Organizational Behavior,* (16), 127–142.

Neck, H. M., Greene, P. G., & Brush, C. (2014). *Teaching entrepreneurship: A practice-based approach.* Northampton, MA: Edward Elgar Publishing.

Nevile, M. (2004). *Beyond the black box: Talk-in-interaction in the airline cockpit.* New York, NY: Ashgate Publishing, Ltd.

Nicholson, L., & Anderson, A. R. (2005). News and nuances of the entrepreneurial myth and metaphor: Linguistic games in entrepreneurial sense-making and sense-giving. *Entrepreneurship Theory and Practice, 29*(2), 153–172.

Perkins, D. N., & Tishman, S. (2006). *Learning that matters.* Project Zero. Harvard University.

Sacks, H. (1984). Notes on methodology. In J. M. Atkinsen & J. Heritage (Eds.), Structures of social action: Studies in conversation analysis. Cambridge: Cambrige University Press.

Statt, N. (2014). Zuckerberg: "Move fast and break things" isn't how Facebook operates anymore. *CNet,* from www.cnet.com/news/zuckerberg-move-fast-and-break-things-isnt-how-we-operate-anymore/

Toffler, A. (1985). *Future shock.* London: Pan.

Twenge, J. M., Campbell, W. K., & Gentile, B. (2013). Changes in pronoun use in American books and the rise of individualism, 1960–2008. *Journal of Cross-Cultural Psychology, 44*(3), 406–415.

Wagner, J. A. (1995). Studies of individualism-collectivism: Effects of cooperation in groups. *Academy of Management Journal* (38), 152–172.

Weick, K. E. (1993). The collapse of sensemaking in organizations: The Mann Gulch Disaster. *Administrative Science Quarterly, 38*(4), 628–652.

Zhou, H., Hills, G., & Seibert, S. E. (2005). The mediating role of self-efficacy in the development of entrepreneurial intentions. *Journal of Applied Psychology, 90*(6).

# 8

# WHAT IF DISRUPTIVE QUESTIONS DIDN'T DRIVE INNOVATION?

## Introduction

Research on entrepreneurship has often focused on the characteristics of the lead entrepreneur (Gartner, 1988). Scholars have studied their risk profiles, educational achievements, socio-economic backgrounds, and other enduring traits for decades (Levine & Rubinstein, 2017; Palich & Bagby, 1995). Much of this work has attempted to identify traits that differentiate entrepreneurs from non-entrepreneurs (Baron, 1998; Baron & Markman, 2003).

In their popular book, *The Innovator's DNA*, scholars Dyer, Gregersen, and Christensen (Dyer, Gregersen, & Christensen, 2011) continue in this vein. They argue that successful and highly innovative lead entrepreneurs ask questions that explore alternative possibilities (e.g., "why not" and "what if") much more frequently than other people do. They claim that by asking provocative questions these individuals synthesize divergent concepts and achieve significant insights that lead to breakthrough products, services, and ventures.

The idea of highly successful lead entrepreneurs asking disruptive questions fits into the model of entrepreneurship as an effectual process. The theory of effectuation asserts that entrepreneurs apply knowledge and control to contend with uncertainties (Sarasvathy, 2001). This kind of non-predictive control in the face of uncertainty requires entrepreneurs to focus on means rather than ends and to leverage unexpected developments as they occur (Wiltbank, Read, Dew, & Sarasvathy, 2009). People who ask questions – especially disruptive questions – are enacting a kind of control. As Sacks put it: "as long as one is in the position of doing the questions, then in part one has control of the conversation" (Sacks, 1992b, p. 54).

By treating the subject of questions in entrepreneurial work as a trait rather than as a practice, previous research has not attended to the context of questioning. Seen through a practice lens, questioning can be understood as a pattern of activities.

Questions are ways of interpreting and interacting, and they are necessary aspects of doing entrepreneurial work. As such, an individual participating in entrepreneurial work engages in questioning activities, but they are not qualities of that individual.

The data behind studies of entrepreneurial questioning tends to come from interviews. However, interviews are not a foolproof method for collecting data, especially about practices. The questions asked and the context of the interview can shape the perspectives that interviewees share (Hammersley & Gomm, 2008). And even well-intended interviewees can misremember or have the interpretations they associate with experiences shift over time (Seale, 1999). Moreover, conventional wisdom about innovative entrepreneurs – that they are heroic visionaries – also can influence how people see themselves and present themselves in interviews (Anderson & Warren, 2011; Kociatkiewicz & Kostera, 2016).

Only by studying the observable language of innovative entrepreneurs in action can the role of questions in entrepreneurial practice be assessed. This chapter uses quantitative CA to investigate the questioning language actually used in the routine work of a successful entrepreneurial team.

## Questions and settings

Because questions are a fundamental part of communication, questions are present in every conversational context. Many academic studies have focused on question practices in institutional settings. Often these settings feature significant asymmetries of knowledge and power between the conversational participants (Arminen, 2005). For example, studies of questioning practices conducted in legal courts, medical offices, and classrooms feature lawyers, doctors, and teachers who are empowered to ask questions and evaluate answers and witnesses, patients, and students who are not. This body of literature plays into our conventional wisdom about questions and agency.

In their review of courtroom questioning practices, Atkinson and Drew (Atkinson & Drew, 1979) illustrated how questions are used by lawyers to make a case. Questions are posed about the features of the case, and these points become accepted as facts as witnesses answer them. Throughout the trial the type of questions asked by lawyers changes: Q-word questions that prompt stories are more common in direct examination whereas polar questions that prompt confirmation tend to occur during cross-examination (Heffer, 2005). The sculpted questions and responses of acceptance create a description of the crime that associates blame with particular entities (Drew & Heritage, 1992).

Questions and responses in medical visits also create a narrative about the patient that influences the diagnostic process and the recommended treatment. While there has been a growing interest in patient involvement in healthcare decision making, doctors still tend to ask the questions and patients tend to respond (Robinson, 2003). While the doctor may start the visit with an open-ended question such as "What brings you here today", s/he typically shifts to more constrained questions to gather medical history and establish a diagnosis (Stivers & Heritage, 2001).

Teachers, too, use questions in their interactions with students. Unlike the doctors, teachers do not ask questions to gather information in advance of making an assessment. Instead, teachers ask questions as a primary means of making evaluations. The three-part sequence in which a teacher initiates a question that is followed by a student response and then a teacher assessment is a fundamental construct in classroom research (Tracy & Robles, 2009).

The institutional nature of a particular workplace interaction can be revealed through participants' attention to "procedural consequentiality" (Schegloff, 1991). Lexical choice as well as the distribution of questioning rights between participants can highlight how tasks are performed in a given setting. For example, the participants in a job interview may opt for professional word choices and grammar as well as a questioning pattern that empowers the interviewer more than the applicant (Llewellyn & Pence, 2009). In short, a workplace is continually co-constructed by the participants and is recognizable by them – and by others, including researchers – through their interactions.

Even though entrepreneurial work is done in places that have been set aside for work, it may retain more informalities than work done in established corporate settings. Behaviors, for example, in a garage, a home office, or even a university-sponsored accelerator, may be less formal than those enacted in a standard office building. Because interactional research in institutional settings tends to feature interactions between people across formal professional boundaries they might not be a model for questioning practices between peers on the same entrepreneurial team. Studies that have focused on questioning language in less structured settings might be more aligned with the interactions that are present in an early-stage entrepreneurial workplace.

## A primer on questions

Questions are commonplace, and they also are socially complex (Goody, 1978). They can signal epistemic advantages and disadvantages, for example. A tourist who is lost may ask a local resident for directions, or, as previously mentioned, a teacher who knows the answer may ask a student a question to evaluate the student's knowledge. In the first case, the person who asks the question seeks the other person's knowledge. In the second case, the person who asks the question already knows the answer and seeks to confirm the other person's mastery of the subject. Questions also can demonstrate meta-stances of affiliation or disaffiliation between the speakers (Heinemann, 2008; Stokoe & Edwards, 2008). Through variations in their construction and delivery, questions can suggest (why don't we go get coffee?), invite (would you like to go get coffee?), request (would you please get me a coffee?), and complain (why don't you ever get me coffee?) (Goody, 1978; Steensig & Drew, 2008).

The structures of questions have been described by detailed taxonomies. Some feature a fundamental categorization of non-verbal and verbal questioning forms (Kearsley, 1976). Non-verbal questioning forms (e.g., a raised eyebrow or a tilted head) can elicit verbal responses or can accompany self-directed questions. Verbal questions include both indirect questions, which are declaratives with an implied interrogative intent, and direct questions which branch into a variety of additional sub-forms and functions (Kearsley, 1976). Alternative taxonomies frame various question forms and functions not as a tree, but as continuum of concerns that range from information sought at one end to information shared at the other (Freed, 1994) and as a spectrum of openness (Waln, 1984).

Three primary question forms dominate the English language: polar questions which seek yes-no answers; "q-word" questions which begin with who, what, where, when, how, or an implied version of these; and alternative questions which articulate a fixed choice of answers (Bolinger, 1957; Quirk, Greenbaum, Leech, & Svartoik, 1985; Schegloff & Lerner, 2009; Stivers, 2010). In all of these cases, the utterances that are understood as questions within a particular conversation prompt an answer from the conversational partner. These "adjacency pairs" – verbal sequences that includes a stimulus with the social expectation of a response (Sacks, 1992a; Sacks, Schegloff, & Jefferson, 1974) – feature prominently in the research on turn-taking sequences.

Once a question has been uttered by the primary speaker, the secondary speaker is socially expected to respond either with an answer. Although the second speaker has a choice in responses, the expectation of some response suggests that questions afford primary speakers an element of control in a given conversation (Goody, 1978; Heritage, 2002).

The responses in context are also meaningful (Schegloff, 1968). Most responses are aligned with the type of question posed (e.g., most polar questions receive yes or no answers without resisting the presuppositions or terms of the question). These fitted responses affirm social bonds through their implicit politeness and immediacy. Non-conforming responses – which might ignore the question type, redirect the conversation, or dismiss the question with silence – occur less frequently in conversation than fitted responses (Clayman, 2002; Heritage, 1984; Raymond, 2003). Non-conforming responses tend to be prefaced by longer pauses than fitted responses. Occasionally, non-conforming responses can play a transformative role, changing the agenda or the terms of the question (Stivers & Hayashi, 2010).

Using these guidelines, the literature can position the disruptive questions that have been associated with innovative entrepreneurial success. The "what if" and "why not" constructions associated with entrepreneurs could be categorized as q-word type questions. The social action related to such questions could be interpreted as an authentic invitation to share ideas and opinions. In such instances, the epistemic advantage could be held by the respondent or by neither speaker at the situated moment of asking. Alternatively, these disruptive questions could be asked in a rhetorical manner as a signal that the speaker is about to share his/her own vision. In these cases, the social action would take an assertive form, and the epistemic advantage would belong to the speaker of the question.

But what kinds of questions do successful innovative entrepreneurial teams actually employ in their routine workplace conversations? How do these questions function in context, and what is their role in the process of creating breakthrough products?

## Observable questions in context

The data comes from the recorded conversations of an innovative entrepreneurial team working on an early-stage venture in a university-supplied private workspace. The team is a dyad – one man and one woman, both American graduate students with technical backgrounds. Neither has been part of a startup before. While this team was involved in a lean startup contest during the time of the data capture, it did not win. However, over a 3-year period, the team did perform well in the real world. It participated in a well-known accelerator and went on to raise venture capital and release a successful, market-making product. They are innovative entrepreneurs by the standards of Dyer, Gregersen, and Christensen (Dyer, Gregersen, & Christensen, 2008).

The analysis of the data began with the transcription of naturally occurring workplace conversations that had been recorded over several days. The grounded analysis continued with the identification of questioning sequences in the data. Words signaling question prompts as well as intonation were used to detect questions. The data then was examined for the question forms and types, the epistemic stances and social actions enacted through the questions, and the sequence and fit of the questions and responses.

Several guidelines from the literature were incorporated to aid in the processes of assessment of social action prompts (Campbell, 2014; Stivers & Enfield, 2010). The coding embraced situated intensions such as requesting information, initiating repair, seeking clarification, making a request, suggestion, or invitation, stating a question to one's self aloud, or asking a rhetorical question that seeks a reaction but not an answer. Similarly, guidelines from the literature also informed the analysis of sequence and fit (Stivers, 2010). Codes were developed to indicate responses, non-answer responses (e.g., "I don't know" or stories independent of the question prompt), and no responses as well as type conforming and transformational responses. Atlas TI was used to code the data.

In all, 1140 sequential turns were examined including 138 questions. The following sections describe the various question types, the range of social actions speakers employ questions to perform, and the patterns of responses that occurred in the data. Distributions of question structure and social actions are compared against the frequency of occurrence in general (non-work) dyadic conversation between native English speakers (Freed, 1994; Stivers, 2010). Transcribed excerpts are presented to highlight response types.

### Question type

The observable questions in the data included approximately 51% polar questions (*n* = 71) followed by 41% q-word (*n* = 57) and 7% alternative (*n* = 10) questions. This is similar to the distribution found in general conversation which has been recorded as including 70% polar, 27% q-word, and 3% alternative question structures (Stivers, 2010). No questions were observed in the data that match the specific constructions of "what if" or "why not".

## Stance and social action

Questions were posed by both members of the team. However, the self-described lead entrepreneur asked 83% ($n$ = 114) of the questions.

The epistemic stance embedded in the questions indicated that the knowledge advantage belonged to the second speaker 86% of the time ($n$ = 119). This is consistent with the social action of seeking information, an intention that dominated the team's conversation. Rarely, only 5% of the time ($n$ = 7), did the knowledge advantage belong to the first speaker. In those cases, the speaker was guiding his partner through the steps he had undertaken to create a piece of technology. He was, in essence, acting as a teacher by confirming his partner's comprehension on the individual steps and identifying where her expectation differed from the work he had done. In several instances ($n$ = 12), the knowledge advantage seemed to be shared if it was present at all. This shared stance was found in conjunction with utterances that were inviting opinions and suggestions.

The social actions enacted through the questions were dominated by requests information ($n$ = 73). The team mates also engaged in efforts to seek clarification ($n$ = 32), invite opinions and suggestions ($n$ = 26), seek confirmation ($n$ = 5), and query oneself ($n$ = 2). (See Table 8.1.) No instances of seeking agreement or rhetorical questions were observed. Information requests and clarification efforts also dominate the social actions associated with general dyadic conversation. However, the recorded workplace conversation of the entrepreneurial team included many more invitations for opinions and suggestions and many fewer requests for confirmation than typically occur in general conversation.

## Sequence patterns and fit

Most of the questions (83%, $n$ = 114) between the team mates received answers. Only 5% of the questions ($n$ = 7) received no verbal answer, and some of those were self-directed questions. It is possible that some if not all of the questions

**TABLE 8.1** Observable language of stance and social action

| Social Action | Observed in this entrepreneurial data | Observed in general dyadic conversation (Stivers, 2010) |
| --- | --- | --- |
| Requesting information | 53% | 43% |
| Seeking clarification or repair | 23% | 31% |
| Inviting opinions and suggestions | 19% | 6% |
| Seeking confirmation | 4% | 21% |
| Querying oneself | 1% | <1% |
| Making assessment | 0% | 2% |

coded as receiving no answer may have received a non-verbal response that was not recognized in the analysis of the audio recording. The remaining 12% of responses ($n = 17$) were non-answers such as, "I can't remember" and "probably". The basic distribution of responses in this team's workplace conversations is similar to those found in general dyadic conversation: 76% answer, 19% non-answer, and 5% no answer.

Of the 131 questions that received answers, 66% ($n = 86$) received answers that directly fit the question type (e.g., polar questions received yes or no answers and alternative questions received answers selected from the choices). Some questions, 16% ($n = 21$), received non-direct conforming responses such as repeats of the question in advance of answering. The remaining questions received transforming responses: answers that challenged the agenda (6%, $n = 8$) or terms (12%, $n = 16$) of the question that had been asked. This is a departure from the patterns found in ordinary conversation with direct conforming responses at 82%, direct non-conforming at 6%, and transformative responses at 12% (Stivers & Hayashi, 2010).

An exchange that challenges the agenda is shown in Excerpt 8.1. Diane has asked a q-word question that prompts an explanation or a description of next steps. Jim's response is direct and immediate, but it does not conform with the agenda suggested by the question. He indicates that he does not have a "plan" to present. With this expression, Jim transforms the focus of the interaction. He will not be sharing a predefined plan. Instead they will be making sense of their situation and forging next steps through their conversation. His utterance transforms the question from one focused on a piece of work he may have done to one focused on work they collaboratively will do. His laugh, followed by hers, signals that this transformation is not posing a challenge to their shared goals or to their affiliation.

## Excerpt 8.1 Changing the agenda in the response

| Line | Speaker | Utterance |
|------|---------|-----------|
| 1 | Diane | What what was your plan for the meter? |
| 2 | Jim | Well I didn't <really <u>have</u>> so much of a plan ((*laughter*)) |
| 3 | Diane | ((*laughter*)) |

Transformative responses can also address the terms of the question as shown in Excerpt 8.2. Diane has asked a polar question, but Jim does not respond with yes or no. After a 4-second pause, Jim starts his response with, "um", the pauses for another 2 seconds before saying, "I don't think we've ever talked about it". He places the emphasis on the word "we've" which suggests he thinks she may have talked with someone else, perhaps an advisor to the venture, about it. His utterance also resists the term "considered". They have not considered the pito tube option because they've not talked about it.

## Excerpt 8.2  Changing the terms in the response

| Line | Speaker | Utterance |
| --- | --- | --- |
| | *Line* | *Speaker* | *Utterance* |

| Line | Speaker | Utterance |
| --- | --- | --- |
| 1 | Diane | Oh um (2) pito tube? Did we ever consider using Pito tube for flow measurement rather than an orphus plate↑ |
| 2 | Jim | (4) Um (2) I don't think <u>we've</u> ever talked about it. I think (.) how would that- |
| 3 | Diane | See (.) the thing is it's <u>not</u> an industry standard thing cause even like when I watched the qed – I watched two presentations by qed – |
| 4 | Jim | Mmhm |
| 5 | Diane | I forget which one it was but one of them said how do you measure your flow. And the options are exactly what you would expect: orphus plate or mass flow meter, the heated wire thing. |
| 6 | Jim | Mmhm |
| 7 | Diane | Nobody ever said pito tube, but pito tube is particularly <u>designed</u> for measuring flow |

The uncharacteristic delay in Jim's response is consistent with non-conforming answers (Sacks, 1973). Time may have been needed to reflect on his experiences or to select which term to address in his response. Jim's response is understood by Diane as disaligned but not disaffiliative (Heritage, 1984). She proceeds without hesitation and starts talking with Jim about pito tubes as a possible solution for their emerging product. Jim's mitigating language of "I think" as well as his delay signals his desire to preserve the affiliation while resisting the constraints of the question (Heritage, 1984; Pomerantz, 1984).

Even though there is a delay in Jim's response, it only lasts a few seconds. While he does pause, he does not disengage. He offers a response that is relevant to the topic. It also is worth noting the exchange illustrated in Excerpt 8.2 is a pivotal moment in the development of the team's emerging product. The pito tube becomes a differentiating feature of the product and contributes to the success of the venture.

## Questions (and responses) as windows into practice

The analysis of this team's use of questioning language extends the investigations of workplace interaction into the entrepreneurial realm. The findings about question type suggest that entrepreneurial workplace conversations are more like non-work encounters than they are like the institutional settings typically associated with questioning language. This is consistent with the idea that founders often select friends to co-founders and early team mates (Francis & Sandberg, 2000).

The observations that the self-described lead entrepreneur asked the majority of the questions and the respondent mostly held the epistemic advantage is consistent with information gathering and clarification – the main social actions undertaken by the team. A stark difference between the team's social actions and those of general conversations emerged in the team's efforts to invite opinions and to seek confirmation. The team mates invited opinions and suggestions much more frequently than general conversationalists do; they also sought confirmation much less. This suggests that despite the informality of entrepreneurial workplace conversations, the team mates share a purpose and goal. Moreover, it suggests that the team mates are invested in working together on the creation of a product. Their infrequent need to seek confirmation may be a factor of their low focus on the self or on a strong sense of connectedness with each other.

Whenever questions are in use, people are attending to layers of social concern (Castor, 2009). While creating a minimum viable project is the team's main objective, they also are navigating social issues of affiliation and identity while engaging in questioning (Shotter, 1993). The team's sequence patterns suggest that the team mates are actively attempting to establish and maintain a bond with each other and a reputation of attentiveness and competence for themselves.

The team's response fit patterns differed from those found in ordinary conversation. Their more frequent use of direct non-conforming responses (such as repeating the question) is another indication of a low focus on the self; each person wants to make sure s/he understands the other person. However, their more frequent use of transformative responses suggests that neither person lacks in status. Both team mates are empowered to address the terms and the agenda of questions.

Transformative responses, like the one uttered by Jim in Excerpt 8.2, disrupt the expected connection between questions and agency. Typically the speaker who asks the question influences the exchange. By posing a question the speaker asserts not only the expectation of a response but also the shape of the response (Schegloff, 1968). When constructed in a manner that preserves affiliation while resisting the terms or agenda of questions, transformative answers shift agency to respondents.

This shift is especially noteworthy in the context of entrepreneurial conversations. Lead entrepreneurs, in particular, are thought to be charismatic and confident visionaries who take charge (Anderson & Warren, 2011; Dimov, 2010; Ogbor, 2000). They score high on self-efficacy, communication skills, and persuasiveness (Baron & Markman, 2003; Baum & Locke, 2004). Given this framing, it would make sense if lead entrepreneurs shaped conversations by asking provocative questions. However, this is not the interaction pattern observed in the data.

If responses also play a meaningful role in the enactment of innovative breakthroughs then the agency of second speakers can wield significant influence in the development of minimum viable products – and ultimately the successful creation of new ventures. This is the language pattern that is observed in the data. Power is not held exclusively by the speaker who asks the question; it is shared.

## Reconsidering questions

This chapter adds to our understanding of what entrepreneurs do and how, in terms of verbal practice, they do it. It demonstrates how people use questions to verbally "do being" a member of an entrepreneurial team (Sacks, 1984a, 1984b). Moreover the chapter illustrates one way that relevant descriptive measures can contribute to the micro-analysis of naturally occurring workplace conversation.

In terms of questioning language, the workplace interactions of the studied team share several features of ordinary conversations. However, they also differ in key ways from ordinary conversation. In terms of social action, they invited opinions and suggestions more frequently and sought confirmation less frequently than general conversations do. And in terms of structure, they used direct non-conforming and transformative responses more frequently than ordinary conversations.

The findings also contrast with the popular belief that entrepreneurs tend to ask provocative questions (Dyer et al., 2008, 2011). While the structure and intent of the questions observed in the data shared some structural traits with disruptive questions, it would be difficult to consider the observed questions in-context to be provocative. This disparity could have many explanations including the experience level of the team which differed greatly from the expert teams in earlier studies. It also is possible that disruptive questions are asked in a particular phase of the innovation cycle. None of this study's recorded data captured the teams' initial ideation conversations, for example; perhaps the status quo challenging "what if" questions (Dyer et al., 2008, 2011) occur primarily within that phase of the innovation process.

This study, of course, has limitations. It analyzes only one case and cannot be overly generalized. However, it does indicate a pathway for future research that uses CA (with or without additional analytical support) to explore and explicate the range of ways in which questions contribute to entrepreneurial practice. Opening up the process of asking and answering questions in routine entrepreneurial work may contribute not only to theories of entrepreneurship as practice but also to the enactment of entrepreneurial innovating and organizing.

## References

Anderson, A. R., & Warren, L. (2011). The entrepreneur as hero and jester: Enacting the entrepreneurial discourse. *International Small Business Journal, 29*(6), 589–609.

Arminen, I. (2005). *Institutional interaction: Studies of talk at work* (Vol. 2). New York, NY: Ashgate Publishing, Ltd.

Atkinson, J., & Drew, P. (1979). *Order in court: The organisation of verbal interaction in judicial settings.* Atlantic Highlands, NJ: Humanities Press.

Baron, R. A. (1998). Cognitive mechanisms in entrepreneurship: Why and when entrepreneurs think differently than other people. *Journal of Business Venturing, 13*(4), 275–294.

Baron, R. A., & Markman, G. D. (2003). Person – entrepreneurship fit: Why some people are more successful as entrepreneurs than others. *Human Resource Management Review, 13*(2), 281–301.

Baum, J. R., & Locke, E. A. (2004). The relationship of entrepreneurial traits, skill, and motivation to subsequent venture growth. *Journal of Applied Psychology, 89*(4), 587.

Bolinger, D. (1957). *Interrogative structures of American English: The direct question.* Alabama: University of Alabama Press.

Campbell, B. (2014). *Entrepreneurship as a conversational accomplishment: An inductive analysis of the verbal sensemaking behaviors of early-stage innovative entrepreneurial teams* (PhD), University of Exeter, Exeter, England.

Castor, T. (2009). It's just a process: Questioning in the construction of a university crisis. *Discourse Studies, 11*(2), 179–197.

Clayman, S. (2002). Sequence and solidarity. In S. R. Thye & E. J. Lawler (Eds.), *Group cohesions, trust and solidarity* (pp. 229–253). Amsterdam: Elsevier.

Dimov, D. (2010). Nascent entrepreneurs and venture emergence: Opportunity confidence, human capital, and early planning. *Journal of Management Studies, 47*(6), 1123–1153.

Drew, P., & Heritage, J. (Eds.). (1992). *Talk at work: Interaction in institutional settings*. Cambridge: Cambridge University Press.

Dyer, J. H., Gregersen, H. B., & Christensen, C. (2008). Entrepreneur behaviors, opportunity recognition, and the origins of innovative ventures. *Strategic Entrepreneurship Journal, 2*(4), 317–338.

Dyer, J. H., Gregersen, H. B., & Christensen, C. (2011). *The innovator's DNA: Mastering the five skills of disruptive innovation*. Boston, MA: Harvard Business Review Press.

Francis, D., & Sandberg, W. (2000). Friendship within entrepreneurial teams and its association with team and venture performance. *Entrepreneurship Theory and Practice, 25*(2), 5–26.

Freed, A. (1994). The form and function of questions in informal dyadic conversation. *Journal of Pragmatics, 21*(6), 621–644.

Gartner, W. B. (1988). Who is an entrepreneur? Is the wrong question. *American Journal of Small Business, 12*(4), 47–68.

Goody, E. (Ed.). (1978). *Questions and politeness: Strategies in social interaction*. Cambridge: Cambridge University Press.

Hammersley, M., & Gomm, R. (2008). Assessing the radical critiques of interviews. In M. Hammersley (Ed.), Questioning qualitative inquiry: Critical essays (pp. 89–100). London: Sage.

Heffer, C. (2005). *The language of jury trial: A corpus-aided analysis of legal-lay discourse*. Basingstoke: Palgrave Macmillan.

Heinemann, T. (2008). Questions of accountability: Yes – no interrogatives that are unanswerable. *Discourse Studies, 10*(1), 55–71.

Heritage, J. (1984). *Garfinkel and ethnomethodology*. Cambridge: Polity Press.

Heritage, J. (2002). The limits of questioning: Negative interrogatives and hostile question content. *Journal of Pragmatics, 34*(10–11), 1427–1446.

Kearsley, G. (1976). Questions and question asking in verbal discourse: A cross-disciplinary review. *Journal of Psycholinguistic Research, 5*(4), 355–375.

Kociatkiewicz, J., & Kostera, M. (2016). Grand plots of management bestsellers: Learning from narrative and thematic coherence. *Management Learning, 47*(3), 324–342.

Levine, R., & Rubinstein, Y. (2017). Smart and illicit: Who becomes an entrepreneur do they earn more? *The Quarterly Journal of Economics, 132*(2), 963–1018.

Llewellyn, N., & Pence, L. (2009). Practice as a members' phenomenon. *Organization Studies, 30*(12), 1419–1439.

Ogbor, J. (2000). Mythicizing and reification in entrepreneurial discourse: Ideology-critique of entrepreneurial studies. *Journal of Management Studies, 37*(5), 605–635.

Palich, L. E., & Bagby, D. R. (1995). Using cognitive theory to explain entrepreneurial risk-taking: Challenging conventional wisdom. *Journal of Business Venturing, 10*(6), 425–438.

Pomerantz, A. (1984). Agreeing and disagreeing with assessments: Some features of preferred/dispreferred turn shapes. In J. Atkinson & J. Heritage (Eds.), *Structures of social action: Studies in conversation analysis*. Cambridge: Cambridge University Press.

Quirk, R., Greenbaum, S., Leech, G., & Svartoik, J. (1985). *A comprehensive grammar of the English language*. New York: Longman.

Raymond, G. (2003). Grammar and social organization: Yes/no interrogatives and the structure of responding. *American Sociological Review, 68*, 939–967.

Robinson, J. (2003). An interactional structure of medical activities during acute visits and its implications for patients' participation. *Health Communication, 15*(1), 27–59.

Sacks, H. (1973). *The preference for agreement in natural conversation.* Linguistic Institute. Ann Arbor, Michigan.

Sacks, H. (1984a). Notes on methodology. In J. M. Atkinsen & J. Heritage (Eds.), Structures of social action: Studies in conversation analysis. Cambridge: Cambrige University Press.

Sacks, H. (1984b). On doing "being ordinary". In J. M. Atkinsen & J. Heritage (Eds.), Structures of social action: Studies in conversational analysis (pp. 413–429). Cambridge: Cambrige University Press.

Sacks, H. (1992a). Adjacency pairs: Scope of operation. In G. Jefferson (Ed.), *Lectures on conversation* (Vol. 2, pp. 521–532). Oxford: Blackwell.

Sacks, H. (1992b). *Lectures on conversation* (Vol. 1 (Fall 1964-Spring 1968)). Oxford: Blackwell.

Sacks, H., Schegloff, E. A., & Jefferson, G. (1974). A simplest systematics for the organization of turn-taking for conversation. *Language, 50*(4), 696–735.

Sarasvathy, S. D. (2001). Causation and effectuation: Toward a theoretical shift from economic inevitability to entrepreneurial contingency. *Academy of Management Review, 26*(2), 243–263.

Schegloff, E. A. (1968). Sequencing in conversational openings. *American Anthropologist, 70*, 1075–1095.

Schegloff, E. A. (1991). Reflections on talk and social structure. In D. Boden & D. Zimmerman (Eds.), *Talk and social structure: Studies in ethnomethodology and conversation analysis* (pp. 44–70). Cambridge: Polity.

Schegloff, E. A., & Lerner, G. H. (2009). Beginning to respond: Well-prefaced responses to wh-questions. *Research on Language & Social Interaction, 42*(2), 91–115.

Seale, C. (1999). Quality in qualitative research. *Qualitative Inquiry, 5*(4), 465–478.

Shotter, J. (1993). *Conversational realities: Constructing life through language.* Thousand Oaks, CA: Sage.

Steensig, J., & Drew, P. (2008). Introduction: Questioning and affiliation/disaffiliation in interaction. *Discourse Studies, 10*(1), 5–15.

Stivers, T. (2010). An overview of the question-reponse system in American English conversation. *Journal of Pragmatics, 42*, 2772–2781.

Stivers, T., & Enfield, N. (2010). A coding scheme for question – response sequences in conversation. *Journal of Pragmatics, 42*(10), 2620–2626.

Stivers, T., & Hayashi, M. (2010). Transformative answers: One way to resist a question's constraints. *Language in Society, 39*(1), 1–25.

Stivers, T., & Heritage, J. (2001). Breaking the sequential mold: Answering "more than the question" during comprehensive history taking. *Text and Talk, 21*(1/2), 151–185.

Stokoe, E., & Edwards, D. (2008). Did you have permission to smash your neighbour's door? Silly questions and their answers in police – suspect interrogations. *Discourse Studies, 10*(1), 89–111.

Tracy, K., & Robles, J. (2009). Questions, questioning, and institutional practices: An introduction. *Discourse Studies, 11*(2), 131–152.

Waln, V. (1984). Questions in interpersonal conflict: Participant and observer perceptions. *Southern Journal of Communication, 49*(3), 277–288.

Wiltbank, R., Read, S., Dew, N., & Sarasvathy, S. D. (2009). Prediction and control under uncertainty: Outcomes in angel investing. *Journal of Business Venturing, 24*(2), 116–133.

# PART IV

# Looking through other lenses

Quantitative CA animated Chapter 7's analysis of question usage by a successful innovative entrepreneurial team. However, quantitative CA can make possible other types of comparisons. Part IV explores the language patterns used by a high- and low-performance early-stage innovative entrepreneurial team and by an elite engineering team (with no entrepreneurial intension).

# 9

# RESILIENCE AS VERBAL PRACTICE

## Introduction

Successful entrepreneurs tend to be resilient (Ayala & Manzano, 2014; Hayward, Forster, Sarasvathy, & Fredrickson, 2010). Their capacity to adapt to changing and challenging circumstances enables them to innovate and ascend amid the uncertainties and setbacks that accompany new ventures (Reinmoeller & Van Baardwijk, 2005).

Resilience refers to the capacity for an individual, team, or organization to bend rather than break in the face of adversity (Bonanno, 2004; Coutu, 2003). Distinct from grit or persistence which can suggest unwavering determination (Van Gelderen, 2012), resilience implies adaptability: the capacity to absorb a jolt, regain equilibrium, and pursue a thoughtfully revised course of action (Sutcliffe & Vogus, 2003). This agility of entrepreneurial teams is associated with their capacity for sensemaking (Cornelissen & Clarke, 2010; Hill & Levenhagen, 1995; Wood & McKinley, 2010).

Sensemaking is a collaborative process used by teams when they face recognizably uncertain, disruptive, or ambiguous circumstances (Weick, 1995) – the typical experience of entrepreneurs (McKelvie, Haynie, & Gustavsson, 2011; Sarasvathy, 2001). Because it is inherently social, sensemaking happens through verbal conversations between team mates (Roberson, 2006). Consequently, sensemaking can be observed through the language used by teams in action (Donnellon, Gray, & Bougon, 1986; Thomas, Clark, & Gioia, 1993; Wilson, 2007).

In his groundbreaking work on sensemaking, Weick (1993) suggests several sources of resilience that may enhance a team's ability to accomplish critical tasks within dynamic circumstances and limited time. Research has linked specific language forms with three of these sources of resilience: improvisation and bricolage, attitudes of wisdom and doubt, and heedfulness (Bandura,1998; Campbell, 1990;

Langer 1992; Caproni, 2001; Langer, 2002; Sutcliffe & Vogus, 2003; Hargadon & Bechky, 2006; Rixon, McWaters, & Rixon, 2006; Wilson, 2007; Barske, 2009; Owens, 2009).

Despite the links between entrepreneurship and resilience as well as those between resilience and language, little empirical evidence exists on the ways that innovative entrepreneurial teams verbally create or access sources of resilience. This chapter explores the role of language in the enactment of entrepreneurial resilience by examining a coordinated set of cases collected from a lean startup contest. Drawing on Weick's sources of resilience and on language forms associated with them in the literature, this analysis compares the naturally occurring workplace conversations of teams that achieve high and low levels of performance. This exploratory work suggests that an innovative entrepreneurial team's capacity to adapt and thrive may be associated with several key verbal behaviors.

## Sources of resilience

### *Improvisation and bricolage*

Improvisation requires the simultaneous design and execution of an act that produces a novel outcome (Baker, Miner, & Eesley, 2003; A.S. Miner, Bassoff, & Moorman, 2001). It implies an unscripted intentionality that is distinct from random expressive acts (Weick, 1996, 1998). It also differs from experimentation and rapid iteration which include deliberate efforts to test and evaluate (Austin & Devin, 2003; Anne S. Miner, Bassof, & Moorman, 2001; Schrage, 1999; Thomke, 1998). People who are skilled at improvisation are said to have a variety of competencies including procedural and declarative knowledge related to the task at hand (Moorman & Miner, 1998).

Bricolage is the practice of using available resources in novel, purposeful ways (Levi-Strauss, 1966). It emphasizes the achievement of sufficient success rather than ideal outcomes (Baker et al., 2003; Baker & Nelson, 2005). People who are capable bricoleurs can recombine a limited set of existing materials and resources to produce something new and useful.

Both improvisation and bricolage are akin to creativity. At the team level, creativity can be enhanced by social practices that include seeking help, giving help, and adaptive framing based on reflection (Hargadon & Bechky, 2006) – acts which can occur, in part, through intra-team conversation. Similarly, the use of conditional forms of language (e.g., could be, might) as opposed to absolute forms of language (e.g., must be, is) can facilitate increased creativity (Langer, 1992, 2002, pp. 216–217). However, in highly uncertain contexts – such as the conditions in which entrepreneurs work – few people are at their creative best (Amabile, Hadley, & Kramer, 2002; Weick, 1993). Instead, in such situations people tend to cling to familiar behaviors even if such actions are not constructive (Raelin, 2001, p. 16; Snook, 2000; Weick, 1993).

Much of the entrepreneurship literature has focused on a linear progression of planning followed by execution (Carter, Gartner, & Reynolds, 1996; Shane, 2003; Shane & Venkataraman, 2000) rather than on acts of improvisation or bricolage. When concepts of improvisation or bricolage are considered in the context of entrepreneurship, they are sometimes positioned as reactions rather than deliberate acts (Senyard, Powell Brown, Davidsson, & Steffens, 2013). However, "improvisational routines" can be a strategic choice for entrepreneurial teams (Baker et al., 2003). Nevertheless, improvisation and bricolage, even when used conscientiously, do not guarantee resilience and success for entrepreneurial teams (Hmieleski, Corbett, & Baron, 2013).

## Attitudes of wisdom and doubt

Humility has become increasingly discussed in the literatures of leadership and organizations (Badaracco, 2002; Cameron, Duttton, & Quinn, 2003; Collins, 2001; Nielsen, Marrone, & Slay, 2010; Weick & Roberts, 1993). Seen as an important quality to be found in leaders and the corporate cultures they create, humility is considered by some to be especially valuable for organizations facing rapid and unpredictable change (Morris, Brotheridge, & Urbanski, 2005; Weick, 2001). Even though changing conditions and uncertainty are inherent in entrepreneurial endeavors, humility is not frequently considered in research on entrepreneurship (Barton, 2010). Instead entrepreneurship research has tended to explore themes of hubris, self-efficacy, confidence, and overconfidence (Baum & Locke, 2004; Hayward, Shepherd, & Griffin, 2006; Hmieleski & Baron, 2008).

Much has been written about the overconfidence bias of entrepreneurs (Busenitz & Barney, 1997; Forbes, 2005). Contexts defined by uncertainty and complexity – such those experienced by entrepreneurs – can intensify the overconfidence bias (Baron, 1998; Hayward et al., 2006; Lichtenstein & Fischhoff, 1977). An abundance of confidence may help entrepreneurs choose to start ventures despite the odds of failure and to persist in challenging situations (Busenitz & Barney, 1997; Hayward et al., 2010; Markman, Baron, & Balkin, 2005; Zhou, Hills, & Seibert, 2005). However, there are limits to the positive impact high levels of confidence can bestow upon entrepreneurs, especially in dynamic environments (Audia, Locke, & Smith, 2000; Bandura & Locke, 2003; Hayward et al., 2006; Hmieleski & Baron, 2008). Some research has suggested training in self-awareness as a possible way to enable entrepreneurs to temper their tendencies toward excessive confidence and respond with more appropriate levels of certainty in uncertain situations (Hmieleski & Baron, 2008).

The contextualized confidence that would be the desired result of such training may have much in common with humility; a "situated humility" (Barton, 2010; Barton & Sutcliffe, 2010) which allows an otherwise confident entrepreneur to acknowledge his/her limitations in a given situation. Humility includes several features, such as an ability to acknowledge self-limitations, appreciate the abilities and contributions of others, maintain a learning stance, and hold a low level of focus on the self (Owens, 2009). These guidelines would suggest that checking assumptions, questioning what you think you know, clarifying information, and referencing the team and the self as part of the team could all be considered verbal expressions of an attitude of wisdom and doubt.

## Heedfulness

Expressions of heedful interactions with team mates include respecting the reports and perspectives of others, being willing to act on the input given by others, and honoring one's own observations and meaning-making while attempting to incorporate the perceptions of others (Campbell, 1990; Weick & Roberts, 1993). While interacting in mutually supportive ways has been shown to improve a team's sense of collective efficacy (Bandura, 1998; Caproni, 2001; Sutcliffe & Vogus, 2003) and collective identity (Cameron et al., 2003; Hardy, Lawrence, & Grant, 2005), heedful interactions are more than demonstrations of respect. To interact heedfully means, in part, to empathize with and anticipate the positions and responses of team mates and to shape your own actions to complement the efforts of the team. This capacity to subordinate one's individual orientation to the service of shared goals is considered by some to be essential to innovation (Dougherty & Takacs, 2004).

Even though face-to-face real-time conversations are a standard part of most entrepreneurial teams' interactions (Amason, Shrader, & Tompson, 2006), the literature on entrepreneurial communication seems to focus mostly on "social skills" (Baron & Markman, 2000). Skills such as reading other people well, creating good first impressions, adapting easily to various situations, and persuading others have been associated with good entrepreneurial team performance. Other research has linked an entrepreneur's ability to garner information and resources with their capacity to read people and situations well and to express their emotions and thoughts clearly and persuasively (Baron & Tang, 2009). Missing in the literature are empirical studies into the enactment of heedful intra-team conversations.

While scholarly interest in entrepreneurial resilience is growing, much research remains based on issues of self-confidence and self-efficacy (Bullough & Renk, 2013; Hayward et al., 2010) rather than on a team's ability to access or create sources of resilience. Outside of entrepreneurship, scholars have posited that intra-team interactions may provide insights into the ways that high-performance teams gain their edge and may yield generalizable antecedents of team performance (Tschan et al., 2006; Waller, Gupta, & Giambatista, 2004). Given that conversation is the means by which team members perform and pursue their shared work (Drew & Sorjonen, 1997; Nevile, 2004), this chapter examines the intra-team conversations of one high-performance and one low-performance early-stage innovative entrepreneurial team in action in an effort to better understand how team members verbally access and create sources of resilience. It is oriented around two exploratory questions: (1) does the naturally occurring language of innovative entrepreneurial teams align with the three aforementioned sources of resilience, and, if so,

2) are there differences in the language patterns used by a high-performance and low-performance innovative entrepreneurial team in the enactment of their work.

## Methodological framework

The research setting is a lean startup contest hosted by an American university with a long history of support for innovative entrepreneurship. Naturally occurring workplace interactions were recorded for many teams throughout the duration of the contest. Data from the final meeting before the contest's conclusion were transcribed for a team that achieved the highest and the lowest ranking. During a phase of "unmotivated looking" (Psathas, 1995), conversational episodes that focused on the teams' efforts to create a viable product were selected for deeper analysis. These episodes included 79 utterances from the high-performance team and 51 utterances from the low-performance team. Data not selected for closer examination included exchanges about contest preparations or gossip. Utterances associated with alignment (e.g., "yeah") also were removed from the analysis.

The episodes were analyzed utterance by utterance with an appreciation for the situated and processual nature of the conversations (Psathas, 1995). In an iterative process, each utterance was coded based on the way it was understood by the speakers in context. These emerging codes were compared with concepts in the literature (Glaser & Strauss, 2009), especially those concepts associated with the enhancement or inhibition of resilience. (See Table 9.1.) The emerging codes

**TABLE 9.1** Integration of resilience traits in the literature and study codes

| Resilience trait | Impact | Language in literature | Attribution | Code informed by micro-analysis |
|---|---|---|---|---|
| Improvisation and bricolage | Enhance | Help giving | Hargadon & Bechky, 2006 | Meaning: Clarify |
| | Enhance | Help seeking | Hargadon & Bechky, 2006 | Information: Seek Information: Reveal Meaning: Clarify Meaning: Reflect |
| | Enhance | Use of conditional and provisional language | Langer 1992, 2002 | Meaning: Conditional |
| | Enhance | *Use of language forms that signal a flexible approach* | *Extrapolated from Langer 1992, 2002* | Meaning: Reflect Action: Levity |
| | Hinder | Use of fixed language forms | Langer 1992, 2002 | Meaning: Absolute |
| | Hinder | *Use of language forms that signal an inflexible approach* | *Extrapolated from Langer 1992, 2002* | Information: Idea |

*(Continued)*

**TABLE 9.1** (Continued)

| Resilience trait | Impact | Language in literature | Attribution | Code informed by micro-analysis |
|---|---|---|---|---|
| Attitudes of wisdom and doubt | Enhance | Acknowledgement of self-limitations | Owens, 2009 | Information: Reveal<br>Information: Seek<br>Meaning: Clarify |
| | Enhance | Appreciation for abilities and contributions of others | Owens, 2009 | Meaning: Reflect<br>Action: Affirm |
| | Hinder | *Lack of appreciation for abilities and contributions of others* | *Extrapolation from Owens, 2009* | Meaning: Influence |
| | Enhance | Learning stance | Owens, 2009 | Information: Reveal<br>Meaning: Conditional<br>Meaning: Reflect |
| | Hinder | *Non-learning stance* | *Extrapolation from Owens, 2009* | Information: Idea<br>Meaning: Absolute<br>Meaning: Influence |
| | Enhance | Low level of focus on the self | Owens, 2009 | Meaning: Clarify |
| Heedful interactions | Enhance | Respect for the reports and perspectives of others | Campbell, 1990 | Information: Seek<br>Meaning: Clarify<br>Meaning: Reflect |
| | Hinder | *Lack of respect for the reports and perspectives of others* | *Extrapolation from Campbell, 1990* | Information: Idea<br>Meaning: Absolute<br>Meaning: Influence |
| | Enhance | Mutual support | Bandura, 1998; Caproni, 2001; Sutcliffe & Vogus, 2003 | Action: Affirm |
| | Hinder | *Lack of mutual support* | *Extrapolation from Bandura, 1998; Caproni, 2001; Sutcliffe & Vogus, 2003* | Meaning: Influence |

also were subject to a peer debriefing to ensure the consideration of alternative impressions of the data. The final set of codes was associated with the data in Atlas TI. After the coding was completed, quantitative measures were derived from the codes and compared across teams.

# Findings

The examination of the naturally occurring conversations of the teams revealed that the high-performance team used language forms associated with the enhancement of resilience more frequently than the low-performance team did. In contrast, the low-performance team used language forms associated with the hindrance of resilience more frequently than the high-performance team did.

The general language patterns differed starkly between the two teams. (See Table 9.2.) The high-performance team consistently the language forms that were associated with the enhancement of resilience whereas the low-performance team consistently used the forms that were associated with the inhibition of resilience. A similar dynamic was found across the three individual sources of resilience as described by Weick. (See Figures 9.1, 9.2, and 9.3, respectively.)

# Discussion

The literature has linked Weick's sources of resilience – improvisation and bricolage, attitudes of wisdom and doubt, and heedfulness – with several language forms. Given that resilience is thought to be an attribute of successful teams, this study considered whether the members of a high- and low-performance innovative entrepreneurial team used the language forms associated with resilience differently in the enactment of their work.

The patterns of observable language revealed by this study lend empirical support to Weick's assertions about resilience (Weick, 1993). In Weick's model, teams who create or access sources of resilience – improvisation and bricolage, attitudes of wisdom and doubt, and heedfulness – tend to be more successful. In this study, the

**TABLE 9.2** Composite of use of language forms associated with resilience

| Language form | High-performance team | Low-performance team |
| --- | --- | --- |
| Information: Idea | 0% (n = 0) | 12% (n = 6) |
| Information: Reveal | 9% (n = 7) | 0% (n = 0) |
| Information: Seek | 3% (n = 2) | 2% (n = 1) |
| Information: Share | 10% (n = 8) | 33% (n = 17) |
| Meaning: Absolute | 8% (n = 6) | 20% (n = 10) |
| Meaning: Conditional | 13% (n = 10) | 8% (n = 4) |
| Meaning: Clarify | 16% (n = 13) | 16% (n = 8) |
| Meaning: Influence | 0% (n = 0) | 2% (n = 1) |
| Meaning: Reflect | 5% (n = 4) | 2% (n = 1) |
| Action: Affirm | 4% (n = 3) | 0% (n = 0) |
| Action: Facilitate | 3% (n = 2) | 6% (n = 3) |
| Action: Levity | 11% (n = 9) | 0% (n = 0) |
| Action: Plan | 14% (n = 11) | 0% (n = 0) |
| Action: Suspend | 5% (n = 4) | 0% (n = 0) |

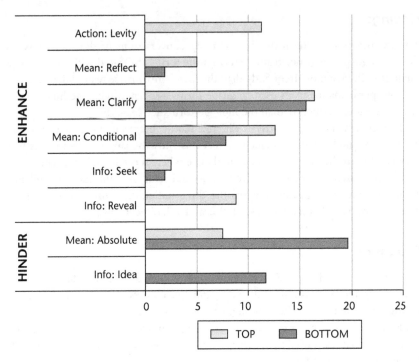

**FIGURE 9.1**  Percentages of utterances associated with language forms related to impro-
vision and bricolage

high-performance team used the language forms associated with the enhancement
of these traits more frequently than the low-performance team. Moreover, the low-
performance team used the language forms associated with the inhibition of these
traits more frequently than the high-performance team.

One of the most distinct differences between the teams' language patterns is
found in their use of claiming language. The low-performance team's tendency to
use fixed, absolute language over flexible, conditional language suggests a somewhat rigid way of approaching the crafting of their product. Their use of absolute
claiming language – along with their exclusive use of utterances coded for Information: Idea and Meaning: Influence – imposes a language of certainty onto an
uncertain situation. Frequent use of absolute language forms may indicate that the
team had denied uncertainties or had made premature cognitive commitments
(Langer, 1992).

In contrast, the high-performance team's tendency to use conditional language
over absolute language suggests adaptability and creativity. Conditional language
has been found to be an asset to teams functioning in uncertain environments
(Krieger, 2005; Weick, Sutcliffe, & Obstfeld, 1999; Wilson, 2007). Conditional
framing (i.e., the use of the word *could* instead of *is*) helps people avoid premature
cognitive commitments and supports their ability to embrace fresh perspectives

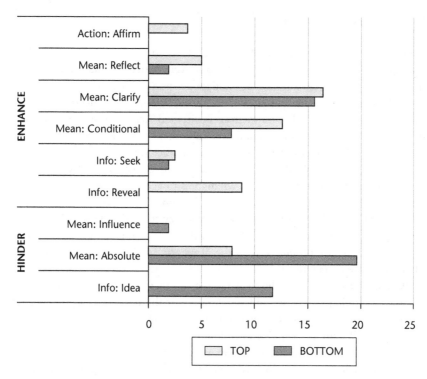

**FIGURE 9.2** Percentages of utterances associated with language forms related to attitudes of wisdom and doubt

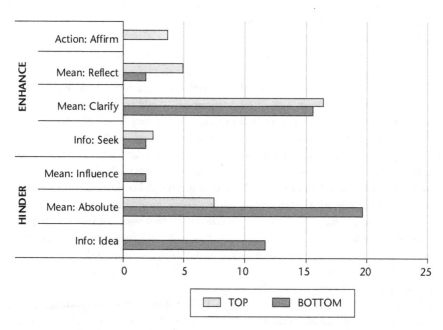

**FIGURE 9.3** Percentages of utterances associated with language forms related to heedfulness

(Langer & Piper, 1987; Langer, 1992, 2002). Conditional language also has been associated with mindfulness – the ability to actively notice and interpret disruptive data while maintaining awareness of multiple perspectives (Langer, 1989, 1997).

Such agility also is demonstrated through the high-performance team's exclusive use of utterances coded for Action: Levity and Action: Suspend. Utterances of Action: Levity present imagined future states that offer alternative, if ridiculous, paths forward. Utterances of Action: Suspend consciously keep a topic or course of action in an unresolved state. Suspending a topic that needs deeper consideration also demonstrates the team's willingness to acknowledge and "access their ignorance" (Lambrechts, Bouwen, Grieten, Huybrechts, & Schein, 2011; Schein, 2009, p. 100); to make time to reconsider what they think they know. Choosing to interrupt and return to a matter rather than dispense with it immediately requires an ability to function productively in the near-term while retaining multiple possibilities for the longer-term.

Whether enabled by conditional framing, levity, or suspension, being able to consider multiple perspectives simultaneously is at the heart of reflective practice (Schön, 1983). In addition to being retrospective, reflective practice also can be anticipatory (Raelin, 2001, p. 19) or unfold in real time (Van Manen, 2006, p. 87). In other words, teams can think and do at the same time (Schön, 1983). A tight coupling of reflection and action is thought to help teams bring to fruition new ideas, actions, and material innovations (Valkenburg & Dorst, 1998, p. 251). The high-performance team's use of language patterns that facilitate the ability to work with multiple perspectives support the claims that reflective practice may be a competence of entrepreneurial teams (Neck & Greene, 2011; Ulvenblad, Berggren, & Winborg, 2013).

Holding multiple possibilities in mind simultaneously suggests that team members are willing and able to adapt to emergent situations and change course productively (Sarasvathy, 2008). The use of relatively inflexible language forms may signal that a team resists the creation of new interpretations that could accommodate all of the relevant, if discordant, information and experiences that they have gathered (Langer, 1992). Consequently, inflexible language may inhibit a team's ability to reconceptualize their emerging product based on feedback that does not support their original vision. Conversely, teams, such as the high-performance team, who frame their work in flexible, provisional language might have a greater ability to discard prototypes lacking market validation or to leverage surprises in customer behavior.

Confidence, sometimes even overconfidence, is often associated with entrepreneurial competence (Hayward et al., 2010). Consequently, asserting that the success of a high-performance team might be enhanced by the use of words such as *might* or *could* may be unexpected. However, because conditional framing can capture the variations and complexities that are present in a dynamic, uncertain context it might be the most accurate – and most success-enabling – way of speaking about innovative entrepreneurial endeavors. In other words, innovative entrepreneurial teams that use conditional language in their intra-team meetings are not necessarily lacking confidence or decisiveness. Rather, the context of their work is full of uncertainties, and they are using conditional language to identify and embrace that. As Badaracco has suggested, people who can maintain an awareness of "the complexities, nuances, and uncertainties around them are likely to do a better job of navigating through them" (Badaracco, 2002, pp. 48–49).

## Conclusion

This chapter explored how innovative entrepreneurial teams verbally access and create sources of resilience. The findings suggest that several conversational moves in particular may be helpful to innovative entrepreneurial teams as they strive to avoid premature cognitive commitments, envision plausible futures, accurately describe their situations, and achieve success.

All studies, of course, have limitations, and this one is no different. The findings come from a very thin slice; from two teams participating in one event. In addition, the teams in the study had different compositions. While they were evenly matched in other ways – maturity and availability of resources among other things – the teams had different sizes and different balances of technical and business expertise. Consequently the findings may have been skewed by this structural difference. But despite these limitations, the data provides an uncommon view into the inner workings of innovative entrepreneurial teams in action. As such, the findings can help answer enduring questions about the micro-foundations of entrepreneurial behavior and the dynamic capabilities of entrepreneurial teams (Shepherd, 2015; Zahra, Sapienza, & Davidsson, 2006).

Future research springing from this exploratory work could continue to investigate sources of resilience. Of particular interest is another attribute of resilience identified by Weick (Weick, 1993); virtual role systems. Perhaps future studies could identify the interactional means by which innovative entrepreneurial teams enhance or inhibit their virtual role systems in action. Such work would speak to the entrepreneurship as practice literature as well as the entrepreneurial resilience literature. It also could have implications for entrepreneurial education.

In summary, this chapter has presented an examination of the language forms associated with resilience as used by early-stage innovative entrepreneurial teams in action. The provisional connections the study has made between language and resilience suggest that several key conversational moves may be an asset to innovative entrepreneurial teams. The chapter also signals how quantitative CA can aid in the study of entrepreneurial teamwork and highlight areas worthy of additional inquiry.

## References

Amabile, T. M., Hadley, C. N., & Kramer, S. J. (2002). Creativity under the gun. *Harvard Business Review, 80*(8).

Amason, A. C., Shrader, R., & Tompson, G. H. (2006). Newness and novelty: Relating top management team composition to new venture performance. *Journal of Business Venturing, 21*(1), 125–148.

Audia, P. G., Locke, E. A., & Smith, K. G. (2000). The paradox of success: An archival and laboratory study of strategic persistence following radical environmental change. *Academy of Management Journal, 43*, 837–853.

Austin, R. D., & Devin, L. (2003). *Artful making: What managers need to know about how artists work.* Upper Saddle River, NJ: Financial Times Prentice Hall.

Ayala, J.-C., & Manzano, G. (2014). The resilience of the entrepreneur. Influence on the success of the business. A longitudinal analysis. *Journal of Economic Psychology, 42*(1), 126–135.

Badaracco, J. L. (2002). *Leading quietly: An unorthodox guide to doing the right thing.* Boston, MA: Harvard Business School Press.

Baker, T., Miner, A. S., & Eesley, D. T. (2003). Improvising firms: Bricolage, account giving and improvisational competencies in the founding process. *Research Policy, 32*, 255–276.

Baker, T., & Nelson, R. (2005). Creating something from nothing: Resource construction through entrepreneurial bricolage. *Administrative Science Quarterly, 50*(3), 329–366.

Bandura, A. (1998). *Self-efficacy: The exercise of control.* New York, NY: W.H. Freeman.

Bandura, A., & Locke, E. A. (2003). Negative self-efficacy and goal effects revisited. *Journal of Applied Psychology, 88*(1), 87.

Baron, R. A. (1998). Cognitive mechanisms in entrepreneurship: Why and when entrepreneurs think differently than other people. *Journal of Business Venturing, 13*(4), 275–294.

Baron, R. A., & Markman, G. D. (2000). Beyond social capital: How social skills can enhance entrepreneurs' success. *The Academy of Management Executive (1993–2005), 14*(1), 106–116.

Baron, R. A., & Tang, J. (2009). Entrepreneurs' social skills and new venture performance: Mediating mechanisms and cultural generality. *Journal of Management, 35*(2), 282–306.

Barske, T. (2009). Same token, different actions: A conversation analytic study of social roles, embodied actions, and ok in German business meetings. *The Journal of Business Communication, 46*(1), 120–149.

Barton, M. A. (2010). Shaping entrepreneurial opportunities: Managing uncertainty and equivocality in the entrepreneurial process (Doctoral Dissertation), University of Michigan, Ann Arbor, MI.

Barton, M. A., & Sutcliffe, K. M. (2010). Learning when to stop momentum. *MIT Sloan Management Review, 51*(3), 69–76.

Baum, J. R., & Locke, E. A. (2004). The relationship of entrepreneurial traits, skill, and motivation to subsequent venture growth. *Journal of Applied Psychology, 89*(4), 587.

Bonanno, G. (2004). Loss, trauma, and human resilience: Have we underestimated the human capacity to thrive after extremely aversive events. *American Psychologist, 59*(1), 20–28.

Bullough, A., & Renk, M. (2013). Entrepreneurial resilience during challenging times. *Business Horizons, 56*(3), 343–350.

Busenitz, L. W., & Barney, J. B. (1997). Differences between entrepreneurs and managers in large organizations: Biases and heuristics in strategic decision-making. *Journal of Business Venturing, 12*(1), 9–30.

Cameron, K. S., Duttton, J., & Quinn, R. E. (2003). *Positive organizational scholarship: Foundations of a new discipline.* San Francisco, CA: Berrett-Koehler Publishers, Inc.

Campbell, D. T. (1990). *Asch's moral epistemology for socially shared knowledge. The Legacy of Solomon Asch: Essays in cognition and social psychology.* Hillsdale, NJ: Erlbaum.

Caproni, P. (2001). *Management skills for everyday life: The practical coach.* Upper Saddle River, Englewood Cliffs, NJ: Prentice-Hall.

Carter, N., Gartner, W. B., & Reynolds, P. D. (1996). Exploring statrtup event sequences. *Journal of Business Venturing, 11*(3), 151–166.

Collins, J. (2001, January). Level 5 leadership: The triumph of humility and fierce resolve. *Harvard Business Review, 79*(1), 66–76.

Cornelissen, J. P., & Clarke, J. S. (2010). Imagining and rationalizing opportunities: Inductive reasoning and the creation and justification of new ventures. *The Academy of Management Review, 35*(4).

Coutu, D. L. (2003). Sense and reliability: A conversation with celebrated psychologist Karl E. Weick. *Harvard Business Review, 81,* 84–90.

Donnellon, A., Gray, B., & Bougon, M. G. (1986). Communication, meaning, and organized action. *Administrative Science Quarterly, 31*(1), 43–55.

Dougherty, D., & Takacs, C. H. (2004). Team play: Heedful interrelating as the boundary for innovation. *Long Range Planning, 37*(6), 569–590.

Drew, P., & Sorjonen, M. L. (1997). Institutional dialogue. In T. A. Van Dijk (Ed.), *Discourse as social interaction: Discourse studies: A multidisciplinary introduction* (Vol. 2, pp. 92–118). London, UK: Sage.

Forbes, D. P. (2005). Are some entrepreneurs more overconfident than others? *Journal of Business Venturing, 20*(5).

Glaser, B. G., & Strauss, A. L. (2009). *The discovery of grounded theory: Strategies for qualitative research.*

Hardy, C., Lawrence, T. B., & Grant, D. (2005). Discourse and collaboration: The role of conversations and collective identity. *The Academy of Management Review, 30*(1), 58–77.

Hargadon, A. B., & Bechky, B. A. (2006). When collections of creatives become creative collectives: A field study of problem solving at work. *Organization Science, 17*(4), 484–500.

Hayward, M. L. A., Forster, W., Sarasvathy, S. D., & Fredrickson, B. (2010). Beyond hubris: How highly confident entrepreneurs rebound to venture again. *Journal of Business Venturing, 25*(6), 569–578.

Hayward, M. L. A., Shepherd, D. A., & Griffin, D. (2006). A hubris theory of entrepreneurship. *Management Science, 52*(2), 160–172.

Hill, R. C., & Levenhagen, M. (1995). Metaphors and mental models: Sensemaking and sensegiving in innovative and entrepreneurial activities. *Journal of Management, 21*(6), 1057–1074.

Hmieleski, K. M., & Baron, R. A. (2008). When does entrepreneurial self-efficacy enhance versus reduce firm performance? *Strategic Entrepreneurship Journal, 2,* 57–72.

Hmieleski, K. M., Corbett, A. C., & Baron, R. A. (2013). Entrepreneurs' improvisational behavior and firm performance: A study of dispositional and environmental moderators. *Strategic Entrepreneurship Journal, 7,* 138–150.

Krieger, J. L. (2005). Shared mindfulness in cockpit crisis situations an exploratory analysis. *Journal of Business Communication, 42*(2), 135–167.

Lambrechts, F., Bouwen, R., Grieten, S., Huybrechts, J., & Schein, E. H. (2011). Learning to help through humble inquiry and implications for management research, practice, and education: An interview with Edgar H. Schein. *Academy of Management Learning and Education, 10*(1), 131–147.

Langer, E. J., & Piper, A. I. (1987). The prevention of mindlessness. *Journal of Personality and Social Psychology, 53*(2), 280.

Langer, E. J. (1989). *Mindfulness.* Reading, MA: Addison-Wesley Pub. Co.

Langer, E. J. (1992). Matters of mind: Mindfulness/mindlessness in perspective. *Consciousness and Cognition, 1*(3), 289–305.

Langer, E. J. (1997). *The power of mindful learning.* Reading, MA: Addison-Wesley Pub. Co.

Langer, E. J. (2002). Well-Being: Mindfulness versus positive evaluation. In C. R. Snyder & S. J. López (Eds.), *Handbook of positive psychology.* New York, NY: Oxford University Press.

Levi-Strauss, C. (1966). *The savage mind.* Chicago: University of Chicago Press.

Lichtenstein, S., & Fischhoff, B. (1977). Do those who know more also know more about how much they know? *Organizational Behavior and Human Performance, 20*(2), 159–183.

Markman, G. D., Baron, R. A., & Balkin, D. B. (2005). Are perseverance and self-efficacy costless? Assessing entrepreneurs' regretful thinking. *Journal of Organizational Behavior, 26*(1), 1–19.

McKelvie, A., Haynie, J. M., & Gustavsson, V. (2011). Unpacking the uncertainty construct: Implications for entrepreneurial action. *Journal of Business Venturing, 26*(3), 273–292.

Miner, A. S., Bassof, P., & Moorman, C. (2001). Organizational improvisation and learning: A field study. *Administrative Science Quarterly, 46*(2), 304–337.

Moorman, C., & Miner, A. S. (1998). The convergence of planning and execution: Improvisation in new product development. *Journal of Marketing, 61*, 1–20.

Morris, J. A., Brotheridge, C., & Urbanski, J. (2005). Bringing humility to leadership: Antecedents and consequences of leader humility. *Human Relations, 58*.

Neck, H. M., & Greene, P. G. (2011). Entrepreneurship education: Known worlds and new frontiers. *Journal of Small Business Management, 49*(1), 55–70.

Nevile, M. (2004). *Beyond the black box: Talk-in-interaction in the airline cockpit.* New York, NY: Ashgate Publishing, Ltd.

Nielsen, R., Marrone, J. A., & Slay, H. S. (2010). A new look at humility: Exploring the humility concept and its role in socialized charismatic leadership. *Journal of Leadership & Organizational Studies, 17*, 33–43.

Owens, B. (2009). *Humility in organizational leadership* (PhD), University of Washington.

Psathas, G. (1995). *Conversation analysis: The study of talk in interaction.* Thousand Oaks, CA: Sage.

Raelin, J. (2001). Public reflection as the basis of learning. *Management Learning, 32*(1), 11–30.

Reinmoeller, P., & Van Baardwijk, N. (2005). The link between diversity and resilience. *MIT Sloan Management Review, 46*(4), 61–65.

Rixon, A., McWaters, V., & Rixon, S. (2006). Exploring the language of facilitation. *Group Facilitation: A Research & Applications Journal, 7*, 21–30.

Roberson, Q. M. (2006). Justice in teams: The activation and role of sensemaking in the emergence of justice climates *Organizational Behavior and Human Decision Processes, 100*(2), 177–192.

Sarasvathy, S. D. (2001). Causation and effectuation: Toward a theoretical shift from economic inevitability to entrepreneurial contingency. *Academy of Management Review, 26*(2), 243–263.

Sarasvathy, S. D. (2008). *Effectuation: Elements of entrepreneurial expertise.* Northampton, MA: Edward Elgar Publishing.

Schein, E. H. (2009). *Helping: How to offer, give, and receive help.* San Francisco, CA: Berrett-Koehler.

Schön, D. A. (1983). *The reflective practitioner: How professionals think in action.* New York, NY: Basic Books.

Schrage, M. (1999). *Serious play: How the world's best companies simulate to innovate.* Cambridge, MA: Harvard Business Review Press.

Senyard, J. M., Powell Brown, E., Davidsson, P., & Steffens, P. R. (2013). *Born unfinished: Boundaries of bricolage effectiveness.* Paper presented at the Australia Centre for Entrepreneurship (ACE) Research Exchange Conference 2013, Queensland University of Technology, Brisbane, QLD.

Shane, S. (2003). *A general theory of entrepreneurship. The individual-opportunity nexus.* Northampton, MA: Edward Elgar Publishing.

Shane, S., & Venkataraman, S. (2000). The promise of entrepreneurship as a field of research. *Academy of Management Review, 25*, 217–226.

Shepherd, D. A. (2015). Party on! A call for entrepreneurship research that is more interactive, activity based, cognitively hot, compassionate, and prosocial. *Journal of Business Venturing, 30*(4), 489–507.

Snook, S. A. (2000). *Friendly fire: The accidental shootdown of U.S. black hawks over Northern Iraq.* Princeton, NJ: Princeton University Press.

Sutcliffe, K. M., & Vogus, T. J. (2003). Organizing for resilience. In K. S. Cameron, J. E. Dutton & R. E. Quinn (Eds.), *Positive organizational scholarship: Foundations of a new discipline.* San Francisco, CA: Berrett-Koehler Publishers, Inc.

Thomas, J. B., Clark, S. M., & Gioia, D. A. (1993). Strategic sensemaking and organizational performance: Linkages among scanning, interpretation, action, and outcomes. *The Academy of Management Journal, 36*(2), 239–270.

Thomke, S. (1998). Managing experimentation in the design of new products. *Management Science, 44*(6), 743–762.

Tschan, F., Semmer, N., Gautschi, D., Hunziker, P., Spychiger, M., & Marsch, S. (2006). Leading to recovery: Group performance and coordinative activities in medical emergency driven groups. *Human Performance, 19*(3), 277–304.

Ulvenblad, P., Berggren, E., & Winborg, J. (2013). The role of entrepreneurship education and startup experience for handling communication and liability of newness. *International Journal of Entrepreneurial Behavior and Research, 19*(2), 187–209. doi:10.1108/13552 551311310374

Valkenburg, R., & Dorst, K. (1998). The reflective practice of design teams. *Design Studies, 19*(3), 249–271.

Van Gelderen, M. (2012). Perseverance strategies of enterprising individuals. *International Journal of Entrepreneurial Behaviour and Research, 18*(6), 630–648.

Van Manen, M. (2006). Reflexivity and the pedagogical moment: The practical-ethical nature of pedagogical thinking and acting. In I. Westbury & G. Milburn (Eds.), *Rethinking schooling: Twenty-five years of the journal of curriculum studies.* New York, NY: Routledge.

Waller, M. J., Gupta, N., & Giambatista, R. C. (2004). Effects of adaptive behaviors and shared mental models on control crew performance. *Management Science, 50*(11), 1534–1544.

Weick, K. E. (1993). The collapse of sensemaking in organizations: The Mann Gulch Disaster. *Administrative Science Quarterly, 38*(4), 628–652.

Weick, K. E. (1995). *Sensemaking in organizations.* London: Sage.

Weick, K. E. (1996). Drop your tools: An allegory for organizational studies. *Administrative Science Quarterly, 41*, 301–313.

Weick, K. E. (1998). Introductory essay: Improvisation as a mindset for organizational analysis. *Organizational Science, 9*(5), 543–555.

Weick, K. E. (2001). Leadership as the legitimation of doubt. In W. Bennis, G. Schweiter & T. Cumming (Eds.), *The future of leadership* (pp. 91–102). San Francisco, CA: Jossey-Bass.

Weick, K. E., & Roberts, K. H. (1993). Collective mind in organizations: Heedful interrelating on flight decks. *Administrative Science Quarterly, 38*(3), 357–381.

Weick, K. E., Sutcliffe, K. M., & Obstfeld, D. (1999). Organizing for high reliability: Processes of collective mindfulness. In R. S. Sutton & B. M. Staw (Eds.), *Research in organizational behavior* (Vol. 1, pp. 81–123). Stanford: Jai Press.

Wilson, D. (2007). *Team learning in action.* Doctoral Dissertation, Harvard Graduate School of Education, Cambridge, MA.

Wood, M. S., & McKinley, W. (2010). The production of entrepreneurial opportunity: A constructivist perspective. *Strategic Entrepreneurship Journal, 4*(1), 66–84.

Zahra, S. A., Sapienza, H. J., & Davidsson, P. (2006). Entrepreneurship and dynamic capabilities: A review, model and research agenda. *Journal of Management Studies, 43*(4), 917–955.

Zhou, H., Hills, G., & Seibert, S. E. (2005). The mediating role of self-efficacy in the development of entrepreneurial intentions. *Journal of Applied Psychology, 90*(6).

# 10

## BRICOLAGE AS VERBAL PRACTICE

### Introduction

Technology doesn't always work the way it should, as the following passage from a recent study's field notes conveys:

> Sitting down at a large table in a bright white conference room Aaron looks distressed: "This is super-mega bummer". He is the lead NASA engineer responsible for some mission-critical technologies related to interplanetary exploration, and a key piece of the system designed for the Mars Rovers unexpectedly has failed a basic test. "Yes" replies Ian, another senior engineer at the table whose facial expression and tone are as serious as Aaron's. More members of the innovation team enter the room, and everyone struggles to understand what they've just seen. Although the team attempts to make sense of the situation, they are unable to identify a clear explanation for the failure. As the conversation continues Aaron leans forward and puts his head in his hands. Technical Manager Claire soon shares her impression of the unfolding discussion: "We're unfortunately going back into a development program". Even though there is money in the budget and time in the schedule to accommodate a short period of re-development and testing, the pressure is on; if they are unable to understand the failure, duplicate it, and quickly develop a functioning system then the mission to Mars could be canceled, wasting years of work by thousands of people. Aaron, looking up and turning to Claire, supports her assessment: "This day means that's where we are".

Whether it thwarts expectations in early development or breaks down in final testing, technology sometimes plunges an innovation team into an urgent problem-solving mode. In some cases, that team must repair or reinvent the technology without the ability to procure additional resources or alter the intended product definition. Such a process of recombining resources to create a specific technological outcome captures the essence of bricolage (Baker & Nelson, 2005, p. 333).

The problem-solving literature outlines what teams in such circumstances tend to do: they formulate the problem and define potential solutions (Schwenk & Thomas, 1983). However, without detailed transcripts of a team engaged in a process of bricolage, researchers have been unable to describe *how* a team verbally accomplishes these acts.

This chapter asks a basic but rarely considered question: what conversational dynamics foster successful bricolage? By analyzing the naturally occurring conversations of an elite innovation team in action, some language patterns have emerged. While interpretive and reflective conversational moves may not seem appropriate for acts of urgent problem solving, the analysis demonstrates that (re)interpretation and introspective reconsideration are present – and potentially critical – in these circumstances.

## The nature of bricolage

Bricolage, a term borrowed from anthropology, is the practice of using available resources in novel, purposeful ways (Baker & Nelson, 2005; Levi-Strauss, 1966). To enact bricolage, a team typically recombines existing materials and resources through an iterative process of tinkering and experimentation. They apply their knowledge about available resources, trust their intuitions, and iteratively alter their theories and practices based on their impressions of their situation as it unfolds (Weick, 1998, p. 353). And, because all teamwork relies on conversation (Donnellon, 1996, p. 6), they are likely to engage in conversation while they grapple with the uncertainties that the problem and the problem-solving process have presented them.

Team mates engage in sensemaking conversations when they have been confronted with uncertainties (Roberson, 2006; Weick, Sutcliffe, & Obstfeld, 2005, p. 1). These conversations in general include the exchange of information, the ascription of meaning(s), and the formulation of next steps (Thomas, Clark, & Gioia, 1993). With regard to bricolage in particular, researchers have posited that verbal gestures such as seeking help, giving help, and reframing can enhance a team's performance (Hargadon & Bechky, 2006). Research also has shown that the use of conditional forms of language (e.g., could be, might) as opposed to unconditional forms of language (e.g., must be, is) can increase creativity and inventiveness in resource-constrained contexts (Langer, 1992, 2002).

While the language markers suggested in the literature are useful guides, questions still remain about the situated language that teams use to understand a problem and to (re)define or (re)invent a piece of technology with limited time and resources. Only by inductively examining the language used by a team engaged in a successful act of bricolage, can we reveal *how* team members use language to identify problems, formulate theories, and accomplish a successful act of bricolage.

## Features of the team and the data

The study follows an innovation team at NASA's Jet Propulsion Laboratory from the moment a piece of technology has failed to the moment a solution has been devised. The seven-person team comprises five NASA personnel and two external consultants. All of the participants have extensive engineering expertise, and the team has worked together on similar projects at NASA before.

The study is based on a set of unedited film footage. After being transcribed, the footage was inductively coded in an iterative process that sought to integrate descriptive codes with formalized codes associated with the literatures of sensemaking and teamwork (Thomas et al., 1993; Wilson, 2007). Thirteen codes emerged.

The footage includes three segments which feature three distinct conversational episodes. The first segment includes interactions that occur immediately after the team has witnessed the technology failure. These are spontaneous gatherings; no one had expected a failure to happen in the test. The second segment is filmed a short time later when the team reassembles to watch and discuss a video of the failure. This is an informal gathering around the video display, not a formal meeting. And the last segment occurs a few hours later when the team meets to review what is known and not known and to develop plans for the next 24 hours. This is a planned meeting with expected attendance that takes place around a conference table in front of a white board. (Shortly after this final segment, one of the team mates begins work on a rough model of the expected solution. His work produces a viable prototype that passes the necessary test. And with that feat, the team is able to successfully conclude their act of bricolage.)

The team grapples with different primary challenges in each of the three segments of footage. Initially they struggle to describe the failure that they've witnessed. Once they are able to verbalize a description of the failure, the team's focus shifts to naming the potential reason(s) for the unexpected failure. By the start of the third and final segment of footage, the team has identified a possible cause, and they are interested in defining ways to test their assumptions.

In the first segment of footage, the team is focused on accurately articulating the observed technological failure. Their quest is to answer the meta-question: *what happened*? As the first conversational episode approaches its conclusion, a side conversation starts between one of the consultants (Earl) and the lead NASA employee responsible for this technology (Aaron). Other team members participate as they begin to articulate what happened.

### Excerpt 10.1 Naming what happened

| *Speaker* | *Utterance* | *Code(s)* |
|---|---|---|
| *Earl* | Well the the the disk certainly wasn't squidding … | *Meaning: Absolute* |
| *Aaron* | Got ya. | *(Acknowledgement)* |

| Claire | *That's right!* | Action: Helping |
| Earl | So you couldn't say the chute was squidding. | Meaning: Absolute |
| Aaron | The BAND was squidding. | Meaning: Reflective |
| Kurt | It was partially inflated and the band . . . | Meaning: Absolute |
| Earl | I I just don't . . . I wouldn't want you to give someone the impression . . . I wouldn't want someone to get the impression that the whole parachute was squidding. | Action: Helping |
| Aaron | Understand; understand; understand | (Acknowledgement) |
| Earl | Which would typically be the case. | Meaning: Provisional |
| Aaron | So it was an aerodynamically stable partially inflated shape. | Meaning: Reflective |

It takes approximately 30 minutes of intense conversation among this elite team to be able to accurately describe the technology failure that they had seen minutes earlier. It takes half an hour for them to articulate a description – "an aerodynamically stable partially inflated shape" – that can be used to generate theories about the cause(s) of that unexpected failure.

Once the team mates are able to verbalize a description of the failure, they shift their focus to the reason(s) for the unexpected failure. In the second segment of footage, the team's conversation probes the meta-question: *what might be the cause(s) of the failure?* Excerpt 10.2 illustrates the team grappling with this implicit question.

## Excerpt 10.2 Exploring the cause(s)

| Speaker | Utterance | Code(s) |
| --- | --- | --- |
| Earl | ((*drawing*)): because I I, uh, I wonder if part of the problem isn't pressure there. ((*Points to a place on his drawing as he finishes speaking.*)) | Meaning: Provisional |
| Aaron | Oh it looks like it is! | Meaning: Reflective |
| Earl | Yeah . . . so that why I was thinking . . . | Meaning: Clarifying |
| Aaron | It's folding it's folding It's even folding the disk in. | Meaning: Reflective |
| Claire | Yes! | (Acknowledgement) |
| Earl | . . . that's why I'm thinking if you started say at the zero diameter right there . . . ((*points*)) | Action: Helping |
| Aaron | Yes! | Action: Helping |
| Earl | . . . and then and, uh, then got the disk inflated you would also be pressurizing that. ((*points*)) | Meaning: Provisional |

Throughout the second conversational episode the team forms theories that could explain the cause of the failure. The episode concludes with a possible explanation; pressure at a particular spot might have been the cause.

By the start of the third and final segment of footage, the team has identified a possible cause, and they are interested in defining ways to test their assumptions. They are striving to answer the meta-question: *how might we test our theories?* Excerpt 10.3 from the third conversational episode conveys the nature of interaction related to this concern.

### *Excerpt 10.3 Considering ways to test theories*

| Speaker | Utterance | Code(s) |
|---------|-----------|---------|
| Claire | Let's assume we already can duplicate this. | *Meaning: Provisional* |
| Aaron | Yes. | *(Acknowledgement)* |
| Claire | Can we then rig up something that will simulate that smaller band on pathfinder? Is there any way to do that? | *Action: Directional* |
| Kurt | No way we can do that. | *Action: Contrasting* |
| Aaron | No, no no no no … we have … we have … THAT's the totally cool thing; We still have … | *Meaning: Reflective* |
| Claire | We still have it; that's right! | *Meaning: Reflective* |
| Aaron | Kurt, please tell me we still have the chute from last week. | *Action: Planning* |
| Kurt | We have everything. | *Action: Helping* |
| Aaron | And it's here. | *Meaning: Clarifying* |
| Kurt | Of course. | *Action: Helping* |
| Aaron | So tomorrow we go into; I mean we go into reefing the chute that failed, reefing the chute that succeeded, and hopefully showing that we know that one passes and one fails in the exact same conditions. | *Action: Directional* |
| Earl | And I think there's one other test you can do there. You can take today's chute and you can alter the permeability of the band by hot cutting some holes in it | *Action: Directional* |
| Aaron | Yes, yes, yes, yes, yes. | *Action: Helping* |

The third episode is comprised of exchanges about the most effective tests that the team can do within the constraints of their available resources.

After all utterances were coded and tallied, several patterns of language use became apparent:

- Meaning-making and flexibility dominate the team's interactions
- Combinations of helping-reflection conversational moves appear at transitional moments

Both of these observations warrant detailed consideration.

## An emphasis on meaning-making and flexibility

The team used utterances related to meaning ascription more frequently than those focused information or action. The team's general language profile consisted of: 29% ($n = 140$) action utterances, 33% ($n = 159$) information utterances, and 38% ($n = 181$) meaning utterances. Within the dominant category of meaning-making, clarifying conversational moves were used most often by the team members. (See Figures 10.1 and 10.2.)

Another pattern is worth noting within the category of meaning-making language use. The three flexible language forms – clarifying ($n = 79$), provisional ($n = 44$), and reflective ($n = 19$) – represented 78% of the team's meaning-making

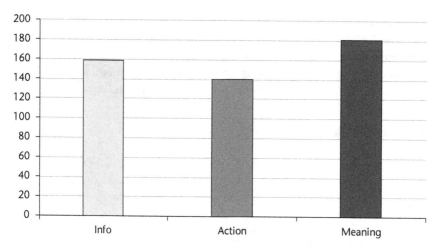

**FIGURE 10.1**   General language profile

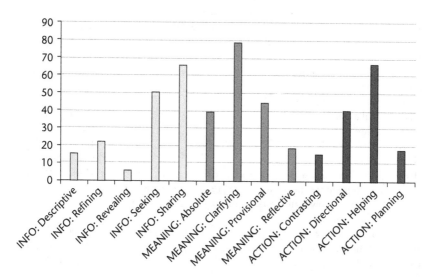

**FIGURE 10.2**   Distribution of conversational moves

moves (*n* = 181) and 31% of all utterances. Unlike utterances associated with the code Meaning: Absolute, which assert inflexible claims with singular interpretations, clarifying, provisional, and reflective utterances are flexible language forms which require a speaker to hold a variety of competing possibilities simultaneously.

## The conversational moves that accompany breakthroughs

Major shifts in understanding and innovating occurred in conjunction with pairings of Action: Helping and Meaning: Reflective utterances. Although the reflective language forms were found relatively infrequently in the data, they were used consistently by this team at transitional moments. Helping language forms, used frequently throughout the data, also were present in these pivotal exchanges.

An example of the loose coupling between these conversational moves in transformative moments can be seen in Excerpt 10.4 from the third episode.

### Excerpt 10.4 Reconsideration in action

| Speaker | Utterance | Code(s) |
| --- | --- | --- |
| Claire | . . . if we can get a system that works without having to go to a mortar firing it allows us much more freedom to investigate this | *Meaning: Provisional* |
| Aaron | Especially if Earl can can rig up some way of decreasing the gap length and then allowing ourselves to increase the gap again and then decreasing the vent diameter. Oo that's going to be a tricky one maybe that's impossible. Maybe that's impossible . . . | *Meaning: Reflective* |
| Kurt | Ah we're not doing that; we're not doing that to here. | *Action: Contrasting* |
| Wagner | No you can fill it in with stuff | *Action: Helping* |
| Claire | Yeah | *Action: Helping* |
| Wagner | You just take some fabric | *Meaning: Clarifying* |
| Aaron | Oooo | *Action: Helping* |
| Kurt | Stuff . . . yeah that's good. | *Action: Contrasting* |
| Wagner | Take it in | *Info: Refining* |
| Kurt | Stuff | *Action: Contrasting* |
| Aaron | Yeah actually | *Meaning: Reflective* |
| Wagner | Sew it in . . . | *Info: Refining* |
| Aaron | That's actually that w that would be the way that we'd do it but we don't have we don't have sew-ers here. So we can only really work on the gap. Does that; Is that accurate? | *Meaning: Reflective* |
| Earl | I think that would be accurate. We can, we can perhaps . . . | *Action: Helping* |
| Aaron | Actually, I'm not sure if we couldn't put something . . . | *Meaning: Reflective* |
| Claire | Yeah. I . . . you can . . . | *Action: Helping* |

Shortly after this exchange, Earl picked up a sewing needle even though he is not an expert in sewing. His stitch-work produced a model of the technology that could pass the necessary performance test. And with that feat, inspired by the exchanges marked by helping and reflective language forms, the team was able to successfully conclude their act of bricolage.

By micro-analyzing the verbal interactions of an innovation team grappling with a technological failure, this inductive inquiry has described the conversational moves associated with an act of bricolage. Meaning-making language forms – especially flexible language forms – are used frequently by this team in their quest to identify technology failures, pose possible explanations for such failures, and test possible remedies to the failures. Loose couplings of helping and reflective language forms – especially language that expresses introspective questioning of perceived limitations of collective agency – tend to be present as the team transitions through the stages of bricolage.

These observations help to explain the conversational work required by acts of bricolage. They contribute to a provisional theory of the conversational competencies necessary to be an innovator and do the work of innovation.

## Understanding these observations

While the observations from this study offer insights into the language used by a team engaged in an act of bricolage, they need to be considered with caution. They are from a single team interacting on one project. However, recordings of naturally occurring conversations of teams engaged in authentic acts of bricolage are extremely rare, and these findings offer a unique and valuable portal into the conversational dimensions of such an act.

Although teams are always sensemaking (Rawls, 2008), they only become aware of their sensemaking efforts when faced with disruptive or ambiguous circumstances (Weick, 1995). In such times, team members make sense of their situation by extracting informational cues and infusing them with (sometimes temporary) meaning before resuming an uncompromised course of action (Thomas et al., 1993). While this team does exchange information and coordinate action, most of their conversational moves are related to the ascription of meaning while they are engaged in this act of bricolage. This suggests that bricolage may be largely an interpretive activity.

Protracting the interpretive process has been associated with an enhanced capacity for innovation (Lester & Piore, 2004; Michel & Wortham, 2009). The team's ability to maintain an interpretive stance may afford them greater creativity in their exploration of possible explanations and potential solutions (Langer, Hatem, Joss, & Howell, 1989). Moreover, their capacity to hold multiple and contrasting interpretations of their situation simultaneously may be central to the team's ability work together and learn together (Drach-Zahavy & Somech, 2001; Schippers, Edmondson, & West, 2014).

The emphasis on meaning-making suggests that the team mates may approach their shared work as an adaptive learning challenge (Heifetz, 1994). Of course, the team does have concerns that can be overcome by new, better, or different information. However, their reliance on the language of meaning-making over the language of information exchange indicates that they understand their main challenge as an adaptive one; a challenge that requires them to not only to know *more* about their situation but to know their situation *differently*. In the end, it is the team's capacity to know differently that catalyzes a successful solution to their problem.

Reframing and conditional framing are especially helpful in the quest to know differently (Langer, 1992, 2002; Hargadon & Bechky, 2006). This team avoids premature cognitive commitment by articulating interpretations with flexible rather than fixed language forms. By using clarifying, provisional, and reflective conversational moves rather than absolute ones, the team members protect their ability to hold multiple interpretations of their situation simultaneously. These conversational moves also permit them to postpone commitments to new frames of meaning until they can do so with high levels of plausibility.

A salient example of cognitive agility can be seen in Aaron's auto-catalytic reconsideration of his assessment of the team's ability to sew. His verbalization of his internal reconsideration prompts critical action. Like the interpersonal reflexivity that is known to help teams overcome challenges (Schippers et al., 2014), this verbal expression of intrapersonal reflexivity propels the team toward a successful remedy for the technology failure.

The literature of bricolage often is focused on material resources and their constraints; on a team's ability to see and use existing materials in unexpected and purposeful ways. Consequently, a review of the physical components related to the technology might be expected to redirect this team's efforts toward a successful outcome. While the team members do engage in such a review, they are not moved in a fruitful direction by it. Instead, this team's pivotal redirection comes from an intrapersonal reevaluation of assumptions and assessments related to the limitations of the team's agency.

A team's ability to spontaneously recognize and rectify a self-imposed barrier to success is not well developed in the existing literature on bricolage. The literature does recognize that a team might expand their arc of agency by using unpolished or self-taught skills (Baker & Nelson, 2005; Fisher, 2012, p. 1027), a tactic that this team employs. For example, when Earl performs the act of sewing even though the team does not have any sewing experts, he is demonstrating the team's willingness to apply amateur skills to accomplish their shared goals. However, the team's reflective conversational moves are not just a call to unconventional action. They are evidence that the team members question the assumptions that they hold about themselves as rigorously as they question assumptions about material resources. Their use of reflective conversational moves in transformative exchanges indicates that the team is able to question not only the data but also their beliefs and behaviors.

The team's use of reflective language is important not only because it is present at key moments leading to their success but also because it is embedded in their active process. Reflection in the innovation process is often associated with retrospection. However, reflection can be anticipatory; enabling active thought about possible alternatives and outcomes (Raelin, 2001, p. 19). Reflection also can be active (and interactive) in real time; giving shape to and being shaped by contemporaneous thought and action as an event unfolds (Van Manen, 2006, p. 87). The team's use of reflective conversational moves demonstrates that they are reflecting and doing at the same time (Schön, 1983).

## The value of this case

This chapter has taken an inductive and exploratory approach to understanding the conversational dynamics that foster technological bricolage. By studying an elite engineering team in action, new details about the role of conversation in urgent problem-solving situations have emerged.

The micro-analysis of this team's interactions has highlighted the importance of several conversational dynamics. Language forms that foster interpretation and flexibility may help teams successfully navigate acts of bricolage. And reflective conversational moves may play a vital role.

Perhaps the chapter's most valuable insight is that transformational moments, at least for the studied team, hinge on loose couplings of expressions of helpfulness and refection. The chapter suggests that successful resolutions to acts of bricolage may spring from introspective reconsiderations that challenge perceived limitations of collective agency. While it would be premature to claim that the re-evaluation of agency is solely responsible for this team's successful outcome, it is possible to posit that reflective conversational moves are a valuable part of the process of bricolage.

Understanding the role that verbal interactions play in acts of bricolage is important, especially in the context of space-related work. Historically, technical malfunctions during an active space mission with a human crew could be addressed by engineers on Earth. The ground team would be responsible for the reinvention of the technology and for eventually instructing the remote crew on the materials and steps required to replicate their work. However, if critical technology were to fail during a deep space mission with a human crew, the traditional transmission model might not be possible; today's communications technology requires between 4 and 24 minutes to send a message from Earth to Mars, for example. Consequently, the remote crew might need to undertake an urgent act of bricolage by themselves.

But even Earth-bound teams care about the timely and successful completion of acts of bricolage. In the rush to solve an urgent problem swiftly, teams might imagine they should focus mostly on the exchange of information and the coordination of action. However, an emphasis on interpretation might serve them better. The micro-analysis of this team's interactions suggests that conversational moves which enhance (re)interpretation are present throughout a process of bricolage, including the most pivotal moments.

Even though the case is focused on an innovation team, it also has relevance for innovative *entrepreneurial* teams. As Chapter 2 argued, an early-stage innovative entrepreneurial venture is synonymous with a validated product. The verbal means by which an innovation team verbally enacts bricolage may not be very different from those used by an innovative entrepreneurial team. At a minimum, the investigation of the NASA JPL team's conversational moves provides a foundation for future studies of bricolage within entrepreneurial teams.

Technologies do fail, and innovation teams need to accomplish acts of bricolage. Subject matter expertise, available tools, and other factors play a role in a team's ability to reinvent a vital piece of technology with limited time and resources. However, conversational dynamics – especially the use of flexible and reflective conversational moves – also contribute to a team's ability to make sense of unexpected failures and productively craft solutions.

## References

Baker, T., & Nelson, R. (2005). Creating something from nothing: Resource construction through entrepreneurial bricolage. *Administrative Science Quarterly, 50*(3), 329–366.

Donnellon, A. (1996). *Team talk: The power of language in team dynamics.* Boston, MA: Harvard Business School Press.

Drach-Zahavy, A., & Somech, A. (2001). Understanding team innovation: The role of team processes and structures. *Group Dynamics: Theory, Research, and Practice, 5*(2), 111–123.

Fisher, G. (2012). Effectuation, causation, and bricolage: A behavioral comparison of emerging theories in entrepreneurship research. *Entrepreneurship Theory and Practice, 36*(5).

Hargadon, A. B., & Bechky, B. A. (2006). When collections of creatives become creative collectives: A field study of problem solving at work. *Organization Science, 17*(4), 484–500.

Heifetz, R. (1994). *Leadership without easy answers.* Cambridge, MA: Harvard University Press.

Langer, E. J. (1992). Matters of mind: Mindfulness/mindlessness in perspective. *Consciousness and Cognition, 1*(3), 289–305.

Langer, E. J. (2002). Well-being: Mindfulness versus positive evaluation. In C. R. Snyder & S. J. López (Eds.), *Handbook of positive psychology.* New York, NY: Oxford University Press.

Langer, E. J., Hatem, M., Joss, J., & Howell, M. (1989). Conditional teaching and mindful learning: The role of uncertainty in education. *Creativity Research Journal, 2*(3), 139–150.

Lester, R. K., & Piore, M. J. (2004). *Innovation, the missing dimension.* Cambridge, MA: Harvard University Press.

Levi-Strauss, C. (1966). *The savage mind.* Chicago: University of Chicago Press.

Michel, A., & Wortham, S. (2009). *Bullish on uncertainty: How organizational cultures transform participants.* New York, NY: Cambridge University Press.

Raelin, J. (2001). Public reflection as the basis of learning. *Management Learning, 32*(1), 11–30.

Rawls, A. W. (2008). Harold Garfinkel, ethnomethodology and workplace studies. *Organization Studies, 29*(5), 701–732.

Roberson, Q. M. (2006). Justice in teams: The activation and role of sensemaking in the emergence of justice climates. *Organizational Behavior and Human Decision Processes, 100*(2), 177–192.

Schippers, M., Edmondson, A. C., & West, M. A. (2014). Team reflexivity as an antidote to team information-processing failures. *Small Group Research, 45*(6), 731–769.

Schön, D. A. (1983). *The reflective practitioner: How professionals think in action.* New York, NY: Basic Books.

Schwenk, C., & Thomas, H. (1983). Formulating the mess: The role of decision aids in problem formulation. *Omega International Journal of Management., 11*(3), 239–252.

Thomas, J. B., Clark, S. M., & Gioia, D. A. (1993). Strategic sensemaking and organizational performance: Linkages among scanning, interpretation, action, and outcomes. *The Academy of Management Journal, 36*(2), 239–270.

Van Manen, M. (2006). Reflexivity and the pedagogical moment: The practical-ethical nature of pedagogical thinking and acting. In I. Westbury & G. Milburn (Eds.), *Rethinking schooling: Twenty-five years of the journal of curriculum studies.* New York, NY: Routledge.

Weick, K. E. (1995). *Sensemaking in organizations.* London: Sage.

Weick, K. E. (1998). Introductory essay: Improvisation as a mindset for organizational analysis. *Organizational Science, 9*(5), 543–555.

Weick, K. E., Sutcliffe, K. M., & Obstfeld, D. (2005). Organizing and the Process of Sensemaking. *Organization Science, 16*(4), 409–421.

Wilson, D. (2007). *Team learning in action* (Doctoral Dissertation), Harvard Graduate School of Education, Cambridge, MA.

# PART V
# Advancing theory and practice

Part V connects the micro-analysis of conversation to enduring puzzles associated with innovation and entrepreneurship. It uses conversational data to address several quests: understanding productive stances toward uncertainty and teaching micro-practices of teamwork.

# 11

# ENTREPRENEURIAL UNCERTAINTY IS A MEMBERS' ISSUE

## Introduction

Contemporary scholarship about entrepreneurial uncertainty is dominated by two main ideas: effectuation and causation (Read, Song, & Smit, 2009; Sarasvathy, 2001; Sarasvathy & Dew, 2005). The effectuation research argues that entrepreneurs acknowledge uncertainties and adapt to them by controlling their means (Baker & Nelson, 2005; Sarasvathy, 2001). In contrast, research with a causal orientation asserts that entrepreneurs take efforts to reduce uncertainties through information acquisition or planning techniques (Cooper, Folta, & Woo, 1995; Delmar & Shane, 2003; Ozgen & Baron, 2007). Entrepreneurs are thought to use both types of logic in their efforts to ascend (Sarasvathy, 2008).

Both of these theories have emerged from studies of entrepreneurial cognition, and both stop short of analyzing uncertainty as a socially enacted feature of entrepreneurial work. As previous chapters have shown, many concepts associated with entrepreneurial cognition can be examined through practices; through an ethnomethodologically informed study of situated and socially shared interactions that evolve over time (Coulter, 1991; Engeström & Middleton, 1996; Lave, 1988; Resnick, Levine, & Teasley, 1991; Suchman, 1987). For example, an earlier chapter illustrated how empathy can be understood not only as an intrapersonal cognitive trait but also as a verbally (re)created interaction between people.

This chapter considers entrepreneurial uncertainty as a members' matter, as a phenomenon that team mates draw upon and orient to in their routine workplace interactions. It touches on the role of epistemic status and stance as evidenced and accomplished in the situated interactions of entrepreneurial teams. It draws on Conversation Analysis (CA) to reveal how entrepreneurial team mates engage with and account for uncertainties – including a lack of knowledge and a lack of confidence in their knowledge and interpretations – in the moment-by-moment details of their workplace interactions.

## Agency and uncertainty

The recent thrust in studies related to effectuation (Sarasvathy, Dew, Velamuri, & Venkataraman, 2005) marks an important transition in the ontological orientation of entrepreneurial research. Simply put, effectuation suggests that entrepreneurial products and ventures are constructed through the sustained efforts of engaged individuals (Bryman & Bell, 2007, p. 23; Sarasvathy, 2004a, p. 292). Entrepreneurial work, then, can be seen as a kind of agentic design work (Sarasvathy, 2004b, p. 9) that emerges "through complex, situated acts of seeing, saying, and doing" (Fleming, 1998, p. 41).

The theory of effectuation (Sarasvathy, 2001) argues that entrepreneurs apply knowledge and control of resources to contend with uncertainties. This kind of non-predictive control in the face of uncertainty requires entrepreneurs to maintain a focus on means rather than ends, on levels of affordable loss, on partnership opportunities, and on the potential benefits of unexpected developments (Wiltbank, Read, Dew, & Sarasvathy, 2009, p. 119). While effectual logic can turn surprises into advantages in some cases, effectuation theory primarily regards uncertainty as an unfortunate externality that should be addressed through a focus on means. It follows that better entrepreneurs should endeavor to (and be able to) contain or minimize uncertainty by thoughtfully controlling their use of time, talent, and other resources.

The types of entrepreneurial uncertainty are many. Entrepreneurs have to grapple with concerns about their product, market, and competition (Shane, 2003). They also have to contend with the inability to calculate probabilities for outcomes, select an optimal direction from a vast array of possible goals, and separate important elements from unimportant ones in their situation (Sarasvathy, 2008). And of course, entrepreneurial team mates have the same challenges as any other human beings in achieving an intersubjective understanding of what is and is not certain (or certain enough) at any point in time (Goffman, 1981).

Each of these forms of uncertainty is connected to a team's knowledge (about their skills, the market's demands, etc.) and their confidence (in their abilities, interpretations, etc.). Given that verbal interactions are the "building blocks of the actual relationships and commitments" that result in entrepreneurship (Dimov, 2018), it is in their intra-team conversations that teams grapple with uncertainties. As a first step, team mates must identify the contours of the uncertainties that they face by verbally addressing imbalances in knowledge between them and ascertaining their level of confidence in their interpretations.

Most studies have explained (re)actions to all forms of entrepreneurial uncertainty as abstract categories of behavior, such as exercise control over resources or focus on means. Rarely have studies analyzed the intersubjectively available processes that teams use to engage with uncertainties in their work, the interactional practices by which team mates display their emerging positions toward uncertainties for each other. An ethnomethodologically informed study can demonstrate how team mates account for limitations of knowledge and certainty in the moment-to-moment organization of their interactions. By focusing on the empirical details of organized interactional phenomena, a study can explicate entrepreneurial practices rather than glossing them. And a focus on practices means that the micro-details of interaction can speak to macro phenomena; the structural underpinnings that make a particular conversation intelligible also make it relevant to other contexts.

Theories of entrepreneurial agency would benefit from empirical studies that show the means by which entrepreneurs enact their own awareness of uncertainty and their situated reactions to it. The literature is missing an explanation of entrepreneurs' ordinary methods for recognizing and responding to uncertainties in context. This chapter begins to unpack the concept of uncertainty as an entrepreneurs' phenomenon by investigating entrepreneurial teams' situated methods and practices for verbally attending to and accounting for uncertainty in their routine work.

## Knowledge and (un)certainty in interaction

One of the basic observations of interaction is that speakers avoid telling people things they already know: "if you've already told something to someone then you shouldn't tell it to them again" (Sacks, 1992, p. 438). Another is that speakers tend to protect a person's pride or "face" if s/he is expected to know something but does not (Goffman, 1955). Both of these guidelines are accomplished and accounted for in the details of ordinary interactions. Speakers draw on what they "know (believe) about the circumstances of their action and that of others" in and through the moment-by-moment sequence of utterances (Giddens, 1984, p. 375). Speakers also must assess a level of certainty in what they know and believe – about the speakers, the content of conversation, and the context of conversation.

The interactional means by which team mates manage relevant differences in knowledge and their certainty in that knowledge constitutes one of the main interests of CA researchers. Increasingly scholars are analyzing the verbal structures and sequences that enable speakers to establish and address the knowledge domains of epistemic status and stance (Heritage, 2012b).

Epistemic status is relational and bounded by particular sets of knowledge. Consequently the epistemic status between speakers will change based on the subject. Other factors also can impact epistemic status (Stivers, Mondada, & Steensig, 2011). If both participants have knowledge about a market segment, the person with more recent information will assume and be afforded higher epistemic status on that matter. Similarly, information acquired through direct access or other appropriate means will be considered more valuable than information gotten through gossip or from unreliable sources. In general, the background experiences and future aspirations of individuals are treated as theirs to own and articulate with authority (Heritage, 2011; Sacks, 1984b). People are recognized as having an enduring epistemic advantage on matters related to their family, friends, and areas of professional expertise.

Epistemic stance is more dynamic. It emerges in the conversation between speakers and is managed turn by turn. As a result, a speaker's stance can shift in a conversation as a result of a specific utterance (i.e., the receipt of a transformative piece of information). Speakers always are working to recognize and address information imbalances in order to established shared understanding. These intersubjective efforts can be observed in the structural facets of a conversation. For example, a speaker who claims a lack of knowledge by taking a stance of not knowing in one utterance can prompt a recipient to respond with additional detail in the next utterance and may signal a coming expansion of sequences on the topic (Heritage, 2012b).

These concepts of epistemic status and stance are relevant to entrepreneurial work. In terms of status, each founder within an entrepreneurial team will have an epistemic advantage on matters pertaining to his/her individual network and to his/her functional area of expertise. And different epistemic stances can be illustrated by the following prompts adapted from the literature (Heritage, 2012b, p. 1): (1) are you with a venture capital firm? (2) you're with a venture capital firm, aren't you? (3) you're with a venture capital firm?

Not only does each of these sentences signal a different level of knowledge (and certainty about the knowledge) on the part of the person who is asking the question, they also prompt different responses. The first option indicates that the person asking the question has no definite knowledge of the recipient's profession. It expects the recipient to give a confirmation or correction. The second option indicates a greater certainty about the recipient's work, and expects the recipient to be able to answer affirmatively. The third option indicates even more certainty on the part of the person asking this declarative statement in place of a question. The speaker is seeking confirmation of knowledge or rendering a context-informed guess (Heritage, 2012b). The recipient is expected to respond affirmatively or perhaps not at all (i.e., the speakers can skip this question and answer because the answer is already known).

CA studies outside of entrepreneurship have demonstrated that epistemic aspects of interaction are recognized and accounted for by participants in the structures of their conversations (Heritage, 2012a, 2012b; Stivers et al., 2011). For example, speakers can verify if their understanding is up to date or outdated by using pre-sequences (Terasaki, 2004), topic announcements (Atkinson & Heritage, 1984), or other structures of "telling" (Schegloff, 2007). Similarly, speakers can signal a lack of knowledge and prompt recipients to offer additional information by sharing the partial understanding that they already possess (Pomerantz, 1980). Epistemic matters also are evident in responses: beginning a second-position response with "oh" signals that the preceding turn contained new information (Heritage, 2002).

Speakers can demonstrate a calibrated level of certainty by downgrading through tag questions (Heritage & Raymond, 2005), ending polar questions with "or" (Drake, 2015), and other means. For example, a speaker's statement, "She is a VC", can be epistemically downgraded by using a conditional verb (e.g., She might be a VC), referencing hearsay (e.g., Pat says she's a VC), or indicating a belief (e.g., I think she's a VC) (Pomerantz, 1984). Epistemic positioning through mitigating language is not limited to establishing an order among the certainty of knowledge speakers;

it also can involve conventional wisdom and "more abstract and socially patterned rights and obligations to knowledge" (Heritage, 2008, p. 309). In this way, epistemic positioning becomes especially relevant to entrepreneurial work which is defined by pervasive limits on knowledge and certainty.

The structural details of interactions also reveal the normative and moral dimensions for a particular context (Stivers et al., 2011). Through their interactions, team mates establish and assess what is possible to know, what is acceptable to know (and not know), and what levels of certainty are permissible in that setting (Buttny, 1993; Shotter, 1984). While the substance of conversations may include these matters, the structural elements are essential for establishing and maintaining a "moral version" of a profession (Silverman, 1987). In entrepreneurial contexts, the structure of a team's interactions reveals what it means to be a good entrepreneur in relation to the persistent uncertainties in their environment. Downgrades and the achievement of epistemic positions expose the preferred entrepreneurial posture toward uncertainty as it is oriented to by entrepreneurs in action.

## Whose uncertainty?

A practice approach to entrepreneurship positions entrepreneurial work as an inter-subjective matter; as a members' phenomenon (Schegloff, 1997). It studies uncertainty through the means by which entrepreneurial team members orient to their own lack of knowledge and lack of confidence in their knowledge and interpretations. CA allows researchers to access this members' perspective on uncertainty by focusing on an entrepreneurial team's naturally occurring interactions and the situated means by which co-founders grapple with lack of knowledge as well as lack of certainty in that knowledge.

Many studies on entrepreneurial uncertainty emphasize the ways the entrepreneurial teams think about acceptable loses, possible alliances, and various contingencies, skills, and resources (Sarasvathy, 2001). However, few studies attend to the verbal means by which entrepreneurs account for (and morally account for) uncertainties in the enactment of their work. By introducing a CA approach, it is possible to add empirical depth to theories of entrepreneurial uncertainty by focusing on the interactional practices actually used by entrepreneurs themselves. It enables researchers to anchor their inquiry in the team's experience of uncertainty; eliminating the concerns about "whose context" (Schegloff, 1997) is really being studied.

The connections between interactional organization and moral order are central to ethnomethodology (see Garfinkel 1963, 1967). Just as ethnomethodology aims to understand social accomplishments through sequences of situated interactions emerging through practical reasoning, it also seeks to understand the interactional foundations by which people recognize, establish, and maintain what is right in a given setting. It does so by focusing on the moral criteria which inform the observable interaction order, the ways in which members formulate practical judgments through their interactions about the right (and wrong) ways to do being on an entrepreneurial team, for example.

The particular attributes that are considered morally acceptable for entrepreneurial team mates can be found in the reciprocity of interactional organization (Rawls, 1990). In other words, if someone were to breach the limits of morally acceptable work in an entrepreneurial setting, a team mate's response would reveal it. Perhaps the team mate would preface the next turn with "well" as a means to mitigate dissonance or engage in other face-saving work (Samra-Fredericks, 2010). Conversely, when team mates are interacting in accordance with the moral boundaries of being on an entrepreneurial team, there is no extra interactional work required. In these ways the moral accountability of entrepreneurial work is made observable through the structure of conversations. Both practical and moral matters are interwoven in the interaction (Jayyusi, 1991). Therefore, the values assigned by entrepreneurs to uncertainty and limitations of knowledge can be observed in the naturally occurring conversations of entrepreneurial teams at work.

To begin to uncover the interactional means by which entrepreneurial teams account for uncertainties, this chapter features several innovative entrepreneurial teams in action. At the time of the data collection, all teams had two members and were very early stage.

The following excerpts demonstrate how teams verbally recognize and account for uncertainty in terms of knowledge imbalances and confidence in their emerging interpretations that are essential to their routine work. The excerpts begin by reviewing how team mates verbally attend to imbalances in the knowledge between them. They also examine what team mates accomplish through their use of epistemic downgrades. And they demonstrate how team mates morally account for persistent lack of certainty in their work.

## Addressing imbalances of knowledge

Heritage and others have argued that an "epistemic engine" functions as a kind of pump to advance the turns in a conversation (Heritage, 2012a). The speakers exchange statements of more (K+) and less (K−) knowledge until equilibrium is created or recaptured between them. There are many variations on the way this seesaw can work depending on whether a topic is initiated from a position of knowing or not as well as from a position of entitlement to know or not. One example of this epistemic back-and-forth can be observed in Excerpt 11.1.

In this exchange Speaker 1 speaks from a not knowing position (line 1). Speaker 2 had epistemic rights to the topic of the antennas that he has been using in the design of their emerging product. After Speaker 1 asks a polar question about the cost of using a particular antenna in terms of power consumption, Speaker 2 follows the format in his response by answering with a "no". He hesitates before saying no, which is consistent with offering dispreferred responses, and offers a detailed answer that repeats a part of the original question and adds clarifying information (line 2). Speaker 1 is still in a position of limited knowledge and asks her question in a direct fashion that prompts a descriptive answer rather than a simple yes or no (line 5). Speaker 2 does not, however, offer a dollar amount when asked about the cost, as might be expected. Instead he uses the response to change the topic to the real problem as he sees it (line 6). He is worried not about the monetary cost of the antenna but about the geometric requirements of the antenna. In this response he asserts his epistemic rights to full set of issues related to the antenna. He also uses this turn to situate the problem of the antenna in an area where Speaker 1 has more knowledge and more rights to knowledge. He accomplishes this through the slight epistemic downgrade he creates through the use of self-depreciating humor. Speaker 1 demonstrates that she now understands the problem by starting her response with "oh" (line 7). She then asserts her epistemic rights on the topic of building the container that can solve their problem. With the imbalance in knowledge addressed, the conversation can move on (and harness interactional energy from a new epistemic pump).

## Excerpt 11.1 The epistemic pump

| Line | Speaker | Utterance |
| --- | --- | --- |
| 1 | S1(k−) | is there a cost to using the high gain antennas in terms of power consumption |
| 2 | S2(k+) | ah no there's no cost in terms of power conception is just that the antenna gain is much higher |
| 3 | S1 | So |
| 4 | S2 | so more of the |
| 5 | S1(k−) | are they more expensive or what is the cost |
| 6 | S2(k+−) | the cost is that I can't figure out how to get everything in the box! (laugh) |
| 7 | S1(k+−) | oh! let me try on that one; that's my job! you tell me what you want in the box and we'll put it in the box |

In this exchange, the back-and-forth between knowing and not-knowing positions is clear. Speaker 1 has less knowledge than her partner about the potential costs associated with the antennas, and her questions openly reveal her position. Speaker 2 transforms a follow-on question with a response that clearly indicates the limits not of his knowledge, but of his ability: he cannot get the various parts to fit the in the box. Speaker 1 indicates the transformation of her understanding with "oh", and the team mates reestablish more equal epistemic positions.

## The utility of downgrades

In other occasions, speakers use downgrades (or upgrades) to save face for their partners or to signal a willingness to realign their own expected knowledge position. Excerpt 11.2 illustrates a downgrade that allows Speaker 1 to demonstrate reverence for her partner's knowledge while also holding a perspective in mind that differs from his. The general topic of conversation is about the use of their resources; the tools for cutting a board.

## *Excerpt 11.2 Downgrade in first position*

| Line | Speaker | Utterance |
|------|---------|-----------|
| 1 | S1 | okay here's another a dumb question can you order them both on the same board with some spacer and cut them in half yourself |
| 2 | S2 | yes we can do that |
| 3 | S1 | because if you do that your set up fee is the same |
| 4 | S2 | yes we'd just have to cut which is |
| 5 | S1 | I'm good at cutting things |
| 6 | S2 | the stuff is really nasty it's it's fiberglass upon epoxy |
| 7 | S1 | what does one normally use to |
| 8 | S2 | I've used a dremel, I've used a hack saw, I've used yeah I mean you know it's fine it just makes this really really fine dust it |
| 9 | S1 | Okay |
| 10 | S2 | that's kind of not the most pleasant stuff |
| 11 | S1 | Okay |
| 12 | S2 | in the world definitely (garble) more than (garble) boards okay |
| 13 | S1 | well shouldn't you be able to use – this is dumb – but the miniature band saw? |
| 14 | S2 | yeah you could do that certainly |
| 15 | S1 | we just happen to have one |
| 16 | S2 | Yeah |
| 17 | S1 | in our nice machine shop |
| 18 | S2 | I know I've never had any of that stuff |
| 19 | S1 | okay let's do that |

Speaker 1 opens a topic about the organization of a circuit board by downgrading her thoughts by calling them "dumb" (line 1). With this utterance she is signaling that she has a vision of how the board might be designed, but she knows her partner has competence on and experience with this matter. She accomplishes this by adopting an initial K– position. Speaker 2 gives a preferred answer that which expresses sensitivity to the downgrade. However, as Speaker 1 continues with an explanation of her thinking, Speaker 2 interjects and asserts his knowledge-based concerns about her initial suggestion; that the material would need to be "cut" (line 4). Speaker 1 declares her knowledge and confidence by interrupting him with a statement about her capabilities, "I'm good at cutting things" (line 5). Undeterred, Speaker 2 underscores his position of knowledge by clarifying why cutting would be undesirable (line 6.) At this point, Speaker 1 takes a different approach. She heeds his knowledge position and asks directly about the tools that are typically used to cut this material (line 7). Speaker 2 offers a list of tools and results that showcase his experience with cutting the material (lines 8, 10, 12). Speaker 1 uses the "dumb" downgrade in her stance and vision again when she asks if a "miniature band saw" could be used (line 13). Speaker 2 offers a preferred answer (line 14) and acknowledges that he has not used that tool (line 18). Speaker 1 then expresses that they have come to an agreement to proceed with the design that requires them to cut the board (line 19).

By downgrading her stance, Speaker 1 was able to engage in an extended exchange about the design of the board. This is a common way that downgrades are used. Speakers are able to engage in detailed conversation to achieve an equal level of knowledge (however limited) about a topic. Downgrades also can be located in second-position responses. Downgraded responses, such as modified repeats, allow respondents to attend to the face issues of the first speaker while inviting additional interaction about the topic.

## Excerpt 11.3 Modified repeat in a downgraded response

| Line | Speaker | Utterance |
| --- | --- | --- |
| 1 | S1 | do we need an advisory board? |
| 2 | S2 | do we need one? |
| 3 | S1 | yeah I mean we need (.) so many people are helping us |
| 4 | S2 | Yeah |
| 5 | S1 | and it's been exceptional um yeah |
| 6 | S2 | I don't know. That's a good question. I I just assume everyone has advisory boards. I don't know what it entails to have an advisory board. Do you have to give out equity like do you |
| 7 | S1 | maybe a little tiny bit |
| 8 | S2 | or is it just a fun project for them |
| 9 | S1 | I think it depends on the person |

Speaker 1 raises the topic of an advisory board while they are looking at text-book example of a business plan. His utterance implies a form of assessment, that a formal board might not be necessary. The combination of this implied assessment and the primacy of having raised the topic both suggest that he has the epistemic rights to this issue related to the presence of committed partners in the ecosystem.

He presents his interest in advisory boards through a yes/no question (line 1). Speaker 2 answers with a modified repeat (line 2) which signals her willingness to receive more information. It is a prompt for elaboration, but it is doing more than requesting additional information. By disengaging from the polar framing of the question and asserting a modified repeat, Speaker 2 is attending to the relational positions between them based on this topic (Heritage, 1998; Raymond, 2003). The modified repeat allows Speaker 2 to manage not just what is known about advisory boards but also who has the right to know more about the topic. This need to establish and maintain relative knowledge rights is thought to be essential to speakers' reputations (and epistemic domains) and their social connections with each another.

Speaker 1 in the third position response downgrades his primacy to know about or direct a conversation on an advisory board by using "I mean" (line 3). His utterance indicates that he is questioning whether they need to formally create a board of advisors given that so many people are informally helping them already. Once he has explained his reasons for bringing up the topic, Speaker 2 offers two pre-sequences before offering her own views on the topic. The two pre-sequences both downgrade her epistemic position about her knowledge of the topic. She then further downgrades her epistemic status and stance by using language such as "I just assume" and a second "I don't know" and by asking a follow on question about advisory board structure (line 6). Speaker 1's responses are again downgraded by his use of "maybe" and "I think" before the topic of conversation moves on (lines 7, 9).

This exchange is concerned with the team mates' social relationship as much as it is about advisory boards. These speakers are attending to each other's sense of self by verbally conveying "an attitude of respect, if not reverence toward each other's 'self'" (Maynard & Zimmerman, 1984, p. 312). Research in other contexts has demonstrated how participants work to verbally maintain their epistemic status in relevant knowledge territories (Heritage & Raymond, 2005). These excerpts from entrepreneurial contexts suggest that entrepreneurial team mates also work on verbally maintaining a downgraded epistemic status; a shared stance of not knowing with certainty.

## Moral version of founders

By using downgrades to save the face of partners and to preserve a shared state of uncertainty, team mates are developing "moral versions" of themselves as entrepreneurs through their workplace interactions (Silverman, 1987). As team mates account for the limits of their knowledge and their (un)certainties as part of their shared work, they begin to define a moral role of an entrepreneur by indicating acceptable levels of not knowing and acceptable limits of (un)certainty through the structure and substance of the intra-team conversations. They hold each other morally accountable for their contributions to their shared work through the sequential organization and epistemic signaling.

In Excerpt 11.4, the team mates have been discussing the investor packet. Having acknowledged the limitations of their knowledge about the packet, Speaker 1 suggests that they might want to "dig deeper on the competitor" materials (line 1). Not only does she downgrade the need to gather this data by using the qualifiers "think" and "little", she also downgrades the expected value of the data by articulating that it will "definitely" not be reflective of their market segment. Speaker 2 validates the uncertainties of their current knowledge of competitors and of the value of gathering more data by simply agreeing with Speaker 1 (lines 2, 4, 6). Both team mates accept a lack of clarity about the competition as a feature of their current work and their expected idea of what is necessary or possible. Thus, the team mates are articulating that the experience of sustained uncertainty is not at odds with being a good founder. Speaker 1 invokes a "moral version" of founders by recognizing uncertainty and by being interested in learning more (even if it does not completely address the lack of knowledge issue) (line 7). Even as uncertainties are named and efforts are planned to address them, the founders recognize that uncertainties will remain.

## Excerpt 11.4 Lingering uncertainties are acceptable

| Line | Speaker | Utterance |
| --- | --- | --- |
| 1 | S1 | yeah yeah I think we need to um dig a little deeper on the competitor side |
| 2 | S2 | Okay |
| 3 | S1 | in terms of what they're market they're markets are and if we can get any sense of how much they sell; their volume of sales |
| 4 | S2 | Yeah |
| 5 | S1 | though it might not be it's definitely not reflective of our market just because we're going after different markets |
| 6 | S2 | Yeah |
| 7 | S1 | but I think it will be directionally interesting to learn |
| 8 | S2 | Alright |

If the lingering presence of limited knowledge and certainty were a breach of doing morally accountable entrepreneurial work one of the team mates would have made a conversational move to correct it. For example, Speaker 2 in line 8 might have prefaced an utterance with "well" or a pause to indicate concern before offering an alternative approach that might have provided a more direct means of addressing the lingering unknowns. The absence of any effort to save Speaker 1's face by prompting a more promising path to greater certainty and asserting an epistemic advantage about the framing for good entrepreneurial work indicates that Speaker 2 is validating activities and moral expectations that accept uncertainties.

Similarly, the team mates in Excerpt 11.5 normalize uncertainty by overtly naming it and through the epistemic interplay between the speakers. The exchange begins with Speaker 1 revealing a lack of knowledge about the patenting process (line 1). Speaker 2 initially holds a more knowledgeable position by explaining the basics of a prior art search (lines 2, 4). Speaker 1 asserts a level of familiarity with the topic by asking a clarifying question about the law which was not mentioned by Speaker 2 in his explanation (line 5), and by speaking in unison (line 7). Speaker 2 then downgrades his claim on knowledge and certainty of knowledge with regard to patents (lines 6, 8). Speaker 1 accepts that he has (and they have) limited knowledge (lines 9, 11). In doing so, she is agreeing that they don't know what they don't know. She also is indicating that their lack of knowledge and certainty are consistent with doing good entrepreneurial work. By simply carrying on with the activity (line 13) she is treating their lack of knowledge and certainty as a normative and morally acceptable matter (Heritage, 1984, p. 102).

## *Excerpt 11.5  Normalizing lack of knowledge and certainty*

| Line | Speaker | Utterance |
|------|---------|-----------|
| 1 | S1 | what's a prior art search? |
| 2 | S2 | a patent search so um prior art does not necessarily define doesn't mean that there's strictly a patent. But you can't patent anything that has been shown to be possible or even an idea in prior art and that is patents, papers, like if a corporate presentation presents something and it gets on the web and it's 3 years old you can't go patent that. Um cause that's prior art then someone already thought about it um |
| 3 | S1 | Interesting |
| 4 | S2 | unless you can prove that you thought of it at the same time before they published their data |
| 5 | S1 | didn't they just change the law on that? |
| 6 | S2 | uh yeah now it's like first to |
| 7 | S1 | to patent |
| 8 | S2 | to patent but prior art still applies and how that matters I don't know |
| 9 | S1 | Okay |
| 10 | S2 | you know I can't go out and (.) no one can patent what I published in my PhD even if we didn't patent it |
| 11 | S1 | Right |
| 12 | S2 | um and I yeah I I dunno that's when you go get lawyers to figure it out |
| 13 | S1 | got you okay |

In this exchange, neither speaker really alters their epistemic position. Just as Heritage (Heritage, 2012a) suggests, this excerpt shows the sequence order that emerges within the process of attending to the epistemic balance between speakers. By signaling an imbalance, as Speaker 1 does in line 1, the utterance starts an interactional sequence that ends when the lack of knowledge or certainty is equalized and jointly acknowledged as such. However, in doing entrepreneurial work, the lack of knowledge and certainty is shared and persistent between team mates. Consequently, an utterance that signals an epistemic imbalance can start a sequence that ends when the imbalance is acknowledged and equalized – but not necessarily minimized or removed as typically happens in non-entrepreneurial contexts.

## Observations at micro and macro levels

Entrepreneurial uncertainty is addressed in and through the routine practices of entrepreneurial work. This chapter's ethnomethodological analysis begins to reveal how team mates interactionally address imbalances of knowledge on matters of consequence – even if the level of confidence in that knowledge remains low. Specifically, this chapter has taken an epistemic approach to investigating entrepreneurial uncertainties. It has examined the roles of relative epistemic status and stance in the enactment of entrepreneurial work. It has considered the importance of downgraded positioning and the implications of sequence order on the moral expectations of entrepreneurial team mates. Glosses, such as focusing on means, cannot capture these intricate practices of epistemic interplay as they relate to entrepreneurial uncertainty.

Three ethnomethodological points are worth emphasizing. First, the constitution of the activity at hand – grappling with entrepreneurial uncertainties – is something team mates do with and for each other by locally attending to the interactional structures that are relevant to their practical work. As with all work, according to Garfinkel, the practices that are essential to identifying and addressing uncertainties are located in the ordered properties of entrepreneurial interactions (Rawls, 2008).

Second, these situated practices rely on each team mate's ability to display what s/he knows (and does not know) and what level of confidence s/he has in that knowledge. Verbal moves, like starting a response with "oh" or downgrading an epistemic position, are not overt rules for entrepreneurial work (or any form of work). Instead these ways of interacting are generally available ways of attending to imbalances of knowledge and confidence in that knowledge. They are recurring, mundane mechanisms that, nevertheless, have a social order and situated organization that are co-produced and recognized in context (Garfinkel & Wieder, 1992).

And third, these epistemic features of entrepreneurial conversation have moral connotations and consequences (Garfinkel & Livingston, 2003). The validation of an entrepreneurial product and the creation of the venture are interactional courses of morally accountable action. Each turn is understood as either carrying on with an activity or departing from it. Either way the utterance is observable and will be held as an accountable property in the next turn. If the utterance breached social expectations in some way it will be treated by the team mate in a "profoundly normative, and morally sanctionable" manner (Heritage, 1984, p. 102). As the excerpts in this chapter have shown, the team mates worked to achieve equal levels of knowledge about relevant topics, but they were able to carry on without concern despite a lack of confidence in that knowledge, despite lingering uncertainties.

By explicating the micro-details of an interaction in a particular activity setting, CA studies like this one can assert broader (macro) claims. This is possible because interaction is rationally organized turn by turn by participants in connection with their social goals (Levinson, 1992). By analyzing the minute recurring interactional *practices* ("oh", modified repeats, etc.), CA studies are able to make claims about a "procedural infrastructure of interaction" that is indispensable to interaction within and beyond a given setting (Raymond, 2018; Schegloff, 2006). CA studies, in concert with their ethnomethodological foundations, explicate interactions and activity settings by revealing the conversational "machinery" that produced them (Sacks, 1984a; Seedhouse, 2004).

Theories of entrepreneurial uncertainty have needed empirical evidence to show if and how teams attend to uncertainty in context. Scholars interested in uncertainty as a members' phenomenon can use CA to reveal more about the actual stances entrepreneurs have toward uncertainties. Future studies in this vein will make it possible to know in what ways traditional theories about entrepreneurial uncertainty aptly represent entrepreneurial practice – and in what ways they might have imposed concepts and values onto the entrepreneurial experience.

# References

Atkinson, J., & Heritage, J. (Eds.). (1984). *Structures of social action: Studies in conversation analysis*. Cambridge: Cambridge University Press.

Baker, T., & Nelson, R. (2005). Creating something from nothing: Resource construction through entrepreneurial bricolage. *Administrative Science Quarterly, 50*(3), 329–366.

Bryman, A., & Bell, E. (2007). *Business research methods* (2nd ed.). Oxford: Oxford University Press.

Buttny, R. (1993). *Social accountability in communication*. London, UK: Sage.

Cooper, A. C., Folta, T., & Woo, C. (1995). Entrepreneurial information search. *Journal of Business Venturing, 10*(2), 107–120.

Coulter, J. (1991). Cognition: cognition in an ethnomethodological mode. In Button G. (Ed.), *Ethnomethodology and the human sciences* (pp. 176–195). Cambridge: Cambridge University Press.

Delmar, F., & Shane, S. (2003). Does business planning facilitate the development of new ventures? *Strategic Management Journal, 24*(12), 1165–1185.

Dimov, D. (2018). Opportunities, language, and time. *Academy of Management Perspectives*.

Drake, V. (2015). Indexing uncertainty: The case of turn-final or. *Research on Language and Social Interaction, 48*(3), 301–318.

Fleming, D. (1998). Design talk: Constructing the object in studio conversations. *Design Issues, 14*(2), 41–62.

Garfinkel, H. (1963). A conception of and experiments with 'trust' as a condition of stable concerted actions. In O. Harvey (Ed.), *Motivation and Social Interaction*. New York: Ronald Press.

Garfinkel, H. (1967). *Studies in Ethnomethodology*. Englewood Cliffs, NJ: Prentice Hall.

Garfinkel, H., & Livingston, E. (2003). Phenomenal field properties of order in formatted queues and their neglected standing in the current situation of inquiry. *Visual Studies, 18*(1), 21–28.

Garfinkel, H., & Wieder, D. (1992). Two incommensurable, asymmetrically alternate technologies of social analysis. In G. Watson & R. Seiler (Eds.), *Text in context: Contributions to ethnomethodology*. Newbury Park, CA: Sage.

Giddens, A. (1984). *The constitution of society: Outline of the theory of structuration*. CA: University of California Press.

Goffman, E. (1955). On face-work: An analysis of ritual elements in social interaction. *Psychiatry, 18*(3), 213–231.

Goffman, E. (1981). *Forms of talk*. Philadelphia: University of Pennsylvania.

Heritage, J. (1984). *Garfinkel and ethnomethodology*. Cambridge: Polity Press.

Heritage, J. (1998). Oh-prefaced responses to inquiry. *Language in Society, 27*, 291–334.

Heritage, J. (2002). Oh-prefaced responses to assessments: A method of modifying agreement/disagreement. In C. Ford, B. A. Fox & S. Thompson (Eds.), *The language of turn and sequence* (pp. 196–224). Oxford: Oxford University Press.

Heritage, J. (2008). Conversation analysis as social theory. In B. Turner (Ed.), *The new Blackwell companion to social theory*. Oxford: Wiley-Blackwell.

Heritage, J. (2011). Territories of knowledge, territories of experience: Empathic moments in interaction. In T. Stivers, L. Mondada & J. Steensig (Eds.), *The morality of knowledge in conversation* (pp. 159–183). Cambridge: Cambridge University Press.

Heritage, J. (2012a). The epistemic engine: Sequence organization and territories of knowledge. *Research on Language & Social Interaction, 45*(1), 30–52.

Heritage, J. (2012b). Epistemics in action: Action formation and territories of knowledge. *Research on Language & Social Interaction, 45*(1), 1–29.

Heritage, J., & Raymond, G. (2005). The terms of agreement: Indexing epistemic authority and subordination in talk-in-interaction. *Social Psychology Quarterly, 68*(1), 15–38.

Jayyusi, L. (1991). Values and moral judgement: Communicative praxis as a moral order. In G. Button (Ed.), *Ethnomethodology and the human sciences*. Cambridge: Cambridge University Press.

Lave, J. (1988). *Cognition in practice: Mind, mathematics and culture in everyday life*. Cambridge: Cambridge University Press.

Levinson, S. (1992). Activity Types and Language. In P. Drew & J. Heritage (Eds.), *Talk at Work*. Cambridge: Cambridge University Press.

Maynard, D., & Zimmerman, D. (1984). Topical talk, ritual and the social organization of relationships. *Social Psychology Quarterly, 47*(4), 301–316.

Engeström, Y., & Middleton, D. (Eds.). (1996). *Cognition and communication at work*. Cambridge: Cambridge University Press.

Ozgen, E., & Baron, R. A. (2007). Social sources of information in opportunity recognition: Effects of mentors, industry networks, and professional forums. *Journal of Business Venturing, 22*(2), 174–192.

Pomerantz, A. (1980). Telling my side:"Limited access" as a "fishing" device. *Sociological inquiry, 50*(3–4), 186–198.

Pomerantz, A. (1984). Giving a source or basis: The practice in conversation of telling "What I Know". *Journal of Pragmatics, 8*(4), 607–625.

Rawls, A. W. (1990). Emergent sociality: A dialectic of commitment and order. *Symbolic Interaction, 13*, 63–82.

Rawls, A. W. (2008). Harold Garfinkel, ethnomethodology and workplace studies. *Organization Studies, 29*(5), 701–732.

Raymond, G. (2003). Grammar and social organization: Yes/no interrogatives and the structure of responding. *American Sociological Review, 68*, 939–967.

Raymond, G. (2018). Which epistemics? Whose conversation analysis? *Discourse Studies, 20*(1), 57–89.

Read, S., Song, M., & Smit, W. (2009). A meta-analytic review of effectuation and venture performance. *Journal of Business Venturing, 24*(6), 573–587.

Resnick, L., Levine, J., & Teasley, S. (1991). *Perspectives on Socially Shared Cognition*. Washington, DC: American Psychological Association.

Sacks, H. (1984a). Notes on methodology. In J. M. Atkinsen & J. Heritage (Eds.), Structures of social action: Studies in conversation analysis. Cambridge: Cambrige University Press.

Sacks, H. (1984b). On doing "being ordinary". In J. M. Atkinsen & J. Heritage (Eds.), Structures of social action: Studies in conversational analysis (pp. 413–429). Cambridge: Cambridge University Press.

Sacks, H. (1992). *Lectures on conversation* (Vol. 1 (Fall 1964-Spring 1968)). Oxford: Blackwell.

Samra-Fredericks, D. (2010). Ethnomethodology and the moral accountability of interaction: Navigating the conceptual terrain of "face"and face-work. *Journal of Pragmatics, 42*(8), 2147–2157.

Sarasvathy, S. D. (2001). Causation and effectuation: Toward a theoretical shift from economic inevitability to entrepreneurial contingency. *Academy of Management Review, 26*(2), 243–263.

Sarasvathy, S. D. (2004a). Constructing corridors to economic primitives: Entrepreneurial opportunities as demand-side artifacts. In J. Butler (Ed.), *Opportunity identification and entrepreneurial behavior: Research in entrepreneurship and management*. Greenwich: IAP.

Sarasvathy, S. D. (2004b). The questions we ask and the questions we care about: Reformulating some problems in entrepreneurship research. *Journal of Business Venturing, 19*(5), 707–717.

Sarasvathy, S. D. (2008). *Effectuation: Elements of entrepreneurial expertise*. Northampton, MA: Edward Elgar Publishing.

Sarasvathy, S. D., & Dew, N. (2005). New market creation through transformation. *Journal of Evolutionary Economics, 15*(5), 533–565.

Sarasvathy, S. D., Dew, N., Velamuri, S. R., & Venkataraman, S. (2005). Three views of entrepreneurial opportunity. In Z. J. Acs & D. B. Audretsch (Eds.), *Handbook of entrepreneurship research* (Vol. 1, pp. 141–160). Boston, MA: Springer.

Schegloff, E. A. (1997). Whose text? Whose context? *Discourse & Society, 8*(2), 165–187.

Schegloff, E. A. (2006). Interaction: The infrastructure for social institutions, the natural ecological niche for language, and the arena in which culture is enacted. In N. Enfield & S. Levinson (Eds.), *Roots of human sociality: Culture, cognition and interaction*. Oxford: Berg.

Schegloff, E. A. (2007). *Sequence organization in interaction: A primer in conversation analysis* (Vol. 1). Cambridge: Cambridge University Press.

Seedhouse, P. (2004). Conversation analysis methodology. *Language Learning, 54*(S1), 1–54.

Shane, S. (2003). *A general theory of entrepreneurship. The individual-opportunity nexus*. Northampton, MA: Edward Elgar Publishing.

Shotter, J. (1984). *Social accountability and selfhood*. Oxford: Blackwell.

Silverman, D. (1987). *Communication and medical practice: Social relations in the clinic*. London: Sage.

Stivers, T., Mondada, L., & Steensig, J. (2011). Knowledge, morality and affiliation in social interaction. In J. Steensig & L. Mondada (Eds.), *The morality of knowledge in conversation* (pp. 3–24). Cambridge: Cambridge University Press.

Suchman, L. (1987). *Plans and situated actions: The problem of human–machine communication*. Cambridge: Cambridge University Press.

Terasaki, A. (2004). Pre-announcement sequences in conversation. In G. H. Lerner (Ed.), *Conversation analysis: Studies from the first generation* (pp. 171–223). Amsterdam: John Benjamins.

Wiltbank, R., Read, S., Dew, N., & Sarasvathy, S. D. (2009). Prediction and control under uncertainty: Outcomes in angel investing. *Journal of Business Venturing, 24*(2), 116–133.

# 12

## TEACHING THE CONVERSATIONAL COMPETENCIES OF INNOVATION WORK

Conversation Analysis in workplace settings has traditionally been used by scholars to add detail to what is known about professional contexts and operations (Arminen, 2005). In recent years CA has moved beyond this neutral role to an *interventionist* one; as a training module to improve workplace interactions (Antaki, 2011). One example of CA influencing a workplace training module is Stokoe's (Stokoe, 2011, 2014) conversation analytic role-play method (CARM). This chapter illustrates how Stokoe's approach can be adapted to entrepreneurship education. This new approach to preparing entrepreneurs complements the practice-based curriculum in accelerators and other learning contexts. It also sets the stage for future innovations in CA-based learning materials for innovators and entrepreneurs.

### Communication in the entrepreneurial curriculum

Adopting a practice-based view of entrepreneurial work means recognizing the interconnected and emergent nature of entrepreneurial actions and interactions (Yamakawa, McKone-Sweet, Hunt, & Greenberg, 2016). It also means embracing a practice-based orientation for the curriculum in accelerators and other learning contexts (Ulvenblad, Berggren, & Winborg, 2013). In order to learn how to be an entrepreneur and do entrepreneurial work, aspiring entrepreneurs increasingly are expected to learn by doing (Kirby, 2007). Instead of studying abstract ideas about new ventures or authoring a fictional business plan, learners are asked to enact the tasks of early-stage entrepreneurs. The learning is thought to emerge from enacting the work (Cope & Watts, 2000), from social interactions (Higgins, Smith, & Mirza, 2013), and from reflection on experiences (Neck & Greene, 2011).

Because the first accelerators were developed by successful entrepreneurs, the core curriculum has its roots in lay theories of entrepreneurship. Drawing on the practitioner-based Lean Startup approach (Reis, 2011), accelerators give entrepreneurs scaffolding to help teams rapidly validate emerging products and raise funding. Accelerators help entrepreneurs in this quest by coaching them on presentation skills and presentation materials. Recent research suggests that training helps entrepreneurs deliver more information in their pitches which increases their ability to convey the opportunity to investors. Training also helps entrepreneurs adhere to more standardized formats for presenting that are recognizable as legitimate by investors (Clingingsmith & Shane, 2016).

Accelerators also aim to develop entrepreneurs' abilities to reflect on their actions. Some scholars claim that reflection may be the most important of the core practices in the entrepreneurship curriculum (Neck, Greene, & Brush, 2014). Through the act of reflecting, entrepreneurs can codify learning (Schön, 1983). By mastering reflection on-action, entrepreneurs can learn to think, act, and interact in ways that will be recognizably and reliably entrepreneurial.

Despite the communicative nature of product validation, pitching, and reflection on-action, accelerators rarely give overt attention to the verbal means by which people talk their ventures into being. Native speakers tend to assume they know how conversation works because it is omnipresent, but often their expectations are only a "caricature" of language (Speer, 2005). They tend to think that talk just exists (Schegloff, 1996); that it is not worthy of examination (or overt reflection). However, CA researchers have shown that social actions are verbally accomplished and understood in ways that defy the assumptions of native speakers despite their comfort with everyday conversation. They also have shown that reflection on the mechanics of naturally occurring conversation can improve interactional practices – and impact workplace processes and outcomes.

## From informing to intervening

Initially CA added new levels of detail to our understanding of the verbal means by which teams accomplished shared goals. While it still is used in this manner, it also is taking on new applied roles. When CA is applied to a naturally occurring act "with the intention of bringing about some sort of change" (Antaki, 2011, p. 1), it becomes an interventional tool that can facilitate change – and learning.

CA has been used to stimulate interventions in various workplace settings. Professional interactions between doctors and patients (Stivers, 2007), second-language teachers and students (Sert, 2013), caregivers and people with intellectual disabilities (Antaki, 2011), and counselors and new mothers (Kitzinger & Kitzinger, 2007) among others have all been the focus of CA research and the beneficiaries of its findings. In aviation, for example, researchers have observed the conversational moves that enable productive communication between the cockpit crew members and also between the cockpit crew and the tower personnel. Aided by data from flight recorders, researchers have been able to differentiate the interactional details that are associated with greater safety. That is, teams with a particular interactional profile are more likely to safely recover from technological failure and human error. Educators have incorporated these findings into aviator training, and safety has improved.

The fundamentals of CA as a process also can be used as a learning tool in professional settings. To continue with the aviation examples, some scholars have coached aspiring pilots to transcribe audio recordings from actual flights and examine the repair problems that occurred in the naturally occurring interactions (Tuccio, Esser, Driscoll, McAndrew, & Smith, 2016). Students then were challenged to listen deeply and to identify the means by which real teams establish shared meaning and negotiate communication gaps. These kinds of interventions help learners gain and retain essential communication skills (Tuccio & Nevile, 2017).

## CARM school

One CA-based intervention used in professional settings is Conversation Analytic Role-Play Method (CARM) (Stokoe, 2014). CARM is a framework for coaching practitioners about the importance of talk-in-interaction in their work. Emerging as a reaction from role-play games in training programs, CARM enables learners to engage with the actual language of practice. It turns the detailed analysis of workplace interactions into evidence-based training materials relevant to that workplace.

Using CARM in the classroom requires access to a computer, projector, and sound system. However, the method begins with the recording of authentic workplace interactions relevant to the professional profile of the trainees. Then selected excerpts from the recordings must be prepared. Specifically, the educator identifies episodes of conversation that capture core challenges of a specific workplace. The educator selects excerpts in which the desired interactional outcome for the recorded speakers is achieved and other episodes in which the intended goal is not achieved. These selected episodes of conversation are transcribed. Both the audio clips and the transcriptions must be made anonymous before incorporating them into a lesson.

With these preparations in order, the educator presents the transcript line by line while playing the sound file (i.e., both forms of data are revealed simultaneously) to learners. The presentation of material is paused after a few turns of conversation are revealed. At this point, the educator encourages learners to discuss the interactional surprises they've heard or seen in the recorded data. A classroom conversation can be directed to focus on potential misinterpretations that are developing between the recorded speakers, the ways that the speakers have repaired any misunderstandings, or any other noteworthy detail that has been observed in the data. Before advancing the sound file and transcription, the educator asks the learners to formulate the next turn in the conversation in terms of the function it will serve for the participants and their shared workplace goals. The educator then plays the next turn of the recorded conversation and asks learners about it: what purpose did the actual turn serve in the conversation; how did the speakers accomplish their purpose through language; and how did the recorded conversation differ from the learner's expectations. A longer classroom conversation can then consider the verbal practices that do and do not work well in a particular professional setting.

The CARM approach works as a learning module because it challenges the assumptions people have about conversation. It helps learners recognize that the mechanical functioning of conversation is beyond their superficial awareness and that their interactions have an internal order that contributes to their shared accomplishments (Sacks, 1992, p. 484). It brings to the foreground the impact a person's utterance has on what utterance comes next – and on what socially constructed action ultimately results.

## Applying CA to entrepreneurship education

A variation of CARM has been developed for use in entrepreneurship courses and workshops. The preparations for the learning module begin by capturing authentic workplace conversations of innovative entrepreneurial teams in action. In the ideal case, these teams include the learners. The educator scans these recordings for instances that capture essential practices associated with entrepreneurial work such as reflection, empathy, or play.

In a future session of the class or as homework, the learners are asked to transcribe the excerpts from their conversations that have been identified by the educator as particularly relevant. At this point it is worth asking the learners what new awareness they have gained about their interactions by writing them down. Their impressions are likely to be more about conversation in general than the practices of entrepreneurial work. However, it is an occasion to build on authentic observations about language that can lead to productive discussions about overlapping speech, unequal turn-taking, and other conversational features that will probably emerge.

In the next class session (or gathering of the accelerator cohort), the educator can play the selected excerpts while projecting the transcriptions for the entire class to hear and see. The presentation is done slowly; pausing after only a few turns have been revealed. Learners are asked to formulate what function the next turn of conversation will serve in context. The educator then plays the next turn of the recorded conversation and pauses again to compare learners' expectations with the data. A class discussion can begin to explore the purpose served by the next turn in context and the verbal means by which the team mates accomplish their goal. A longer classroom exchange can probe more deeply into the conversational moves that contribute to entrepreneurial practices.

---

### Alternative recordings of teams in action

If the participants in the class are not actively working on a venture, one class session can be devoted to a design-thinking exercise. Many such exercises can be found online. After you download and distribute the instructions or have students stream the exercise video, you can begin the activity with your class.

Each team will be recorded while it is enacting the design exercise. Before the next session, the educator can scan the recordings for instances of essential practices associated with entrepreneurial work such as reflection, empathy, or play. In the next class session, teams are told a set of time markers in their recording, and they are asked to collaboratively transcribe that episode turn by turn. (This transcription activity can also be assigned as homework.) In the next class, the educator can play the selected excerpts while projecting the transcriptions for the entire class to hear and see (and follow the lesson plan as described in the section on CA in entrepreneurship education).

This method is useful in entrepreneurship courses and workshops because it brings attention to the means by which teams talk their ventures into being. It helps learners understand how practices are verbally enacted. This is critical: becoming an entrepreneur requires learners to experience and understand how practices matter in context. While experiencing approximations of practice is instructionally better than just informing students about practices, both are insufficient. The CA-based learning module provides the scaffolding that aspiring entrepreneurs need to be able internalize the practices associated with entrepreneurial prowess.

## Follow on opportunities

Given that a significant amount of effort goes into creating, selecting, and preparing the episodes for educational use, it is important to maximize the value the leaners can gain from the CA-oriented materials. Several additional opportunities for reflective learning are possible. Learners can consider turn-taking equity in their team's interactions as well as epistemic and pronomial orientation.

To prompt a class activity with a focus on turn-taking, the educator asks the learners to start by noticing how many turns each person on their team had. After the team mates have had a chance to calculate that, they share their turn-taking balances with the class. At this point a group discussion can explore whether the teams felt like their conversations were more or less balanced in the moment than they actually were. The goal of this conversation is not to advocate a particular balance of turns, but simply to notice the proportional structure of turns.

Next, the learners are asked to sketch an interaction map. To do this exercise it is helpful to have large sheets of paper and colored markers. However, it also can be done on the whiteboard, digitally in a software program for drawing, or on a small sheet of paper. The drawing of the map begins by marking a node to represent each person on the team. Every next turn is marked by a line that connects the person whose turn just finished with the person whose turn comes next. After the interaction maps are rendered, each team makes its map visible to the whole class and explains it briefly. Do some pairs of team mates have a thicker lines between them than others? Do some team mates not have any lines between them? Why might that be? A conversation can be had to explore whether the teams' expected participation levels matched or differed from the maps. Again, the goal is not to suggest an optimal pattern of interaction. Instead, it is to raise awareness of the value of looking deeply at the verbal construction of work; what people actually do in practice can be very different from what they think they do.

And for a final exploration of turn-taking, learners can be asked to identify how the next speakers knew to take a turn. This may require the learners to listen again to their episodes and to discuss their recollections of the conversations as they happened. Some turns may be overtly marked (i.e., a next speaker is named directly). However, most of the turns probably begin and end in other ways. Teams can discuss how instances of overlapping speech were resolved; why one speaker continued and one dropped off. Following time for these intra-team discussions, the class can reassemble to engage in a group dialogue about their observations and hypotheses. This is a chance to look for links between these observations and the ones from the earlier turn-taking exercises. For example, is the person who tends to keep speaking after an overlap also the person who took the most turns? The session can conclude with a conversation (or brief writing assignment) to summarize how a detailed look at turn-taking added to the learners' understanding of conversation in entrepreneurial work, and what new insights have they had about their own participation in team talk.

Similar learning activities can be executed to focus on other easily recognized features of the teams' prepared data. For example, teams can be asked to consider the use of pronouns in their exchanges. After reviewing the data with this interactional feature in mind the class can discuss what is going on when they use "we", what is going on when they use "I" or "you", and what is the relationship between individual contributions of work and shared work as a team.

These follow on learning activities enable aspiring entrepreneurs to recognize that they have agency in even the most micro-details of their socially constructed work. The utterances they contribute to their workplace conversations function based on an orderliness that lies outside of their conscious decision making. However, every utterance influences what comes next in the conversation – and next in their quest to achieve their shared social accomplishments of creating new products and new ventures.

## CA and pitching

In addition to helping learners become competent in entrepreneurial practices such as play, empathy, and reflection, accelerators and other contexts for entrepreneurial learning help teams develop and deliver pitches for investors. Pitches are constructed, at least in part, from prepared and rehearsed points. They are performed for potential investors and tend to be monologues more than dialogues. Presentations also are given to inform or influence listeners rather than to explore a topic collaboratively; they are intended to persuade.

A rich body of literature exists on pitching. Investigations have revealed that narratives and metaphors are used persuasively by entrepreneurs to build legitimacy and entice people to invest (Chen, Yao, & Kotha, 2009; Larty & Hamilton, 2011; Martens, Jennings, & Jennings, 2007). Research also indicates a positive link between storytelling and fundraising (Chen et al., 2009; Lounsbury & Glynn, 2001; Martens et al., 2007; O'Connor, 2004). Stories may convey information about the new venture's unique identity, market validation, cultural legitimacy, and future promise in a way that demonstrates personality and builds rapport – and contributes to the "gut feel" that guides some early-stage investors (Zacharakis & Shepherd, 2007).

Most scholars agree that the "social competence" of the entrepreneurial team is critical to the team's ability to raise funding (Balachandra, Briggs, Eddleston, & Brush, 2013). However, few studies utilize CA to investigate the verbal machinery of doing a pitch (Chalmers & Shaw, 2017). Bringing a micro-analysis of language to pitches could lead to minimal but fundamental changes in the way teams prepare and deliver pitches. For example, CA research in medical settings found that by instructing doctors to ask "Is there something else you'd like to address in your visit" instead of "Is there anything else you'd like to address in your visit" strongly reduced the incidence of unmet concerns for patients (Heritage, Robinson, Elliott, Beckett, & Wilkes, 2007). It is possible to imagine that a similar verbal shift in a pitch (or in the question and answer session after a pitch) could impact an entrepreneurial team's ability to address the concerns of investors – and ultimately raise money.

Similarly, many workshops on entrepreneurial pitching capture video of teams practicing pitches, but only a few look at that recorded data through the lens of CA. Instead the recordings of practice pitches tend to be used to offer coaching on matters such as nervous fidgeting and speed of delivery. However, the coaching rarely includes overt calls to reflect on language.

A CA-based lesson plan easily can emerge from video recordings of teams pitching. Its value lies in its ability to showcase how the structure of language enables people to verbally do persuasion or do legitimacy. For example, contrast structures have been shown to be powerful persuasive devices in many contexts (Atkinson & Heritage, 1984; Heritage & Greatbatch, 1986; Pinch & Clark, 1986). In other words, speakers who establish credibility by verbally "doing ordinary" first are better able persuade someone to adopt an exceptional idea.

A class session demonstrating this dynamic in pitches could be organized around the exploration of videos and transcripts. As in the earlier lesson descriptions, the educators could collect the data from the teams in the class or workshop. Alternatively, the educator could incorporate online videos and transcripts of successful pitches. The educator can show the video and transcript simultaneously and guide a sentence-by-sentence discussion about the verbal machinery of pitching.

As an example, an anonymized version of an elevator pitch that won a recent university-sponsored contest is presented below.

> Hey, I'm Josh. 500,000 people go to the hospital every year because of an allergic reaction to nuts. I have been one of the 500,000, and it was the

scariest experience of my life. Typically, when I go out to eat I tell the waiter or the person taking the order that I have a nut allergy. And the person responds, "Well we cannot guarantee nuts have not been in contact with our food". The information about ingredients and the supply chain just isn't available to servers or consumers. So my team is developing an app called Nut Free Food. It takes menus from major restaurants, puts them on one app, and all the things you can't eat disappear, leaving only the things that are safe for you to choose from. The beauty of this is that all this information already exists in the supply chain. It's just not in a form that can be used by consumers. So we are putting it in an app. You can have it on your phone and use it every time you eat. Thank you.

This brief pitch includes what other forms of research about successful pitches have observed. It tells a story. It demonstrates knowledge of market size. It even claims the special advantage of lead-user status. However, CA's attention to sequence order reveals yet another feature of this successful pitch: the entrepreneur "does ordinary" before asking the investors to imagine and accept the extraordinary solution of his app. He establishes his identity as an ordinary guy who goes to restaurants before contrasting that with his vision for a new product. By using a contrast structure, he incorporates a verbal means of persuasion that has nothing to do with the compelling features of his market or product.

## Ongoing developments

All of the described learning activities are oriented toward raising awareness about the dynamic role of language in entrepreneurial work. They encourage learners to reflect upon their own interactional and entrepreneurial practices. They stop short, however, of prescribing a complete list of best verbal practices for entrepreneurial work. While the early studies entrepreneurship as practice that draw on CA are beginning to identify language patterns that differentiate high- and low-performance teams, more research needs to be done to fine-tune and extend these patterns.

The most challenging aspect of the learning exercises described in this chapter is the capture and preparation of the data for educational use. It is not only cumbersome to collect and prepare, it also is limited in its relevance; there is no guarantee good examples of core entrepreneurial practices will be observable in the convenient sample of data that is available to the class.

In order to make in-depth language examination a robust part of the entrepreneurship as practice curriculum, more data from authentic entrepreneurial teams in action is needed. From this growing collection of recordings, exemplary examples of entrepreneurial talk-in-action can be prepared and then used and reused in many future classes. Finding these "trainables" (Tuccio & Nevile, 2017) is difficult because it requires what Garfinkel dubbed "unique adequacy" (Garfinkel, 2002); it requires that researchers are competent in the work enacted in the research setting. Given that few scholars of entrepreneurship are also practitioners of entrepreneurship, great care must be taken to attend to the intersubjectivity of the entrepreneurial research setting as it is understood and (re)created by entrepreneurial participants. Great care also must guide the assertion of any conversational competencies; the discovered language patterns must be meaningful to practitioners and to their understanding of the successful accomplishment of entrepreneurial work.

The fundamental condition that underlies all interventionist CA applications – the existence of a recurring interactional problem for practitioners in their routine work (Antaki, 2011) – is abundantly present in entrepreneurial work. And as self-recording and self-publishing technologies become more ubiquitous the ability to collect large sets of raw data from authentic entrepreneurial teams in-action will get easier.

As data from teams becomes available, it will need to be treated according to the CA traditions of micro-analysis. It also will need to be treated with a grounded approach to qualitative coding. Using qualitative data analysis software, data is examined utterance-by-utterance and assigned descriptive codes. These codes are iteratively evolved to better represent the categories of language in-action. The coding helps to identify the episodes that can be featured in entrepreneurship learning activities. And because the codes can be considered in a quantitative manner, they also facilitate comparisons (between teams of different performance levels, the same team over time, etc.) as a large collection of data is assembled.

Scholars and educators in contexts outside of entrepreneurship have begun developing largescale repositories of CA-oriented data for purposes of research and training (Tuccio & Nevile, 2017). While institutions interested in entrepreneurship research and education currently are investing in new forms of data and expanded means of access to data, no organization seems to have begun a largescale collection of recordings and transcripts of pitches and of naturally occurring entrepreneurial conversations. Such a body of data would be a boon to scholars of entrepreneurship as-practice, scholars of CA, educators of entrepreneurs, and entrepreneurs themselves.

As the number of recordings of naturally occurring entrepreneurial interactions increases, researchers and creators of educational materials will find new opportunities. In particular, the availability of many authentic episodes of workplace interaction makes distribution patterns of language structures observable. With access to many instances of the same phenomena, researchers can make comparisons that incorporate features such as culture and organizational maturity (Arminen, 2009). Quantification of CA-oriented data is a sensitive matter. However, if it is done with attention to the situated details of each interaction, it can highlight the interplay between language patterns and wider social concerns. Moreover, it can yield results in a form that allows the research to reach additional audiences.

## Concluding thoughts

Over time, more naturally occurring interactions will be collected in entrepreneurial workplaces and analyzed using CA. More pitches also will be gathered and micro-analyzed. Analysis of this growing set of data will yield episodes that can be used as trainable examples of core entrepreneurial practices. It also will demonstrate patterns of interaction that can directly influence entrepreneurial learning goals – and new venture success.

The verbal practices of entrepreneurial work, like all practices, are learned by engaging in and reflecting on them. CA-based learning materials hone in on the situated and authentic verbal work of entrepreneurs in action. They can reveal to entrepreneurs how the structures of their conversations (and pitches) can influence their ascendency. And they can help educators provide the scaffolding necessary for aspiring entrepreneurs to master the conversational competencies of entrepreneurial work.

## References

Antaki, C. (Ed.). (2011). *Applied conversation analysis: Intervention and change in institutional talk.* New York, NY: Palgrave Macmillon.

Arminen, I. (2005). *Institutional interaction: Studies of talk at work* (Vol. 2). New York, NY: Ashgate Publishing, Ltd.

Arminen, I. (2009). On comparative methodology in studies of social interaction. In M. Haakana, M. Laakso & J. Lindström (Eds.), *Talk in interaction: Comparative dimensions.* Helsinki: Finnish Literature Society.

Atkinson, J., & Heritage, J. (Eds.). (1984). *Structures of social action: Studies in conversation analysis.* Cambridge: Cambridge University Press.

Balachandra, L., Briggs, A., Eddleston, K., & Brush, C. (2013). Pitch like a man: Gender stereotypes and entrepreneur pitch success. *Frontiers of Entrepreneurship Research, 33*(8).

Chalmers, D., & Shaw, E. (2017). The endogenous construction of entrepreneurial contexts: A practice-based perspective. *International Small Business Journal, 35*(1), 19–39.

Chen, X. P., Yao, X., & Kotha, S. (2009). Entrepreneur passion and preparedness in business plan presentations: A persuasion analysis of venture capitalists' funding decisions. *Academy of Management Journal, 52*(1), 199–214.

Clingingsmith, D., & Shane, S. (2016). *Training aspiring entrepreneurs to pitch experienced investors.* Case Western Reserve University.

Cope, J., & Watts, G. (2000). Learning by doing: An exploration of experience, critical incidents and reflection in entrepreneurial learning. *International Journal of Entrepreneurial Behaviour and Research, 6*(3), 104–124.

Garfinkel, H. (2002). *Ethnomethodology's program: Working out Durkheim's aphorism.* New York, NY: Rowman and Littlefield.

Heritage, J., & Greatbatch, D. (1986). Generating applause: A study of rhetoric and response at party political conferences. *American Journal of Sociology, 92*(1), 110–157.

Heritage, J., Robinson, J., Elliott, M. N., Beckett, M., & Wilkes, M. (2007). Reducing patients' unmet concerns in primary care: The difference one word can make. *Journal of General Internal Medicine, 22*(10), 1429–1433.

Higgins, D., Smith, K., & Mirza, M. (2013). Entrepreneurial education: Reflexive approaches to entrepreneurial learning in practice. *The Journal of Entrepreneurship, 22*(2), 135–160.

Kirby, D. (2007). Changing the entrepreneurship education paradigm. In A. Fayolle (Ed.), *Handbook of research in entrepreneurship education.* Northampton, MA: Edward Elgar.

Kitzinger, C., & Kitzinger, S. (2007). Birth trauma: Talking with women and the value of conversation analysis. *British Journal of Midwifery, 15*(5), 256–264.

Larty, J., & Hamilton, E. (2011). Structural approaches to narrative analysis in entrepreneurship research: Exemplars from two researchers. *International Small Business Journal, 29*(3), 220–237.

Lounsbury, M., & Glynn, M. A. (2001). Cultural entrepreneurship: Stories, legitimacy, and the acquisition of resources. *Strategic Management Journal, 22*, 545–564.

Martens, M. L., Jennings, J. E., & Jennings, P. D. (2007). Do the stories they tell get them the money they need?: The role of entrepreneurial narratives in resource acquisition. *Academy of Management Journal, 40*, 1107–1132.

Neck, H. M., & Greene, P. G. (2011). Entrepreneurship education: Known worlds and new frontiers. *Journal of Small Business Management, 49*(1), 55–70.

Neck, H. M., Greene, P. G., & Brush, C. (2014). *Teaching entrepreneurship: A practice-based approach*. Northampton, MA: Edward Elgar Publishing.

O'Connor, E. (2004). Storytelling to be real: Narrative, legitimacy building and venturing. In D. Hjorth & C. Steyaert (Eds.), *Narrative and discursive approaches in entrepreneurship* (pp. 105–124). London: Edward Elgar.

Pinch, T., & Clark, C. (1986). The hard sell: "Patter Merchanting" and the strategic (re) production and local management of economic reasoning in the sales routines of market pitchers. *Sociology, 20*(2), 169–191.

Reis, E. (2011). *The lean startup*. New York, NY: Crown Business.

Sacks, H. (1992). *Lectures on conversation*. Oxford: Blackwell.

Schegloff, E. A. (1996). Confirming allusions: Toward an empirical account of action. *American Journal of Sociology, 102*(1), 161–216.

Schön, D. A. (1983). *The reflective practitioner: How professionals think in action*. New York, NY: Basic Books.

Sert, O. (2013). Integrating digital video analysis software into language teacher education: Insights from conversation analysis. *Procedia – Social and Behavioral Sciences, 70*, 231–238.

Speer, S. (2005). The interactional organization of the gender attribution process. *Sociology, 39*(1), 67–87.

Stivers, T. (2007). *Prescribing under pression: Parent-physician conversations and antibiotics*. Oxford: Oxford University Press.

Stokoe, E. (2011). Simulated interaction and communication skills training: The "conversation-analytic role-play method". In: C. Antaki (Ed.), *Applied conversation analysis*. London: Palgrave Macmillan.

Stokoe, E. (2014). The conversation analytic role-play method (CARM): A method for training communication skills as an alternative to simulated role-play. *Research on Language and Social Interaction, 47*(3), 255–265.

Tuccio, W., Esser, D., Driscoll, G., McAndrew, I., & Smith, M. (2016). Interventionist applied conversation analysis: Collaborative transcription and repair based learning (CTRBL) in aviation. *Pragmatics and Society, 7*(1), 30–56.

Tuccio, W., & Nevile, M. (2017). Using conversation analysis in data-driven aviation training with large-scale qualitative datasets. *Journal of Aviation/Aerospace Education & Research, 26*(1), 1.

Ulvenblad, P., Berggren, E., & Winborg, J. (2013). The role of entrepreneurship education and startup experience for handling communication and liability of newness. *International Journal of Entrepreneurial Behavior and Research, 19*(2), 187–209.

Yamakawa, Y., McKone-Sweet, K., Hunt, J., & Greenberg, D. (2016). Expanding the focus of entrepreneurship education: A pedagogy for teaching the entrepreneurial method. *Journal of Business and Entrepreneurship, 27*(2).

Zacharakis, A. L., & Shepherd, D. A. (2007). The pre-investment process: VCs' decision policies. In H. Landstrom (Ed.), *The handbook of research on venture capital* (pp. 177–192). Cheltenham, UK: Edward Elgar.

# AFTERWORD ON THE DEMOCRATIZATION OF INNOVATION

## The new relevance of an old question

Because studies of practice are studies of interactions, a practice orientation highlights features of entrepreneurial work that tend to be overlooked – such as the materiality of learning spaces or the role of prototypes. It also frames familiar concepts in new ways. For example, a practice orientation allows us to think of sensemaking not as a cognitive epiphany, but as a conversational accomplishment. Similarly, it allows us to think of cognition not as an invisible process inside the brain of an individual entrepreneur but as an "interactive organization of knowledge" (Goodwin, 1996, p. 399) that emerges in situated conversations between people (Nevile, 2004).

Studies of practice also assist educators of entrepreneurs. The verbal means by which entrepreneurial teams enact their routine backstage work can be made explicit and coached. The settings for entrepreneurial learning can be designed to facilitate community as well as agency. And through these small changes, studies of practice begin to bridge the gap between the work of analysts and the work of entrepreneurs.

But who are these entrepreneurs?

Decades ago, Bill Gartner productively argued that "Who is an entrepreneur" is the wrong question to ask (Gartner, 1988). Up to that point (and for a long time after) many scholars were trying to define entrepreneurs in terms of their psychological or cognitive traits. Few scholars, as Gartner made clear, were focused on the actions of entrepreneurs or the interactive contexts of entrepreneurial work.

Drawing on Gartner's insights, a set of scholars were inspired to investigate the behaviors, activities, and relationships of entrepreneurs – and the research trajectory now known as entrepreneurship-as-practice got its start. This recognition of practice as the heart of entrepreneurial work is, at least in part, responsible for the surge of interest in practice-based learning and the growth of accelerators. However, despite their prevalence and popularity, accelerators have not changed the demographics of entrepreneurship. People of color, women, rural populations, and working class communities remain underrepresented. That old question of "who" is worth asking again; this time in terms of equity and inclusion.

American entrepreneurs are 80% white, 65% male, and mostly urban and young (Morelix, Hwang, & Tareque, 2017). Moreover, founders of high-growth ventures, which generate nearly half of the new jobs each year in the United States (Decker, Haltiwanger, Jarmin, & Miranda, 2014), tend to be white and male with economically advantaged families and a background that includes minor illicit acts during their youth (Levine & Rubinstein, 2017). Some well-known entrepreneurs fit this profile (Kushner, 2012).

Although no accelerator would encourage criminality, entrepreneurship education does vigorously promote the Schumpeterian ideal of disruption (Schumpeter, 1942). Universities are celebrated for entrepreneurship programs that encourage bold behavior. For example, in 2017 the Association to Advance Collegiate Schools of Business recognized 35 business schools for delivering exceptional entrepreneurial learning opportunities. The logo for the Entrepreneurship Spotlight Challenge features the words "Visionary", "Creative", and "Brave", and the announcement of the winning schools begins with this introduction: "entrepreneurship isn't a buzzword – it's a mindset. A passion. An instinctual drive that blends visionary, creative thinking with a bit of bravery – all while embracing risk in the pursuit of great reward" (AACSB, 2017).

Because business education can engage personal identities (Ruth, 2016), it is worth considering the various meanings that can be associated with concepts such as bravery and risk. The meanings of these concepts might be very different for an MBA student at Stanford, for example, than they would be for an individual on the Standing Rock Sioux Reservation or in the Ninth Ward of New Orleans. For people who identify with the dominant group, educational opportunities that position entrepreneurs as brave risk-takers might be attractive (Burgelman & Grove, 2007; Zhang & Arvey, 2009). However, this framing may be less compelling to people who have different definitions of bravery and risk or different historical and economic associations with rule-breaking and its consequences.

Addressing the enduring lack of diversity is critical given the links between innovative entrepreneurial work, prosperity, and well-being (Nanda, 2008; Shepherd & Patzelt, 2017; von Hippel, 2005). If the current answer to "who is an entrepreneur" tends to exclude so many, then it is time to ask questions of why and what can be done.

Fortunately, entrepreneurship-as-practice scholars already are invested in understanding the social, cultural, and political dimensions of entrepreneurial work. Calls for studying entrepreneurship in contexts not traditionally considered and with methodologies not classically used have been made (Welter, Baker, Audretsch, & Gartner, 2017; Welter & Gartner, 2016). Studies of entrepreneurs affiliated with specific demographic groups have been recognized as relevant to entrepreneurship research more generally (Baker & Welter, 2017). And we are committed to closing the gap between theory and practice. Consequently, we are positioned to undertake important arcs of inquiry that can reveal what entrepreneurs do not only in understudied cultures around the world, but also in underrepresented communities around the corner.

Both scholars and practitioners have argued that more diversity fuels innovation and fosters a healthy economy (Boone, Brouwer, Jacobs, Van Witteloostuijn, & De Zwaan, 2011; Hewlett, Marshall, & Sherbin, 2013; Lakhani & Panetta, 2007). And a growing body of research describes the positive impact that entrepreneurial work can have on our communities (Steyaert & Hjorth, 2006; Zahra & Wright, 2016). Only by understanding authentic entrepreneurial practices and evolving the learning pathways to entrepreneurial careers can we make entrepreneurial work a viable option for people from all backgrounds.

By micro-analyzing the naturally occurring conversations of teams in action, this book has offered some new ways to approach the study of entrepreneurial work. It also has presented some new observations about what entrepreneurs actually do as they talk their ventures into being. In these and other small ways, the book has contributed to the discussion of entrepreneurship as practice and the ways that practice can inform contexts for informal learning about entrepreneurial work.

Of course, much of the research presented in the preceding chapters is exploratory in nature. Additional studies that embrace CA in combination with other ethnomethodological forms of inquiry can refine the ideas of this book and build on them by zooming in and out on practices. Similarly, more research needs to be done to understand the relationships between communities, identities, and learning in accelerators; to understand the interdependent factors that influence diversity and equity in entrepreneurial work.

Decades of practice-based inquiries into science have generated changes in the scientific workplace and in the education of scientists (Garfinkel, Lynch, & Livingston, 1981; Latour & Woolgar, 1979; Lynch, 2001). Future research on entrepreneurship as practice eventually may impact our understanding of entrepreneurial work, the means by which aspiring entrepreneurs are taught, and ultimately the demographics of the innovation economy.

## References

AACSB. (2017). *Entrepreneurship Spotlight Challenge*. Retrieved from http://www.aacsb.edu/esc

Baker, T., & Welter, F. (2017). Come on out of the ghetto, please! – Building the future of entrepreneurship research. *International Journal of Entrepreneurial Behavior and Research*, 23(2), 170–184.

Boone, C., Brouwer, A., Jacobs, J., Van Witteloostuijn, A., & De Zwaan, M. (2011). Religious pluralism and organizational diversity: An empirical test in the city of Zwolle, the Netherlands, 1851–1914. *Sociology of Religion*, 73(2), 150–173.

Burgelman, R., & Grove, A. (2007). Cross-boundary disruptors: Powerful interindustry entrepreneurial change agents. *Strategic Entrepreneurship Journal*, 1(3–4.), 315–327.

Decker, R., Haltiwanger, J., Jarmin, R., & Miranda, J. (2014). The role of entrepreneurship in US job creation and economic dynamism. *Journal of Economic Perspectives, 28*(3), 3–24.

Garfinkel, H., Lynch, M., & Livingston, E. (1981). The work of a discovering science construed with materials from the optically discovered pulsar. *Philosophy of the Social Sciences, 11*, 131–158.

Gartner, W. B. (1988). Who is an entrepreneur? Is the wrong question. *American Journal of Small Business, 12*(4), 47–68.

Goodwin, C. (1996). Transparent vision. In E. Ochs, E. H. Schegloff & S. Thompson (Eds.), *Interaction and grammar*. Cambridge: Cambridge University Press.

Hewlett, S., Marshall, M., & Sherbin, L. (2013). How diversity can drive innovation. *Harvard Business Review, 91*(12), 30.

Kushner, D. (2012, May 7). Machine politics: The man who started the Hacker Wars. *The New Yorker*.

Lakhani, K. R., & Panetta, J. (2007). The principles of distributed innovation. *Innovations: Technology, Governance, Globalization, 2*(3), 97–112.

Latour, B., & Woolgar, S. (1979). *Laboratory life: The social construction of scientific facts*. London: Sage.

Levine, R., & Rubinstein, Y. (2017). Smart and illicit: Who becomes an entrepreneur do they earn more? *The Quarterly Journal of Economics, 132*(2), 963–1018.

Lynch, M. (2001). Ethnomethodology and the logic of practice. In T. Schatzki, K. D. Knorr-Cetina & E. von Savigny (Eds.), *The practice turn in contemporary theory* (pp. 131–148). London: Routledge.

Morelix, A., Hwang, V., & Tareque, I. (2017). Zero Barriers: Three mega trends shaping the future of entrepreneurship *State of Entrepreneurship*. Kansas City, MO: Kauffman Foundation.

Nanda, R. (2008). *Cost of external finance and selection into entrepreneurship*. Working paper. HBS entrepreneurial management. Cambridge, MA: Harvard Business School.

Nevile, M. (2004). *Beyond the black box: Talk-in-interaction in the airline cockpit*. New York, NY: Ashgate Publishing, Ltd.

Ruth, D. (2016). What is your MBA for? What's the story? *Management Learning, 48*(1), 7–22.

Schumpeter, J. (1942). *Capitalism, socialism, and democracy*. New York, NY: Harper.

Shepherd, D., & Patzelt, H. (2017). Researching the inter-relationship of health and entrepreneurship. In D. A. Shepherd & H. Patzelt (Eds.), *Trailblazing in entrepreneurship*. Basingstoke: Palgrave Macmillan.

Steyaert, C., & Hjorth, D. (Eds.). (2006). *Entrepreneurship as social change* (Vol. 3). Cheltenham, UK: Edward Elgar.

von Hippel, E. (2005). *Democratizing innovation*. Cambridge, MA: MIT Press.

Welter, F., Baker, T., Audretsch, D. B., & Gartner, W. B. (2017). Everyday entrepreneurship – a call for entrepreneurship research to embrace entrepreneurial diversity. *Entrepreneurship Theory and Practice, 41*(3), 311–321.

Welter, F., & Gartner, W. B. (Eds.). (2016). *A research agenda for entrepreneurship and context*. Northampton, MA: Edward Elgar Publishing.

Zahra, S. A., & Wright, M. (2016). Understanding the social role of entrepreneurship. *Journal of Management Studies, 53*(4), 610–629.

Zhang, Z., & Arvey, R. (2009). Rule breaking in adolescence and entrepreneurial status: An empirical investigation. *Journal of Business Venturing, 24*(5), 436–447.

# APPENDIX: TRANSCRIPTION CONVENTIONS

Jeffersonian notation (Jefferson, 1984, 2004) includes markings such as the following.

| Symbol | Name | Indication |
|---|---|---|
| [text] | Brackets | Start and end points of overlapping speech |
| = | Equals sign | Break and continuation of a single utterance |
| (# of seconds) | Timed pause | A number indicating seconds of pause |
| (.) | Micropause | A brief pause, less than 0.2 seconds |
| ↓ | Down arrow | Falling pitch or intonation |
| ↑ | Up arrow | Rising pitch or intonation |
| , | Comma | Temporary rise or fall in intonation |
| – | Hyphen | Abrupt halt or interruption in utterance |
| >text< | Greater than/Less than | Speech delivered more rapidly than usual for the speaker |
| <text> | Less than/Greater than | Speech delivered more slowly than usual for the speaker |
| ° | Degree symbol | Quieter speech |
| ALL CAPS | Capitalized text | Louder speech |
| underline | Underlined text | Emphasized or stressed speech |
| (hhh) | | Audible exhalation |
| (hhh) | | Audible inhalation |
| ((*italic text*)) | Double parentheses and italics | Annotation of non-verbal activity |

# References

Jefferson, G. (1984). Transcript notation. In J. Heritage (Ed.), *Structures of social interaction.* New York, NY: Cambridge University Press.

Jefferson, G. (2004). Glossary of transcript symbols with an introduction. In G. H. Lerner (Ed.), *Conversation analysis: Studies from the first generation* (pp. 13–31). Amsterdam/Philadelphia: John Benjamins.

# INDEX

Page numbers in *italic* indicate a figure and page numbers in **bold** indicate a table on the corresponding page.